Augsburg College
Lindell Library
Minneapolis, MN 55454

D1786647

The Politics of Ethnicity in Settler Societies

Also by David Pearson

RACE, CLASS AND POLITICAL ACTIVISM
ECLIPSE OF EQUALITY (*with David Thorns*)
JOHNSONVILLE: Continuity and Change
A DREAM DEFERRED: The Origins of Ethnic Conflict in New Zealand

The Politics of Ethnicity in Settler Societies

States of Unease

David Pearson
Reader in Sociology
Victoria University
Wellington
New Zealand

palgrave

© David Pearson 2001

All rights reserved. No reproduction, copy or transmission of this publication may be made without written permission.

No paragraph of this publication may be reproduced, copied or transmitted save with written permission or in accordance with the provisions of the Copyright, Designs and Patents Act 1988, or under the terms of any licence permitting limited copying issued by the Copyright Licensing Agency, 90 Tottenham Court Road, London W1P OLP.

Any person who does any unauthorised act in relation to this publication may be liable to criminal prosecution and civil claims for damages.

The author has asserted his right to be identified as the author of this work in accordance with the Copyright, Designs and Patents Act 1988.

First published 2001 by
PALGRAVE
Houndmills, Basingstoke, Hampshire RG21 6XS and
175 Fifth Avenue, New York, N.Y. 10010
Companies and representatives throughout the world

PALGRAVE is the new global academic imprint of
St. Martin's Press LLC Scholarly and Reference Division and
Palgrave Publishers Ltd (formerly Macmillan Press Ltd).

ISBN 0–333–63687–2

This book is printed on paper suitable for recycling and made from fully managed and sustained forest sources.

A catalogue record for this book is available from the British Library.

Library of Congress Cataloging-in-Publication Data
Pearson, David, 1945–
    The politics of ethnicity in settler societies : states of unease / David Pearson.
      p. cm.
    Includes bibliographical references and index.
    ISBN 0–333–63687–2 (cloth : alk. paper)
    1. Nationalism—Case studies. 2. Ethnicity—Political aspects—
—Case studies. 3. Multiculturalism—Case studies. I. Title.
JC312 .P43 2000
320.54—dc21

00–067095

10 9 8 7 6 5 4 3 2 1
10 09 08 07 06 05 04 03 02 01

Printed and bound in Great Britain by
Antony Rowe Ltd, Chippenham, Wiltshire

To the memory of Charlotte, and for John

Contents

Acknowledgements	viii
1 Introduction	1
2 Nations without States	25
3 States without Nations	51
4 Migrations	77
5 Management, Accommodation and Resistance	102
6 Multi-Culturalisms	129
7 Nationalisms	154
8 Beyond Nations and States?	180
Notes	205
Bibliography	209
Index	220

Acknowledgements

The writing of a book rests on many shoulders and tries the patience of more than a few. A project taking several years, and crossing and re-crossing several countries, magnifies the process. I will not attempt to name all the persons and institutions who assisted in getting material, supplied ideas and criticism, and provided hospitality, solace and support. Some people must be mentioned for going well beyond the call of duty. Donald Baker, Gale Burford, Ken Dempsey, Augie Fleras, Kathleen Hugesson, Rosemary Ommer, Daiva Stasiulis and Kevin White, and their families and friends, were welcoming hosts abroad. Closer to home, John Morrow can be blamed for getting me started, and others who frequented the 'Southern Cross' both aided, and hindered, its completion. My colleagues and students in Wellington can be seen in the same light.

I would like to thank the publishers, ISER books, for permitting me to draw on my Occasional Paper *Canada Compared: Multiculturalism and Biculturalism in Comparative Perspective*, in Chapters 6 and 7; and the editors of *The International Migration Review* (and my co-author Patrick Ongley) for allowing me to use some material from 'Post-1945 International Migration: New Zealand, Australia and Canada Compared', in Chapter 4. Acknowledgements are also due to Victoria University, which assisted with various grants and periods of leave along the way, and a Memorial University, Newfoundland, ISER Fellowship (in 1994) helped put the idea of this book into my head. Donald Baker, Kevin Dew and Patrick Ongley, read all, or most, of the manuscript at various stages. Others read particular chapters. My thanks to all for their comments, most of which I addressed. Thanks too, to Jane McKinlay, for helping check the bibliography.

T. M. Farmiloe, at Palgrave, deserves mention for having faith in the project, and Heather Gibson and Jo North took it through to its completion.

As always, Suzette and Joy made sure an often solitary occupation was not endured alone. I hope my love and gratitude were not marred too often by other traits. Finally, this book is dedicated to Charlotte and John. Charlotte's memory was a constant inspiration to get it finished.

1
Introduction

Many nations are currently exhibiting states of unease. In the European Old World, to recoin a phrase whose currency, quite literally, is in the process of being revolutionised, states are said to be suffering from recurring crises as the boundaries of identity – personal, national and global – are radically transformed. Yet, in New World societies, these upheavals have added twists, only partly attributable to the changing relations between conceptually dubious elderly and youthful nation-states.

Not so long ago Chinese men who came to dig for gold in Australasia or wield a pick and shovel on the Canadian railroad were subject to harsh immigration controls and the opprobrium of lowly esteemed 'race aliens'. Racism has hardly disappeared today, as a glance at Brisbane, Vancouver or Auckland newspapers will reveal, but the headlined anger or anxiety is directed at new Asian migrants, as likely to be Hong Kong or Taiwanese professionals or investors as South East Asian refugees.

At the turn of the nineteenth century, Indians, Aborigines and Maori were viewed as 'dying races'. A fate greeted with indifference, relief and the occasional spark of sadness among white settlers or their descendants. They saw the indigenes as 'a problem' rather than a threat, although in many parts of their countries, particularly the cities, they did not see them at all, unless one ventured into slum areas or viewed depictions of them and their cultures in museums. Nowadays, in much of North America and the Pacific, aboriginal peoples are still peripheral populations, but, politically speaking, they have come 'out of the margins'. Despite their small numbers aboriginal peoples have become a potent powerful force. Their renewed demands for material reparation and political autonomy strike at the very heart of 'traditional' conceptions of state sovereignty, while their recognition as 'first nations' give them a prominent position in public iconography and within the recast foundational myths of majorities in post-settler states.

Changes in, mainly post-Second World War, immigration patterns and the self-determinative politics of aboriginality are vital sources of unease in post-settler societies, with Canadians having the additional *frisson* of relations with Quebec. Status anxiety among dominant elites, the 'chattering classes', and possibly the masses, are also attributable to twentieth-century shifts in geopolitics. Groups that once saw themselves as epitomes of 'Britishness' within the Empire have seen the mother country slip down the league of imperial teams; while the United States, once seen, at least through British eyes, as an upstart colony in the settler stakes, seeks to retain its exceptionalism in power terms at the head of the medal table. Rearrangements in the rise and fall of nation-states have coincided with other forces from within and without that threaten the idea of independent states with neat boundaries of identity.

Since the Second World War the internationalisation of labour and capital has been striking, although one can hardly argue that money and workers, paid or unpaid, were not transportable in earlier eras. Transnational corporations are now more important game players than many nation-states in an increasingly integrated world market with an international division of labour. Massive innovations in technology have globalised information systems and transformed population movements. Immigration officers can retrieve information about arrivals by pressing a few keys. State policy makers and members of ethnic associations affected by such policies can confer with one another and their counterparts in other nation-states by E-mail. Images of carefully orchestrated or spontaneous 'ethno dramas', reflecting the clash of interests and values, and, quite possibly, more physical encounters, are beamed into living rooms around the world.

Such developments both shaped and were influenced by a wave of social movements – feminist, environmental and civil rights for example – that swept much of the world in the 1960s and continued to reverberate in a variety of local forms through subsequent decades. Transformations in Soviet–American relations, moves towards the unification of Western Europe and the fragmentation of its Eastern counterpart, and shifting balances between old and new imperialisms in Africa and Asia are only a few major trends that come to mind.

Recent debates about postmodernity and the fluidity of ethnic identities and boundaries raise further questions about the relevance of modernist conceptions of 'nation' and 'state'. Outdated 'master narratives' about nation and state building, modernisation and national identity have seemingly given way to a new relativism in which national and ethnic boundaries are viewed as discourses in flux and cultural identities are multiple imaginings in what is often viewed as post-colonial times. Heralding the end of the nation-state however, is somewhat premature. Some identities are more pervasive and enduring than others, and the 'post' in post-colonial requires some thought. The nation is still the chief bulwark against the globalisation process and the state the most effective agency in managing the divisions between sexes, classes and ethnic categories. While modernist, and in some instances pre-modern, historical trajectories continue to shape the post or late modern world, particularly in societies where long-standing ethnic conflicts remain unfinished business.

Empire and colonisation

Between the late fifteenth and nineteenth centuries 'Europe spun a web about the world, and in the process the world was remade' (Cornell 1988a: 11). The British, Portuguese, Spanish, French and other European powers were the imperialist weavers of this mesh of diverse movements of peoples, capital, technology and ideas, and they all developed overseas empires of different dimensions and endurance in what they were to call Africa, the Americas, the Pacific and Asia. Such empires were merely the latest example in a world history of states seeking to control the political sovereignty of other political societies. Indeed, these European powers often had histories of being trapped within the imperial webs of earlier empire builders. Nevertheless, the sheer size of their global ambitions was unprecedented. Particularly the British pattern of geopolitical acquisition, whose post-seventeenth-century imperialist ventures were to prove a movement of unparalleled expansion.

Millions of emigrants left the shores of the various nations that formed the British state for a variety of individual and institutional reasons. Some were forced out by famine or poverty, political or religious intolerance, by the order of a court official or the point of a sword; others left to seek a better life for themselves, and possibly their families. The lure of a job, land, the prospect of 'getting on', combined in a matrix of social and geographical mobility. For the state, or more accurately, those elites who shaped and implemented its policies, emigration became the panacea for economic, political and social ills and a means of seeking or cementing international trading and geopolitical gain. Rational strategy, whether individual or institutional, however, was always laced with serendipity, and once the web was established, traditions were created that renewed or expanded the migratory networks of empire. These networks created decidedly fuzzy boundaries between 'us' and 'them' (Cohen 1994). The borders outlined on maps rarely matched social barriers between peoples, so the ambiguities and uncertainties of the frontiers between the English and Celtic fringes were often as hazy as the distinctions drawn between more distant British supranational identities. But much depended on the form and content of imperial linkage.

British colonisation took a variety of forms over time and space. Colonisation refers, in O'Sullivan See's terms, to 'the control of a specific territory by a non-indigenous group through either limited or massive settlement' (See 1986: 20). Colonies of limited settlement, characteristic of the imperial expansion of Western European absolutist states in the fifteenth century, were originally designed to assert military and administrative dominance over regions seen as having strategic importance and/or valuable natural resources. Metropolitan powers established economic or military bridgeheads to forestall indigenous reaction and to facilitate the extraction of primary resources for processing in their own societies, but in many parts of Africa and Asia, for example, the form of colonial control was indirect. Metropolitan administrators and soldiers maintained a colonial presence but relied on the manipulation and collaboration of local political elites to preserve their interests. Whether the focus was on geopolitical imperial advantage or economic exploitation, military outposts and/or entrepots required only a 'skeletal infrastructure' to maintain the colonial presence of a 'thin white line' (Weitzer 1990: 25).

In other colonial settings an extensive manufacturing, mining or agricultural infrastructure was introduced by more sizeable settler populations, requiring the forced or voluntary labour of the indigenes or imported workers and a full-scale administrative structure. Plantation economies are an obvious example. In these colonies, despite the continued emphasis on sojourner status, the metropolitan influence was far more intrusive. In some settings the word 'intrusion' hardly seems appropriate. The indigenes in various parts of the Caribbean, for example, were wiped out and replaced with varying degrees of brutality by the institutions of slavery and indentured labour.

In other parts of the Empire there was a more extensive pattern of settlement from Britain itself. In North America and the Pacific we have examples of mass settler colonies. Initially Europeans intent on economic gain visited these societies with little thought of settlement. The whalers, sealers, fur trappers, adventurers or explorers who visited their shores in the initial period of European/aboriginal contact often came and went, sometimes with the tide, depending on the mixed fortunes they experienced. In each society, however, subsequent limited settlement gave way to mass colonisation.

Massive colonial settlement is a by-product of more limited forms, either because, for example, limited settlement fails to secure control over territory or the metropole seeks to solve its own labour problems by encouraging colonial emigration. The most distinctive feature of mass settler colonisation, therefore, is that most European colonists, after lengthy or somewhat shorter periods of transition, settled permanently. Original sojourners became settlers, or migrants set out with firm intentions of staying put.

Settler societies

Settler societies were born out of the colonisation of territories and peoples by, in this case, European migrant groups who had intentions to settle and to build 'self-sustaining states' (Weitzer 1990: 24) with their own newly minted nationhood. Such motives demanded, often their initial, but invariably subsequent, political domination over indigenous populations and their control of immigrant Others. As Stasiulis and Yuval-Davis remark, settler states are: 'Societies in which Europeans have settled, where their descendants have remained politically dominant over indigenous peoples, and where a heterogeneous society has developed in class, ethnic and racial terms' (Stasiulis and Yuval-Davis 1995: 3). The balance of power described in this definition appears to support the phrase 'white settler colonies', but, as the authors observe, this expression disguises more than it reveals. To dwell over-narrowly on 'whites' hides the differences within this racial category, neglects important aspects of the dynamics of relations between various groups within and beyond 'the colony', and effectively banishes the study of the societies within the territory that was 'settled' into the realms of prehistory.

A full understanding of ethnic politics in settler societies demands that equal attention be devoted to heterogeneous aboriginal and settler populations and to other immigrants who arrived after the initial contact between indigenes and colonisers. It also requires recognising that aboriginal, settler and immigrant populations all have their prehistories. Pre-contact histories become intimately linked to, but are still separable from, the process of intermingling and the foundational myths that resulted within a territory that becomes a homeland displaced or created for respective indigenes and arrivals.

We cannot parcel the spatial and temporal encounters of these groupings into a neat 'settler society' conceptual package since the dividing line between such societies and other colonial situations is indistinct. Colonial societies of settlement took on a variety of forms in different settings at different times with varying degrees of permanence. Moreover, the process of settlement has to be placed within a broader context than relations between a colonial power and settler colony. Indigenous peoples had their own relations of contact, embracing co-operation and conquest, before the arrival of Europeans. Both European colony and metropole were part of wider geopolitical global relations that consistently shaped their destinies.

A counsel of perfection would require me to confront a wide array of European settler situations in all their multidimensional internal and external aspects over several centuries. But this level of ambition is unattainable in a single, brief volume. Hence my decision to examine a few, similar cases throughout the text and use them to explore the internal relations between majority and minority populations within a framework that embraces the key external state relations that shaped such societies. The key sites of exploration will be those societies that have been called British 'colonies of settlement' or 'dominion societies'. In the following pages Australia, Canada and New Zealand will be used as core case studies. These societies are quintessential mass settler nation-states, not only in terms of their origins and subsequent relations of ethnic dominance and subordination, but also because of the enduring influence of their ethnic foundations, mythical or otherwise, and the current design of ethnic politics that have resulted from a mix of continuities and changes.

Dominion societies reflect a commonality of experience through their creation by the global expansion of a specific (British) empire; a varied history of nation-building and state formation with a common thread of continued semi-dependency on the initial coloniser and, subsequently, other core players in the global system of states. Consequently, relations with Britain and the United States will be recurrent themes in the shaping of ethnic relations within our featured nation-states. The 'dominion societies', unlike many 'settlements' in, for example, Africa, South America and South Asia colonised by Britain and other European imperial powers, emerged from mass settlement and the subsequent *de jure* politically independent creation of settler nation-states. Their legal self-governance, however, was and still is, circumscribed by *de facto* economic and political semi-dependency within a global system of state relations.

There are problems with the term 'semi-periphery' given the heterogeneity of states with diverse economic and political histories that could and have been so categorised. And the pack gets shuffled in different ways if we are drawing economic or political cards to reflect a positional hand. Nonetheless, heuristically speaking, the term neatly captures settler and post-settler states who have been consistently controlled or influenced by powerful core states, but have histories that distance them from the political economies of 'Third World' peripheries. Australia, Canada and New Zealand, while hardly constituting 'pure' states, and reflecting important differences fluctuating over time (Boreham et al. 1989), are epitomes of intermediacy along a continuum of autonomy and control in world economic and political terms. All states wear masks of the exploiter and exploited in the double mirrors of history, but they particularly blur the imagery of our core case studies. Settler states, particularly Australia and New Zealand, experienced what Denoon (1983) calls relations of 'unforced dependence' with Britain, while, simultaneously, maintaining internal control over aboriginal populations and external sway over the peoples within their own small domains.

This long-standing semi-peripherality, I suggest, distinguishes such societies from the United States, although this country's British settler origins and subsequent aboriginal and immigrant policies, with the striking exception of extensive black slavery, are comparable to other colonies of settlement. And the fledgling, disunited 'states', clearly modelled many of their institutions on those of their parents. American foundation myths were shaped primarily by memories of an early severance of the umbilical link with the mother country and the rejection of British national liberalism based around a strong, centralised form of governance and a core of national, cultural traditions. American individualist, political liberal traditions and myths of origin about being a heterogeneous, 'country of immigration' was based on 'the supersession and transvaluation of European cultures' (Heller 1997: 53).

If Australia, Canada and New Zealand's semi-peripherality hinged on their 'special relationship' with Britain and its Empire, and its peculiar condition of privileged dependence, the United States swiftly moved to core status, cementing autonomy in economic and political terms, and acquiring its own imperial sway along the way. Ultimately, such dominance, particularly with respect to Canada, but hardly unimportant in Australia and New Zealand, saw one Northern American offspring of Britannia replacing its parent in its sphere of hegemonic influence over other siblings around the Pacific Rim. The United States, therefore, diverged in important respects from the 'dominions' and relatively swiftly attained an exceptional position among post-settler states.

Australia, Canada and New Zealand also share much in common with South Africa and Zimbabwe, particularly if we reintroduce the suspect 'white settler colony' tag. But South Africa and Zimbabwe are closer to the limited, indirect settler control models noted above. Despite the establishment of coercive internal security systems and particularly authoritarian forms of 'caste-like' state domination (Weitzer 1990) the small settler elites in these states were unable to control armed struggles and the eventual political overthrow, in the case of Rhodesia, or major transformation towards political power sharing (in South Africa) of 'white' state control. The histories of South Africa and Zimbabwe, although clearly enwrapped in somewhat similar foundational myths and institutional forms of imperial diasporas, and figuring importantly in the ethnic politics of other 'dominion settlements', reveal very different historical trajectories of state formation and nation making. And their contemporary patterns of ethnic and racial political arrangements diverge considerably from the 'bi' and 'multi' cultural models of ethnic politics on display in the Antipodes and North America.

Even if we are distinguishing Australia, Canada and New Zealand from the United States and African settler colonies, the similarities between our core case studies should not be overdrawn. Australia, for example, began its history of British settlement as a gaol where those deemed undesirables were transported and temporarily deprived of their liberty, and whose relations with heterogeneous indigenes were frequently remote and hostile. Canada grew out of a long period, close on three centuries, of interdependence between Europeans and equally diverse 'First Nations', and the conflict between competing British and French colonisers. Only in New Zealand did one treaty signify a relatively rapid move towards an unstable rapprochement between the most culturally homogeneous sets of aboriginal and settler peoples of our three colonies. Nevertheless, our core case studies exhibit sufficient commonalities to provide a viable comparative platform from which to examine a number of important themes that this book will address. The remainder of this chapter will briefly rehearse some of them, providing an entrée for the main courses that follow.

State formation and nation-making

Nation-statehood is not easily achieved in settler and post-settler societies. There is a constant tension between three linked historical trajectories. First, the process of colonisation resulting in aboriginal dispossession. Second, the process of settlement within which settler elites, at least in the early decades of settlement, are as attached to their societies of origin as to the societies they are in the process of transforming in their own image – and in societies like Canada there are competing colonisers which complicate the situation. Thirdly, the process of 'foreign' immigration which brings added populations with equally problematic allegiances into the society of settlement. These historical trajectories, in cumulative fashion, continue to influence the shape of contemporary ethnic politics. And when one acknowledges the class, gender and other points of division within these processes, the establishment of the 'nation' as a unified 'abstract community' (James 1996) is rendered even more difficult.

Colonising elites, seeking to resolve these tensions and to manage diverse internal and external forces, saw the early establishment of a centralised state within a unitary or federal political structure as an essential prerequisite for establishing law and order, acquiring and controlling territory and for capitalist development to be introduced and sustained (Pearson 1991: 197). Elites in Australia, Canada and New Zealand tried to move as quickly as possible to the formation of a unified territory, economy, mass education system and common legal rights: the foundations of a modern nation-statehood (Smith 1989). They also sought to gain early political autonomy from the imperial metropole, thus effecting greater control over the indigenes in their midst and the immigration process.

Settler elites were scarcely undivided among themselves, particularly in federally organised states. And the vast territorial sweep of North America and Australia posed problems of control of a different order to those encountered in New Zealand. Nevertheless, state making was relatively swiftly expedited by using a British bureaucratic template. Governmental, judicial, militarist (both internal and external policing) and educative institutions were established and the state agencies of political rule, legitimate violence and surveillance (Giddens 1985) spread their tentacles of mass influence steadily outwards from the initial bridgeheads of limited settlement.

Ideally, for settler elites, a developing sense of common nationhood should reinforce these institutional components of statehood. Where political elites are ideologically successful, the identities and ways of life gradually match the demands of the state and support its growth. The material, territorial and the symbolic order should be as one. The nation-state should form a unitary whole – one people in one polity in one territory. State formation is a vital prerequisite for nation creation in mass settler colonies, but we should be wary of suggesting that states simply beget nations. The institutions of governance and control help promote the setting within which national consciousness may emerge. Nevertheless, other ingredients are necessary to produce a recipe for successful nationhood. An 'ethnic core' is an important constituent for nation-building and survival (Smith 1986). Elites, therefore, seek to use the state to achieve a linkage between state formation and 'ethnic' components of nationhood. The construction of a symbolic order, a collective identity that becomes articulated in a system of ideas of who we are as a people, is also what promotes the coincidence of nation and state. So civic and ethnic factors are important for nation-state formation, and they are so interwoven as to be only analytically distinguishable (Smith 1995: 99).

Both civic and ethnic nationalisms are based on imaginings of 'peoplehood'. In the ethnic sense of nationhood, the 'people' are regarded as a 'popular community of descent and vernacular culture'; while, civically speaking, they are 'a territitorialized community of citizens bound by common laws and a shared public culture and civil religion' (Smith 1995: 111). Achieving harmony between both conceptions of 'peoplehood' is the central task for nation-state builders and renovators, and the achievement has its own peculiar qualities in settler societies. I have noted above that state formation precedes the emergence of 'new' nations in these settings, so settler societies, in my view, are state-nations rather than nation-states for much of their histories. The move from state-nation to nation-state is intimately linked to nationalisms with their civic and ethnic traces.

Nationalisms, and the plural is noteworthy, are systems of ideas that shape the social construction of the nation and legitimise its outcome. These ideologies are not simply a gloss on an objective reality but are themselves constitutive of what is deemed to be 'real'. Any sense of 'the nation' must, therefore, be viewed as a constructed rather than essentialist phenomena, although essentialism, strategic or otherwise, is frequently embedded in nationalisms. Nationalisms provide putative explanations of departures, arrivals and destinations. In settler societies myths of origin and destiny are drawn upon to create, sustain or recapture a unity of present identity and experience. Settler elites seeking to create independent nations, imposed identities and politico-economic cultures upon people who did not necessarily share their vision. Class and gender imagery and practices were sites of contestation within their own ranks, while myths of ethnic and 'racial' difference were key shapers of insider/outsider relations between settlers, indigenes and aliens. Ethnic myths are about group boundary creation and maintenance based on a collective naming of self and others, beliefs of common origin and/or destiny, a shared sense of place, and 'real' or imagined cultural distinctiveness (Smith 1986: 32). Beliefs about the existence of 'races' and how these signify supposedly immanent boundaries of biological and cultural inferiority are the stuff of racial myths. Together these myths underpin nationalist political projects that make claims for a contiguity between ethnic/racial boundaries, territory and political control. Such claims encompass the process of the creation or remaking of a settler controlled sovereign and autonomous nation-state, but they also include the quest for some forms of 'self-determinative authority' within a nation-state by indigenous or immigrant political forces.

Settler elites commonly develop myths of origin that have discrete starting points coinciding with historical moments of colonial conquest or the beginnings of mass settlement. Even if aboriginal populations are incorporated into such discourses they inevitably relegate them to the prehistory of the settler nation-state (Stasiulis and Yuval-Davis 1995: 4). Myths of ethnic origin are not, however, confined to elites, nor the dominant 'mass' settler population. Minorities, aboriginal or immigrant, also construct them, as they are forcibly or voluntarily incorporated or excluded from the 'nation' and/or the state.

Several forms of state-nation-building need to be considered, relating to what I call 'mythic sites of invention'. First, there is the process of establishing an institutional template that links settlers with their 'mother country' through linguistic, legal, economic and political ties, and conceptions of 'Home'. These links introduce the civic underpinnings of a national community based on metropolitan practices and align them with an ethnic 'core' of British sentiments. Secondly, and subsequently, there is the process of creating and recreating myths and memories that denote a reshaping, attenuation or rupturing of the links between new and mother countries. A conception of 'Home', for example, shifts through time. Initially, 'Home' is a sense of the society one has, at least geographically speaking, left behind. Subsequently, there is a dualistic, and not necessarily in tension, sense of 'Home past' and 'Home present', until, eventually, there is a rupture between these conceptions. 'Home' becomes firmly identified with where one is, rather than where one was.

A glance through the calendars on sale in North American and Antipodean malls reveals the regular reconstruction of symbolic markers – National Days – that reproduce the past and seek to cement a common

destiny in the future. Some days denote the literal timing of independencies, a claimed uniqueness. Others, like the observance of Queen's Birthday, display, at least for some, the memory or maintenance of metaphorically maternal links between metropole and dominion, whilst days like Anzac remembrance, evoke mixed memories of common cause and separate wills across neighbouring Antipodean states. Thirdly, there is the process of appropriation of cultural symbols from aboriginal peoples and other 'national minorities'. National maps reveal the initial or later retention or revision of 'original' place names, while the coins and notes in our pockets or the stamps on our envelopes reflect other usages of indigenous images in the creation and reproduction of everyday 'banal nationalism' (Billig 1995) Finally, borrowings from other ethnic collectivities are woven into nationalist tapestries. The introductions of new cuisines and sporting heroes immediately come to mind.

These multiple strands of cultural extension and appropriation illustrate how nationalist discourses in settler and post-settler societies will shift over time according to changes in the composition, distribution and relationship between ethnic categories and groups both within and beyond the nation-state. Such discourses are both constitutive and reflective of the policies and practices of elites, and the state agencies they have most influence over, and the struggles between dominant and subordinate groups to shape and reshape events and identities. This point brings us to a preliminary discussion of the construction of ethnic minorities and how best to conceptualise 'the majority'.

Aboriginal and immigrant minorities

There is no neutral language we can use to describe persons and positions of aboriginal and immigrant status. Words like 'aboriginal' and 'immigrant' are political constructs as well as cultural artefacts that are products of human imagination in particular historical circumstances. Likewise 'minority' is hardly uncontested, but I still find it a useful heuristic device to describe the position of groups that are relatively powerless by dint of lack of numbers, resources and political influence compared with the more powerful, numerous and resourced majority populations that dominate them in various ways. Neither minorities nor majorities should be perceived as static or undifferentiated. They are always divided by gender, potentially by class and ethnicity, and much else besides, and their boundaries and composition defy finite measurement. Nevertheless we can, I believe, usefully distinguish between what I call aboriginal and immigrant minorities.

Aboriginal minorities, in Robert Paine's words, are native societies, in the sense of autochthonous, who find themselves: 'encompassed within states formed by subsequent populations that reached their territories' (Paine 1984: 213). These minorities are formed out of coexistence with the majorities who created them, so the concept 'aboriginal' is fully modernist in tenor, drawing its original meaning from state-organised colonisers who wished to describe and impose a particular social, political and economic relationship between themselves and what they perceived as the 'primitive' polities and peoples they encountered during colonisation (Werther 1992).

The dispossession of territory is the hallmark of aboriginal minorities. If Britain was long the 'mother country' for many settlers, Australia, Canada, the United States and New Zealand became a stepmother for Aborigines, Indians and Maori. If relations between settlers and metropole represent external relations of colonialism in a world of states, relations between settlers and aboriginal peoples can be depicted as internally colonised. The indigenes became captives within their own territories. The colonial process takes place within the same (nation?)-state between a majority population and aboriginal minorities, with the degree and form of boundedness between them being highly problematic. Relations between dominant and subordinate are core/peripheral in economic and political terms and these statuses are frequently compounded by territorial separation and socio-cultural and physical distance.

In contrast to aboriginal minorities who are formed through the internal colonial process within states that contain their homelands, immigrant minorities are categories or groups who move externally across state borders into different societies. Members of these minorities may be free or unfree labour, and voluntary or involuntary arrivals, and they may reflect a variety of legal statuses. The racialised 'guest worker', penniless refugee or illegal asylum seekers represent various points on continua of juridical, economic and social variation. Such immigrants bring limited economic resources, often lack full legal and civic citizenship rights, occupy inferior positions in the labour market, and experience various forms of discrimination. The majority often perceive them as culturally and possibly phenotypically distinctive. To a point where minority group members, particularly those from non-English speaking backgrounds or categorised as 'visible' minorities, may be labelled as 'true ethnics' along a scale of 'migrantness' used by majority groups to measure the distance between themselves and others. Once labelled the tag may be difficult to remove. Ethnic markers, real or imagined, can override the fact that the person so categorised, or, indeed, their parents, may be native to the society of settlement. As a result 'immigrants' as 'ethnics' may still be deemed to be outsiders, despite the common eventuality that they are full *de jure* citizens by birth and have become acculturated to majority group mores. Their status therefore presents them with problems of inferior life chances, a marginal political and social status, and discrimination in formal and informal settings.

Such characteristics of immigrant minority status are shared with aboriginal minorities, as are many other features of their existence that derive from how minorities are constituted and reconstituted by the process of state inclusion and exclusion. Colonisation is one possibility. But whereas some immigrants, or their ancestors, may still wear a cloak of stigma because of past or present colonial relations between societies of origin and societies of settlement, all aboriginal populations are colonised within what used to be their own societies. What distinguishes aboriginal and immigrant minorities is not the quality of being or not being ethnic, although the perception of such by majority and minority alike has to be accounted for. Nor is the quality of being 'native' a concrete divider, despite the common use of 'indigenous peoples' as a phrase to distance such persons from more recent arrivals. Where one is born or the cultural boundedness of one's group is not a straightforward guide to different minority statuses. Even the claim to 'being here first' is contestable by different historical interpretations of the archaeological and oral evidence drawn upon by various groups to substantiate original occupancy. Aboriginality, however, in the historical and legal sense noted above, is a status that clearly divides persons so categorised from subsequent immigrants. Only aboriginal minorities can claim aboriginal rights based on being *in place* at the time of European colonisation.

A dominant diaspora?

One of the great ironies of the minority/majority model is its depiction of the population with most power and numerical supremacy as a residual category. The majority is simply what is left over after minorities are defined. This will not do. Although I will continue to use 'majority' as a general descriptor, as a general principle the use of this concept demands greater theoretical precision, especially since these groups in the colonies of settlement had specific noteworthy characteristics. The latter distinguished them from the minorities in their midst and, ultimately, separated them from the metropolitan populations they were so intimately linked with in their ancestral homes. The recently coined concept 'imperial diaspora' (Cohen 1997) might serve a useful purpose here.

At first glance the use of the term diaspora seems inapposite since it may conjure up immediate thoughts of the involuntary dispersion of minorities – notably the Jewish diaspora. But recent scholarship provides a persuasive case for using the term diaspora in a wider sense to describe the 'multidirectional dispersal' of peoples whose motives for migration span a broad spectrum of possibilities from 'the prudent calculation of opportunity' to forcible removal (Akenson 1995: 381), and whose position in at least some societies of settlement were not ones of numerical and political disadvantage. Indeed, even in situations where diaspora became immigrant minorities this did not preclude the possibility of them displacing indigenous peoples and colluding with majorities in the oppression of aboriginal minorities. In this light a more flexible definition of diaspora becomes attractive.

Cohen argues: 'all diasporic communities settled outside their natal (or imagined natal) territories, acknowledge that "the old country" – a notion often buried deep in language, religion, custom or folklore – always had some claim on their loyalty and emotions' (Cohen 1997: ix). Imperial diasporas resulted from a widespread tendency among powerful European nation-states to further their imperial plans by settling abroad for colonial or military purposes. These diaspora retained a connection with the homeland and deferred to and imitated many of the mother country's social and political institutions. The diasporic community, particularly its elites, saw themselves as a 'chosen race': part of a global mission to bring civilisation to colonised Others within a plan of grand imperial design that fostered the status of both ancestral and settler territories.

The Anglo-Celtic imperial diaspora was particularly pervasive and enduring and the English-speaking majority groups that formed in Australia, Canada and New Zealand were 'prime examples of colonies of settlement that emerged as part of the second British empire' (Akenson 1995: 395). In these societies the imperial diaspora eventually formed an anglicised cultural *mélange* with their own distinctive ethnic and cultural characteristics. They came from a multinational British Isles and sought to develop a national consciousness that has to be viewed globally as part of the history of their homeland of ancestry, the evolving homeland of settlement, other imperial diaspora, and other societies beyond these confines. This conception of nationhood raises intriguing questions about whether 'Britishness' was a quality that emerged in settler states rather than being an importation from Britain, and at what point 'Britishness' coexisted and/or gave way to Australian, Canadian and New Zealand national identities. The interplay of relations between 'Anglo-Celtic' imperial (and post-imperial) diaspora and immigrant and aboriginal minorities are an integral part of the answer to these questions. Not least in the recent attempts of the majority to develop multi-cultural national identities that not only achieve a sense of autonomy from an imperial past but also potentially alter the fate of minorities in a post-colonial future.

Categories, groups and communities

The histories of settler societies are in part stories of displacement, disruption, journey and resettlement in strange places (Pettman 1992: 1). Colonisation disrupts old identities and social relations but forges new ones enabling further relations and categories to be devised. The aboriginalising of diverse peoples through the process of external and internal colonisation and the ethnicising of later arrivals deemed to be other 'Others' coincides with the making or remaking of 'Britishness' for settler populations. Each of these processes is interwoven within another layering of identity and categorisation. The national identifiers 'Australian', 'Canadian', 'New Zealander', for example, came into being as part of the process of movement and change and the way in which categories like nation, 'race' and ethnicity are constructed and reconstructed by majority populations *in relation with* the aboriginal and immigrant minorities they created. These relations are contained within broader geopolitical and symbolic world orders where neighbouring or more far-flung significant others shape the making and remaking of national identities. To name oneself a New Zealander now, in contrast to past eras, is more likely to be a statement of being not British; to call oneself Canadian is a disavowal of being American. To say what one is, is therefore a statement of what one is not – and the latter may be a somewhat easier task than the former in many circumstances.

Nationality, 'race' and ethnicity are not natural categories or predetermined identities, they are political constructs with shifting memberships and meanings. They are ways of naming oneself and others, of representing identities and interests within different orders of collectivity. Categories are not necessarily groups, and not all groups are communities. This maxim, oft-stated, is still all too easily forgotten. Categories are abstractions, analytical constructs used to describe and classify collections of individuals who may, unwittingly or otherwise, be wrongly attributed groupness. Groups are living, breathing social collectivities that form out of interaction and awareness. Some groups are sufficiently close-knit and conscious of each other to display a communality of kind. Categories, groups and communities display different layers of relations between 'us' and 'them' the texture of which may vary according to their 'racial', 'ethnic' or 'national' content. The politics of categorisation, group affiliation and communal action is what this book is primarily about. We will readdress definitional matters in more detail at appropriate points in the text. But as a general rule of thumb I will be using 'race' and the more useful word, 'racialisation' (see Miles 1993) to denote, respectively, a category and the process through which that category comes to shape group identifications and relations. To be racialised is to be categorised, initially by others, but possibly subsequently by ourselves, as socially distinct based on imputed biological and/or phenotypical characteristics. One can also be ethnicised, with the locus of control over the process more likely to stem from internal identification than external categorisation, although both sides of the equation need to be considered. To be ethnicised is to identify oneself, and/or be identified by others, as putatively having the same descent, history, sense of place and cultural symbols and attributes. At a minimal level, as Cornell and Hartmann argue, 'an ethnic or racial group is simply a self-conscious ethnic or racial category' (Cornell and Hartmann 1998: 85), with part of that process being a relational awareness of 'us' to 'them'. A community, ethnic or otherwise, implies a deeper solidarism arising out of shared common interests, institutions and cultural mores. If part of the self-consciousness of ethnicity and/or 'race' is focused on the project of establishing or reproducing a form of *political* autonomy, unity and identity, then we are describing nationalism (Hutchinson and Smith 1996: 5). Are nations simply politicised, self-governing ethnic groups, or, far more likely, clusters of such groups? Often but not always should be the reply. Cultural nationalist projects, and we will encounter several in this book, may not have statehood in mind, and even if this aim is pursued, non-ethnic bases for unity may prevail: for example, political national models deliberately designed to knit together a civic-based weave of common (national) sentiments that extend beyond the alternative inclusivities and exclusivities that perception of ethnic and racial differences promotes.

Ethnic, racial and national categorisations have material consequences for those so named and represented. Such categories are also devices for drawing boundaries denoting belonging and not belonging. Resultant borders may be seen as sites of struggle over ideological collectivisation, language formation and the mobilisation of identity and action (Pettman 1992: 3). Boundaries of inclusion and exclusion are always constructed within and through relations of dominance and subordination, although national, racial and ethnic boundaries are not simply imposed from above, they are resisted, subverted and exploited from below. Both aboriginal and immigrant minorities were named, constructed and reconstituted by the process of state inclusion and exclusion and such minorities, in turn, accepted, modified and contested this process within the dynamics of positioning and counter-positioning.

Inclusion and exclusion

Minority/majority concepts, however defined, point us towards positions of consistent relative disadvantage. Colonisation is always a complex balance of domination and resistance. The colonised are never simply pawns in an overarching 'game' of control. Paradoxically, the process of state formation fosters conditions that furnish even the most powerless of peoples with possibilities for frustrating the plans of the powerful.

As noted earlier, state formation is an essential prerequisite for nation making in settler societies. In common with historical patterns in much of 'the West', the 'modernising' state, as Mann (1984) suggests, seeks to expand what he calls its infrastructural power to a point where it intrudes into most areas of society, enforcing its control by surveillance and direct coercion, over progressively tighter measures of units of population and territorial boundaries. This neatly describes the process of colonial state making in mass settler societies as well as the transition from feudal to capitalist states in the metropolitan experience. Mann also contends that, in contrast to the absolutist states of past eras, the modern (Western) state is infrastructurally strong but despotically weak, particularly in federal coalitions. However, in the early stages of state making in settler societies, neither infrastructural nor despotic strength can be relied upon, particularly where settler elites are isolated from the support of the metropolitan state and where the strength of resistance, within and beyond their own ranks, curtails their desire for imperious control. Hence the tendency for state elites to use policies of co-optation, limited self-regulation or devolution to maintain their ascendency over class, gender and ethnic subordinates. The 'spaces' created by these policies become the sites of struggle within which ethnic minorities seek to achieve more control over their lives. The pattern of differential political and economic incorporation of minorities depends on the historical distribution of power between ethnic categories/groups and the shape of ethnic stratification. This is likely to vary depending on whether we are talking about aboriginal minorities formed from internal dispossession, or immigrant minorities created out of the control of new arrivals from outside settler societies.

State policies of inclusion and exclusion and the forms of, often racially ascriptive, categorisation used to facilitate these policies were and are partly designed to solve the problem of what Weaver (1985: 114) calls 'representivity'. All states need to be able to 'name' the groups they deal with and they require 'representatives' to act for those so named. The process of naming and providing a system of representation not only maintained the control of the state over aboriginal and immigrant minorities, but also constructed and incorporated subordinate categories to the point where new political points of resistance were created. The politics of boundary making, to extend two major examples, constructed the Other in a way that transformed diverse autochthonous, stateless societies into 'tribal' and pan-tribal political alliances, and created 'ethnic' and/or 'immigrant' constituencies within or across the array of regional, linguistic, and inwardly stratified populations that entered these societies in increasing numbers, particularly since the Second World War. This historical construction of the Other as dispossessed, colonised aboriginal populations ('Indian', 'Aborigine', 'Maori'), and immigrant 'ethnics', promoted a sense of identity and difference through imposition and opposition (Pettman 1992: 117).

With increased industrialisation, bureaucratisation, and urbanisation the Other, moving in from the margins in a geographical, economic, political and symbolic sense, came into closer proximity and more intense and visible competition with the majority group and other ethnic minorities. The shape and goals of ethnic politics in this type of scenario are multifarious, contingent upon the character of individual and collective agenda within particular societies, but all hinge on linked questions about membership, degrees of participation, and degrees and forms of authority in the political and national community. The use of the word 'community' should alert us to the amorphous character of both concepts. Who or what makes up 'the community' in the senses of membership, participation and control?

Culturalisms and colonialisms

Who are we, and what should we be? These questions are of increasing concern, at least among those with intellectual pretensions to render their thoughts in texts. 'We are all multiculturalists now', answers Nathan Glazer (1997) in his recent analysis of cultural difference in the

United States. The phrase is not meant to imply a wholehearted embrace, there is hardly a lack of contestation about the issue, but, for Glazer, multiculturalism is the latest, and most potent, evocation of a concern to 'manage' cultural diversity. In ethnic political terms, there has been a recent requestioning in the United States of what used to be taken as an article of faith – the value of immigration. Calls for immigration restrictions, particularly on migrants from Third World sources, and the denial of citizenship to 'illegal aliens', conjure up remembrances of the restrictive immigration climate of the 1920s, with such memories strengthened by the fact that California legislators are at the forefront of recent debates about 'Asians' and 'Hispanics' in their midst. If immigration debates have an air of *déjà vu* about them, other racial fault-lines are equally familiar. The old sores of slavery and dispossession remain unhealed. African-American and Native American 'shadows of race' (Heller 1997) still fall across the face of a nation and state that espouse '*e pluribus unum*'.

Multiculturalism is also an issue in Britain, although the histories and discourses of immigration and slavery have very different resonances on the other side of the Atlantic. As in the United States multiculturalism is a word that conjures up debate, if that is not too polite a term, about the position of ethnic and racial minorities within state institutions, notably education and social welfare agencies. But Britain is a classic society of *emigration*. Consequently, debates about a multiethnic Britain hardly have the same ring about them when only 5 per cent of Britons are classed as belonging to ethnic minorities. Such persons are primarily in Britain because Britain was in their homeland. The 'Other' is no longer geographically at a distance, but resides within. So the anxieties in British urban heartlands have some ingredients of the enduring American dilemma. Additional, broader questions of sovereignty and national unity, however, signal rather more particularistic forms of unease. Who are 'the British', or should that be 'the English', now that the Empire has unravelled, union with Europe has arrived, and the 'Celtic Fringe' shows persistent and new signs of departing?

Between these American and British benchmarks of waxing and waning metropoles, Australia, Canada and New Zealand portray their own variants of 'culturalist' ideologies and institutional arrangements and we can see them as particularly striking illustrations of multi-culturalisms (note the hyphen and plurality that denote a mix of 'bi' and 'multi' possibilities) deriving from the specificities of these settler and post-settler states. Paradoxically, states that were once quintessential examples of attempts to form new nations based on a narrowly conceived ethnic core have moved in recent decades to dualistic and/or multiple imaginings of national membership. States that once guarded their monocultural underpinnings with vigilant immigrant gatekeeping and strict control of their indigenes are now officially denouncing assimilation and lauding the merits of cultural pluralism.

Faced with the spiralling climate of demands for expanding social citizenship rights that governments faced after the 1960s, multi-culturalisms became strategies for the regulation and institutionalisation of ethnic conflict. Are these policies and ideologies indicative of innovative ethnic political arrangements, possibly global in scope, that will eventually see the demise of modernist conceptions of citizenship and sovereignty within outdated states? Or are we seeing the peculiarities of post or late modern states within which premodern and modernist ethnic political pathways are still apparent? These questions will loom large in the final section of this book.

In ex-dominion settler states current 'culturalist' struggles reflect a loosening of the ties to societies of origin for majority group members and their internally divided attempts to renew or create 'old' and 'new' nationalisms, while ethnic minorities, aboriginal and immigrant, within the 'new nation' seek to assert greater control over that process by pursuing their own imaginings. This conjunction of ethnic forces shares something of the experience of Britain and the United States. Recent Australian, Canadian and New Zealand nationalisms grew out of a colonial and post-colonial history that, initially, sought an intimacy of British relations but over time veered closer to the American path. With the result, some would argue, that in so doing national imaginings risked replacing the first site of influence and locus of control with the other. Yet the settler and post-settler societies that comprise the core case studies in this book illustrate rather novel forms of ethnic and national frameworks that are in the forefront of attempts to devise social democratic solutions to the ethnic conflicts that beset us. Australia, Canada and New Zealand reflect an array of multi-culturalisms that bear only a partial resemblance to some aspects of American ethnic politics, whilst diverging sharply from much of the British experience.

The recent history of settler societies might imply a decolonising of First Worlds to set beside the Third in the same untangling Empire. Post-settler states are, arguably, post-colonial, having undergone a process of change in which 'majority' groups in ex-dominions finally reached a destination where their American counterparts had long ago arrived. Semi-peripheral histories, however, introduce and maintain ambiguities.

Settler societies occupy an uneasy position between oppressor and oppressed, particularly when the dynamics of internal colonisation are set within its external manifestations. The ex-dominions' role within the colonising enterprise set against their moves for independence placed them in an ambivalent zone between Euro-American metropoles and their less privileged colonies. Postcoloniality and post-colonialism, the former an ongoing process of becoming, the latter an outcome contentiously achieved (Boehmer 1995: 3), are therefore beset with delicate counterpoints depending on whether we are examining, for example, aboriginal or post-imperial diasporic nationalisms. Are the self-determinative aims of aboriginal peoples in any way reconcilable with the national imaginings of the ancestors of those settlers who dispossessed them? Not forgetting, in Canada, 'First Nation' quests for 'sovereign' status are complicated by the ethnoregional ambitions of Quebec. And where do immigrant minorities fit into these national, and possibly statist, visions?

Citizenship and sovereignty

Such questions strike at the heart of current debate about citizenship and sovereignty in nation-states increasingly influenced by global forces. How can 'the nation', as an ideological framework utilised by dominant elites and national minorities, be sustained when the traditional vehicle for its dissemination, the state, is being reconstructed and rolled back; when the culminations of historically embedded ethnic conflicts are openly displayed; when globalisation threatens, some say dissolves, any sense of bounded community and state authority? Perhaps new conceptions of citizenship within and across nation-states can provide innovative avenues for new forms of social democracy: or do they still reflect trajectories of historical inequalities embedded in the frameworks of current ethnic politics?

Ethnic and national categorisations, alongside gender and class distinctions, have been persistent bases for inclusion/exclusion within a variety of citizenship models across space and time. Elites, often with passive or active acquiescence from the masses, have used immigration controls, in tandem with differential citizenship rights and obligations, for filtering or excluding persons. The degree of cultural and/or physical distance from majority group norms has been a common yardstick for rules of admittance, but immigration policies and practices in settler states have always been constrained by internal political and market considerations and international geopolitical and trading relations.

But citizenship, as this book shows, is not only about movement between international territories. The rights and obligations of aboriginal populations, or explaining their absence within settler and post-settler societies, also claim our attention. Discussion of aboriginality extends debates about immigration and citizenship into questions about other areas of political and territorial confinement and movement and raises profound issues about communal rights (and responsibilities). Aboriginal peoples have successfully asserted their special, reparative and collective rights as 'first nations' within settler states, while, at the same time, they are individual members of society, sharing much in common with other citizens.

Legal and political/civic rights and duties, relating to suffrage or military service for example, and the degree of access to property and labour markets, education provision and social welfare, are important examples of sites of contested material rights and obligations for ethnic minorities, aboriginal and immigrant. Equally salient is how citizenship status affects the symbolic place of immigrant groups and aboriginal peoples in the wider polity and 'nation' (Breton 1984). Citizenship is (thus) both an instrument and an object of intersecting material and symbolic closure (Brubaker 1992: 23). This conception has general utility in studying ethnic politics *per se*, but once again the peculiarity of settler and post-settler states and nations is brought into focus.

Turner, for example, argues that whilst citizenship should be seen as a quality of modernity in all 'Western' states, including 'dominion societies' modelled, at least initially, on the political and legal institutions of 'the mother country', these offspring had their own unique characteristics (1986: 67). They did not follow the broad path of civil, political and social rights mapped out by T. H. Marshall in his seminal, if still much debated, evolutionary model of British citizenship. Marshall, writing in an era of frozen nationalisms and domestic welfare expansion (Joppke 1998), saw British citizenship *in situ* as a progressive evolution of rights protecting the (male) working classes from the vagaries of capitalism. Settler capitalism, at least within the areas of the British Empire we shall be concerned with, was forged in the heat of meetings between non-feudal indigenes and post-feudal settlers and the speed of transformation contrasted with the slower changes in Europe. Class struggles, war, migration and egalitarian ideologies were still, as Turner (ibid.) suggests, major components of the modernisation of both metropolis and satellites, but the weighting and content of these factors in the contest for real, substantial citizenship varied in the core and semi-periphery. While recent post-settler state experiments in seeking pluralistic solutions to the confluence of aboriginal, immigrant and majority group nationalisms have their own distinctive flavour, despite the increasingly global links that extend beyond nation-state borders.

The above themes suggest that in order to go forward we need, at first, to go back. The business of seeking solutions to ethnic conflicts in post-settler states is as much a question of unfinishing as it is of moving onwards. Consequently, the next three chapters, in turn, will address the historical shape of aboriginal/settler relations, state-nation formation, and migration patterns in order to provide a backcloth for a more intensive examination of various aspects of ethnic politics in the last few decades that follows.

2
Nations without States

'Aboriginality must be understood as an artefact of the colonial encounter. Both native and settler began to articulate it in the process of coming to terms with one another's presence and redefined it as the local and global context of their interaction changed' (Beckett 1989: 118). Beckett has Australia in mind, but his remark is equally pertinent to the meetings between indigenous peoples and Europeans in other settler societies. When French persons stepped ashore along what is now called the St Lawrence river in Canada, and their British counterparts alighted on Antipodean shores, they encountered diverse peoples with their own polities, economies and social mores. These were richly tied within complex belief systems embracing all aspects of their lives and the environments within which they and their ancestors had lived from time immemorial. After differing periods of initial contact, reflecting varying degrees of mutuality and highly localised variations in social and political relations, such peoples were to endure a strikingly similar series of experiences. The result was the formation of what I have called aboriginal minorities. This chapter describes the processes through which 'aboriginality' and 'the aboriginal' were created, and how their minority status was established despite ongoing competing definition and resistance among those whom these processes affected. Initially, let us look at our case studies to sketch in particular patterns of political relations and then turn to broader comparative questions of similarity and difference.

Canada and North America

The explorers and traders who arrived in North America in the sixteenth century were preceded by Vikings, Basques and other European visitors who made fleeting contact with the peoples and resources on the continent. But the arrival of the French was the starting point of a train of events leading to a clash between modernising states and pre-modern 'nations'. This encounter completely transformed the global position of what was to become Canada and the United States and irrevocably changed the nature of the lives of the indigenes and their internal relations. The process of invasion and settlement of North America was a lengthy one. By the early nineteenth century much of the continent still remained substantially unsettled by Europeans with the indigenous peoples in the far north of Canada isolated from incursions until the Second World War, when, ironically, joint Canadian and United States government initiatives to establish military bases and refineries to safeguard their states against the threat of an external invasion, finally brought full-scale internal invasive forces into native territories.

The French, English and, for a time, Dutch, who competed for trade and political influence in the sixteenth and seventeenth centuries had to negotiate with powerful Iroquoian and Algonkian speaking peoples. These societies with their own shifting political alliances had traded, fought, and formed their own ethnocentric evaluations of each another, long before European arrival, so the subsequent fur trade and relations between the French and English severely compounded rather than created political tensions in the area.

Initially, settlers relied on aboriginal people for 'advice, support, technology and foodstuffs', in their roles as trading partners, military allies and enemies (Coates 1999: 143). Many Europeans, particularly the Jesuit missionaries, saw 'Indians' as eminently civilisable. The indigenes, in turn, were eager to trade in furs for material goods, but were less impressed with the idea of exchanging their souls. Ultimately, mutual interdependence and cautious regard waned. By the mid-eighteenth century, the power balances between natives and settlers had shifted in line with declining demand for furs, greater settler self-sufficiency as their numbers grew, and the eventual military and political victory of the English over the French. Yet the ascendancy of the British state was hardly assured. Aboriginal peoples were still able to mount political and military resistance to settlement despite the depredations of introduced pathogens, the death toll from internecine use of muskets, and the wholesale disruption of their economies and ecologies by the inroads of capitalism.

The Royal Proclamation of 1763 was designed to kill several political birds with one juridical stone. It sought to placate Indian dissatisfaction with British rule in North America by seeming to offer official recognition of Indian sovereignty and protection of their lands and resources; provide a base line for Crown governance and control over future territorial acquisitions in the pursuit of 'orderly settlement'; and, more specifically, in Canadian terms, established the constitutional and territorial limits of French control in Quebec. As history was to repeat on many occasions, the gap between *de jure* sentiments and *de facto* actions was considerable, particularly relating to that most valued commodity – land.

The pursuit of land and the conflicts between British Crown and settlers loomed large in the American Revolution and the split between the Thirteen Colonies and British North America, and were the prime motives for the policies of Indian containment that resulted in the establishment of a confederal Canadian state in 1867. British and local elites supported the British North America Act ushering in the dominion of Canada because of their envy and fear of American expansionary aims of 'Manifest Destiny' and their desire to emulate the search for prosperity through immigration and technological development. Indigenous peoples, including some whose traditional territories were bifurcated by the new states line, sought to avoid the 'twin evils of starvation and armed conflict' they knew had devastated buffalo and peoples on the plains to the South (Coates 1999: 151). Some European and aboriginal leaders were equally mindful of the dangers of unfettered settlement and returned to treaties to negotiate a resolution.

Treaties had been made between aboriginal peoples and imperial representatives before confederation. Colonial officials designed these primarily to establish peaceful relations and access to territory and resources at a time when the indigenes often called the political tune. By the mid-nineteenth century the balance of power had firmly swung the other way. Following confederation treaty making became a far more deliberate instrument of mass settlement, and the shape of these 'agreements' had lasting repercussions. The Robinson and Douglas treaties,[1] for example, reserved lands for 'Indians' in their own territories. Subsequent 'numbered treaties'[2] set up reserves clustering different peoples together in territories they may never have previously occupied. Such distinctions were to prove important in the future when conceptions of aboriginal title were tied to ideas about permanent 'traditional' occupancy and the diversity of peoples on reserves had implications for the strength and type of political solidarity. Nevertheless, the immediate, overall result was much the same. The transfer of administration of Indians from the imperial to the colonial government signalled the end of conciliation and co-operation. By the 1880s most aboriginal peoples were relegated to small, marginal reserves and effectively controlled by the Indian Act and federal state.

The Indian Act epitomised the creation of an aboriginal minority. Political resistance to invasion was not halted by the establishment of a centralised bureau of control. Indeed, as we will see later, this agency, paradoxically, laid some foundations for eventual renewed and effective political solidarity. Nor did the panoply of federal state policies necessarily get enforced consistently at the regional and local level given the exigencies of social and geographical distance and varied processes of inclusion and exclusion. Aboriginal peoples were neither completely assimilated nor destroyed by the state. Nevertheless, the Act and the offices set up to administer it, categorised and codified 'Indians' and controlled most aspects of their lives. Blood and place were the key indicators of Indian status. The Métis, of 'mixed' French and Indian ancestry, and 'Eskimo' (Inuit) who remained isolated from European contact were not 'Indians'. Aboriginal peoples on reserves were. Those persons who fell between these parameters were in socio-legal limbo. In effect, 'Non-status Indians', who made up a substantial proportion of Canadian indigenes, were rendered bureaucratically invisible.

The Indian Act (1876) laid down prescriptions for reserve management by Canadian officials and local councils of 'chiefs'. These councils represented 'bands', artificial political amalgams bearing little relation to traditional political mores, particularly since many reserves were populated by clusters of indigenes removed from their homelands. Schooling, welfare and justice provisions of the Indian Act laid down prescriptions for Indians to be civilised, Christianised and controlled by persuasion or coercion. Indians became wards of local and federal states within a system of 'coercive tutelage' that was not based on contractual agreement nor negotiated understanding (Dyck 1992: 24). Indigenous peoples were to be Europeanised by missionaries, schoolteachers and reserve agents. If successful in attaining a level of middle-class Victorian accomplishment and rectitude few settlers had accomplished, they could be enfranchised and granted private property (Miller 1991: 190). They could not be British, later Canadians, *and* Indians. If the constitutional line between these categories was legally crossed there was no going back. Few Indians accepted the proffered hand of 'acceptance' into British North America. The price to be paid, a complete abrogation of one's traditional identity as a distinct people, was too great.

Reluctance was met with further restrictive legislation and practices. As Foster notes, the coercive edge of the Indian Act was significantly sharpened between the 1880s and 1930s (Foster 1999: 364). There was a steady increase in the powers of the Minister over Indian lives, land and resources as Indians refused to assimilate. When Indians persisted in electing traditional chiefs to reserve councils and maintaining a parallel system of aboriginal politics alongside the bureaucratic one imposed upon them, laws were introduced to depose elected leaders and deny their re-election. When reserve-based education was seen as ineffective in loosening tradition, parents were forced to send their children to off-reserve schools (Miller 1996). When few Indians leapt at the chance of becoming citizens and individual landowners, their collective grip on reserve lands was loosened by other means. Band consent to land sales was bypassed or their territory was directly appropriated. When Indian belief systems persisted, despite efforts to Christianise them, their ceremonies, the potlatch and Sun Dance for example, were banned.

These legislative changes were often ineffective. State strategies of surveillance and control were hampered by the vast geographical expanse of jurisdiction, varied local effectiveness in implementing it, and ongoing resistance. Regional diversity was still a consistent feature of the national picture. In the more settled parts of southeastern Canada 'Indians' were becoming a category of persons one occasionally read about but rarely saw, while in some prairie towns aboriginal numbers were more significant but receding in the face of new waves of settlement. Canada's much vaunted nineteenth-century settlement ambitions had to wait until American westward expansion faltered as most prime agricultural land was seized. It was not until the first two decades of the twentieth century that substantial numbers of potential farmers could be lured from the States or northern and eastern Europe. In 1901 the Canadian prairies had 400 000 settlers; by 1920 this had reached two million. The harsh climate and terrain of the North still protected indigenes from mass settlement, although the Klondike gold rush in the late 1890s and capitalist development of parts of northern Manitoba, Ontario and Quebec inexorably extended the boundaries of settlement. Not all subsequent contacts were negative for the indigenes, and impoverishment was not an inevitable consequence. Settlement and expansion enabled some Indian farmers and small business persons to thrive, and the numbers of aboriginal full-time wage labourers continued to rise (Dickinson and Wotherspoon 1992). Yet these were exceptions hardly disproving the rule. In the main native peoples were swept aside and pushed to the physical, economic and political margins of territories they had once controlled. By 1926 when Canada moved from being an indirect colony of Britain to a position of formal political independence, most aboriginal peoples had been reduced to a small, fragmented population on remote reserves or in tiny enclaves within or on the outskirts of Canadian towns and cities. They had become a minority in both political and numerical senses of the term.

Australia

One of the founding myths of the Canadian state and nation was that 'Canada' treated aboriginal people fairly and with little of the violence marking relations between native and settler Americans. If one is measuring hostilities in terms of direct military aggression, we may sustain the latter sentiment, but notions of 'fairness' rest on rather dubious assessments of comparative advantage rather than intrinsic tests of justice and freedom. Relative peace was ensured in Canada because of the long legacy of the fur trade and strategic economic and political alliance, centralised forms of government-led control preceding mass settlement, and the initiatives of aboriginal peoples themselves (Coates 1999: 156). Resistance of indigenes to invasion is a universal quality of settler societies, but the form of initial contact and the relationship between central and regional control of aboriginal peoples in Australia was very different from the Canadian situation.

The British state's earliest contacts with aboriginal peoples in Australia still arose from estimates of strategic economic and imperial advantage. But whereas North America was always seen as a rich bounty of resources waiting for commercial exploitation, Australia was also viewed as a potential offshore prison for the criminal classes. The British government had already sent thousands of English and Irish 'undesirables' to its North American and Caribbean colonies, but by the end of the eighteenth century the Thirteen Colonies were lost to the Empire, the British West Indies' labour demand was being met by black slaves, and the Canadian political economy lacked the facility (plantations) or need (fur trade) for penal settlement (Perry 1996: 162).

Like Canada, a very long settled and diverse set of peoples already populated pre-European contact Australia. They also occupied a vast territory, much of which was unsuitable for arable cultivation. Within this diversity, however, there was a greater uniformity of small, nomadic or semi-nomadic hunting and gathering peoples with highly sophisticated systems of coexistence with the land and the cosmos. Each people had a sense of territory related to topography and the location of sacred sites, and drew firm distinctions between themselves and strangers. Hostilities between groups were common, but they were usually minor in scale and often dampened by mobility and avoidance. There were no examples of the type of indigenous military and political coalitions, and extensive trading, the French and English encountered in their earliest contacts in North America.

The British state had always believed that acknowledgment of sovereignty in the far corners of its Empire depended on notions of agriculture, property ownership (preferably private) and architecture as measures of civilisation. Land had to be used and altered in order for its occupants to be accorded political recognition. Few, if any, of the aboriginal peoples in North America met these criteria in full, hence the need for tutelage, but in Australia the indigenes and their lifestyle were often viewed as irremediably primitive. In Canada, non-status Indians were bureaucratically erased by 1867. In Australia, most aboriginal peoples were deemed to be politically invisible from the outset. Adopting the legal principles of *terra nullius* (vacant, unoccupied land): 'The British treated Australia not merely as a land lacking a sovereign power, but almost as a land literally empty of people' (Markus 1994: 22).

When Cook set out in the *Endeavour* in 1776, he was directed, following the imperial conventions of the day, only to take possession of inhabited territories 'with the consent of the natives'. Natives were certainly sighted in Australia, but Joseph Banks, who sailed with Cook, informed a British parliamentary committee on transportation on his return, that the sparse native population was confined to coastal areas. Furthermore, they were indifferent to, or incapable of, being negotiated with, and could be expected to 'speedily abandon the Country to the New Comers'. Consequently, the first Governor of New South Wales arrived with no instructions about treaties or purchase of aboriginal land. In a sense, as Markus notes, 'there was no government policy towards Aborigines for almost fifty years, except for ad hoc measures to deal with resistance and some isolated acts of charity' (Markus 1994: 22).

Humanitarianism and notions of the nobility of savagery *were* found among British explorers, missionaries and some colonial officials. Many of whom considered the march out of barbarism was an easier route for natives than it was for convicts. In the contact era of imperial and military rule there *were* attempts to civilise, educate and even co-opt aboriginal peoples. But the earliest decades on 'the Fatal Shore' were generally marked by the unwillingness or inability of local officials to control the colonists, despite the concern of the humanitarian lobby and the Colonial Office in Britain. The indigenes also showed little inclination to adopt alien mores. The result was a period of settlement between the late eighteenth and nineteenth centuries marked by, often bloody, confrontation, in some cases to the point of premeditated genocide.

Ex-convicts and new settlers all too readily took up arms, and aboriginal people, lacking the resources to engage in direct warfare, resorted to guerrilla tactics. Despite resistance, the processes of loss of territory and decimation of population continued. The indigenes were outnumbered, outgunned and found invaders rapidly depleted their food sources. Between 1790 and 1860 the settler population swelled from approximately 2000 to more than a million. Estimates of aboriginal numbers in the late eighteenth century vary from 300 000 to five times that figure. A century later it is estimated only 60 000 aboriginal people remained (Day 1996: 130). Introduced pathogens, some deliberately spread, and the escalation of local hostilities as settler encroachment led to clans being pushed into others' territories, all took their toll. The dual depredations of settler terror and alien diseases are reminiscent of similar conflicts in the United States during the mid-to-late nineteenth century, but in Australia sporadic frontier violence stretched from the late eighteenth century until the 1920s.

Having established a bridgehead on the eastern and southern coastlines, the invaders pushed into the hinterland, with extensive squatting on what was seen as prime pastoral land. The Colonial Office sought to control the violence and rampant land grabbing by seeking to introduce a system of pastoral leases that set aside reserves, and some minimal protection for aboriginal hunting areas. The system preserved some semblance of aboriginal title and occupation in more established areas, but 'the frontier' was out of reach of any, even mildly benevolent, restraining hand. The threshold of settlement was 'shifting, contextual, negotiated, moved in and out of, enacted and suspended' (Wolfe 1994: 95). The complex tenor of relations between aboriginal and non-aboriginal persons, belie models of fatal impact *and* revisionist attempts to see resistance to invasion at every turn. 'Aborigines' were subject to homicide, sexual abuse, disease and starvation, but there were also relations of reciprocity, even respect. As in North America, opposition and accommodation to European invasion were frequently interwoven. Within the colonial process aboriginal people were used as guides, interpreters, protectors of explorers, police and troopers, and were engaged in a wide range of regionally and seasonally varied labour for meagre wages or, more often, rations and accommodation (Wolfe 1994: 100). In the cattle industry aboriginal people were a vital component of capitalism, but work relations were decidedly unfree.

The patterns of interactions between colonists and indigenes aroused, at best, individual settler recognition of some semblance of a shared humanity perpetuating the 'contradictions between conscience and belief in British supremacy' (Broome 1982: 26). Generally, settlers viewed aboriginal land as a far more important commodity than the persons who lived on and with it. Colonial ethnocentrism, laced with Social Darwinian-inspired racism, became entrenched by the end of the nineteenth century. Aborigines were a pest or irrelevance doomed to inevitable decline. By the end of what Wolfe calls the 'confrontation period', most aboriginal persons had become 'decimated and largely pacified survivors improvising a variety of livelihoods in the pores of the now-established settler society' (Wolfe 1994: 99).

As formal control over land and aboriginal policy steadily shifted from London to Australian state colonial capitals in the decades leading up to federation, the fate of aboriginal peoples rested even more squarely with local political interests. After federation (in 1901), the Commonwealth polity deferred to State Governments on most aspects of aboriginal affairs.[3] Consequently, in contrast to Canada and the United States, in Australia there was no nationwide bureaucracy, nor overarching federal government responsibility for 'aborigines'. The constitutional cornerstone of the new Australia was cemented in place with scant legal recognition of the original occupants. Having decided the land was unoccupied there was a brutal logic in virtually ignoring aboriginal peoples in the founding document, to the point where they would not even be counted in the census. Aborigines in the arid heart of the country remained isolated from constitutional questions and still preserved some de facto autonomy. Those who lived on the fringes, or within the zones of white settlement, became further entrapped within the authoritarian control of local state legislatures. Between 1869 (in Victoria) and 1910 (Northern Territory) various Aborigines Protection Acts and Boards were introduced to 'protect a dying race'.

The Australian emphasis on regional state-based policies and practices introduced a greater degree of variation in categorisation and treatment than the Canadian Indian Act. Nevertheless, the measurement of 'aboriginality' by 'blood quantum', and the growing agitation among European Australians about the 'half-castes' problem', were nationwide trends having all the hallmarks of coercive wardship in North America. The result was equally or more severe. Legislation, firmly in place across Australia by 1915, and strengthened in the 1930s, led to thousands of 'mixed-blood' children being forcibly removed from their parents and home territories by official will. Thus developed a familiar pattern of local contingencies within an overarching framework of persistent control. Some indigenous persons continued to live in traditional ways in the more isolated parts of the continent in areas adjudged, for the moment, to be of little or no economic value to white settlers. Those Aborigines in greater contact with the dominant society, lived in a variety of situations:

> A minority lived in institutions such as children's homes, supervised government reserves, and church-run missions, others on reserves with minimal supervision. Some worked within the European economy, the greatest number in the pastoral industry. Some lived on the margins of 'White Australia', in camps on pastoral properties, or on the outskirts of missions or country towns, frequently near the garbage tip, generally in material poverty. There were major variations in the treatment accorded Aborigines within each of these major categories. (Markus 1994: 139)

What overlaid this diversity of lifestyles and relationships was the invariance of the structural placement of aboriginal peoples in Australia as a minority characterised by political powerlessness.

New Zealand

There is much debate about when the two main islands now comprising New Zealand were first sighted and settled by Polynesian navigators, theories ranging from 500 to 1150 AD. Whatever the date of arrival, the indigenous peoples were less culturally diverse than their North American and Australian counterparts, and they occupied territories much smaller, and climatically and physically less hostile to humankind. Maori, as they came to call themselves after European settlement, were agriculturalists, hunters and gatherers. Despite important differences in dialect and custom, they broadly had the same language and way of life. People lived in kinship units of differing sizes and regional concentrations, tracing their descent back to a common ancestor on the original canoes. The key political and economic unit was the *hapu*, although larger groupings formed, often temporarily, when *hapu* joined together for common advantage in times of war and peace. Group categories of common descent affiliations linking scattered hapu were called *iwi*.

The three engines driving pre-colonial Maori societies, much like those among the peoples the French first encountered in Canada, were the pursuit of status (mana), food and technology, and political and territorial ascendancy (Belich 1996: 81). Thus the dynamics of co-operation and conflict continually redrew the lines between *hapu* and *iwi* as marriage, trade or military alliances were made and remade. This dynamism was both the political saviour and undoing of Maori after European settlement. Initially, the military strength and material and spiritual acquisitiveness of the indigenes worked to their advantage. When the Dutch, in the guise of Abel Tasman, visited in 1642, the resulting skirmish between explorers and indigenes prompted a hasty departure. Many of the British encounters in the late eighteenth century with 'the New Zealanders', including several visits by Cook (from 1769 to 1777), were also uneasy and conflictual. Nevertheless, many voyagers stayed around long enough to be impressed, not only by the qualities of the 'natives', but also the trading and settlement potential of the lands they occupied (Salmond 1997). The resultant progression of economic, cultural and political goods and actors, inserting New Zealand into a global orbit of trade, faith and empire, was not viewed by the indigenes as totally intrusive. Often, they eagerly seized and adapted them within existing patterns of practice and belief.

Seals, whales, timber and sex, were only some of the commodities sought, and exploited, with Maori assistance (Belich 1996). Even the missionaries found a reception seemingly propitious for the propagation of converts. Muskets and measles were the initial danger to Maori, not European might or ministrations. Both led to depopulation in the decades before mass settlement. Neither completely undermined a fragile coexistence resting on the military supremacy of Maori and the material advantages of Pakeha. The land-buying forays taking place in the 1830s threatened this delicate balance of power, as Sydney speculators, and Wakefield's New Zealand Company, already influential in South Australia, eyed the possibilities elsewhere in the Antipodes. The British government, mindful of the lessons of uncontrolled settlement in North America and Australia, and nervous of the expansionary aims of the French in the Pacific, sought to exert Crown control. In doing so they had, again, to tread a political tightrope between the competing interests of settlers and indigenes. The Colonial Office, influenced by the 1837 Select Committee on Aborigines in British Colonies, and vocal anti-slavery and pro-aboriginal lobbies, was now sceptical of the long-term benefits of a coercive reserves policy. Knowing they did not have the resources, or, in some quarters, the will, to enforce marginalisation of Maori, they opted for a policy of gradualist containment combining some elements of aboriginal self-government within a framework of benevolent paternalism, assimilation and control.

These principles are discernible in the treaty Governor Hobson and *hapu* and *iwi* leaders, attending or after the Waitangi ceremony in 1840, signed.[4] The motives and meanings of the signatories of the 1840 documents (the plural is deliberate given different versions in Maori and English) are still hotly debated, but the British state's intentions at the time seem clear. Crown officials saw Article 1 of the Treaty establishing British sovereignty. Article 2 facilitated orderly economic development by enforcing a Crown monopoly on land sales, and proffering an ambiguously worded form of Maori autonomy through its allusions to the protection of chiefly authority and the resources they controlled. Article 3 foreshadowed juridical and political incorporation of the indigenes through the granting of British subjecthood.

Following a long-established colonial convention, treaties bought time until the balance of power shifts towards the colonisers. The Treaty of Waitangi was no exception, although its single, consolidated nature eventually proved to be a more durable and widespread foundation for myths of national origin and destiny than many treaties with aboriginal peoples elsewhere. The nature of the treaty also epitomised a society in which the relative homogeneity of settlers and indigenes, and the size and topography of the country, enhanced the possibilities of the swift implant of a unitary state and the co-option and control of aboriginal peoples within it.

Gradual assimilation was the primary aim of the policies pursued while New Zealand remained a Crown colony. Given Maori had proved themselves adept at agriculture and trading, appeared to have accepted much of the Christian faith, and had acquired a level of literacy ahead of many white settlers, conditions seemed ripe for the indigenes to be evangelised, educated, incorporated into capitalism, and made subject to the British rule of law. Early attempts to set up negotiated *hapu*- and *iwi*-based local justice systems, and village *runanga* (councils), and the pursuance of a conservative land purchase policy, reflected the gradualist idealism of colonial officials and missionaries. The idealism was often genuine, but it was fatally flawed by European attitudes of racial and cultural superiority and their false assumption that Maori would gratefully assent to the workings of introduced institutions (Ward 1973). Reactions to the European legal and political process varied greatly between individuals and across regions, but the general pattern was one of selective acceptance and suspicion of the underlying intent of colonial policies and practices. Their suspicion was not misplaced.

In the 1850s, Governor Grey's forced 'amalgamation' policies, the premature establishment of a centralised settler assembly and constitution upholding European concepts of authority and property rights, and the twin problems of an expanding settler population and contracting

Maori land base, provoked an inevitable conflict. The encroachment of settlers and the problem of controlling 'the tendency of individual chiefs to sell their community's patrimony' (Ward and Hayward 1999: 384) provoked the formation of larger tribal assemblies and the development of new, regional, syncretic political and religious movements. The *kingitanga*, or King movement, for example, centred on the Waikato, effectively blocked further land sales in the middle of the North Island, and provided a base for resistance against further alienation in neighbouring regions. Resistance ultimately took a military form in the so-called 'Maori' or 'New Zealand' wars that, at their height in 1864, saw ten British regiments aided by colonial and Maori troops quell the opposition of what were deemed, by the state, to be rebels against the Crown. Guerrilla warfare continued in the bush-clad interior until the mid-1870s. The 'wars' were not a simple conflict over territory by two opposing peoples. They were 'a contest for authority, for mana and the question of whose law was to prevail' (Sorrenson 1981: 175). The South Island, and much of the North, was not directly involved in hostilities, although its outcome affected all regions. The combatants, particularly on the 'Maori' side were not clear-cut. *Hapu* and *iwi* fought or did not fight, and chose different sides to align with, depending on their perception of past disputes and current and future political gains.

Despite the winning of several battles, the eventual loss of the 'wars' proved pivotal in the shift from imperial control to settler interests, and a consequent move from attempts at peaceful and voluntary incorporation of Maori subjects to their forced marginalisation. A flurry of legislation in the mid to late 1860s established a Native Land Court and Maori justice provisions bringing tribespeople fully within the same property and legal codes as the settlers. Special Maori schools, with compulsory English tuition, provided an education designed to fit indigenes for restricted roles in capitalist society. The provision of four special Maori parliamentary seats and the granting of Maori male suffrage (in 1867) gave the indigenes an unprecedented political representation in settler society.

Such moves seem to show that the victors in the wars were at least prepared to make a place for respected foes in the state and polity. On a comparative scale, Maori were not ignored, swept aside or confined to reserves or missions. Local and international assessments of relations between 'the two races' supported a 'genial myth' of New Zealand as 'a notable exception in the annals of European expansion and indigenous retreat' (Denoon 1983: 184). What was exceptional were the precise political form and degree of acceptance and incorporation into setter society, but the overall position of the indigenes was comparatively much closer to their Canadian, and even Australian counterparts, than local settlers were prepared to concede. In the closing decades of the nineteenth century, some *hapu* were relatively wealthy. Particularly in more isolated areas, cultural heritages and local tribal organisation remained largely intact. There were still enough signs of a religious and political vigour to retain some autonomy in the face of increasing settler domination, but after the 1860s most Maori had a much firmer Hobson's choice than at the time of the signing of the Treaty of Waitangi with Captain William.

Maori could seek to hold on to their land through the Land Court, and thus, inevitably, be drawn into the European notion of viewing land as a marketable commodity, or risk losing that land by other means. They could accept an often inferior level of education and enter the labour force at its lowest end, or eke out an existence on the small, agriculturally marginal land bases left in their hands. They could either accept their status as subjects of the Crown or be, at best, totally ignored.

By the turn of the nineteenth century the bulk of the Maori population was relegated to a peripheral existence on the fringe of a rapidly expanding settler population. The indigenes, who had still been in a numerical majority at the end of the 1850s, had been reduced to a mere 4 per cent of the total New Zealand population by the early 1900s. In the mid-nineteenth century Maori still controlled most of the land and people in the North Island. By the end of that century less than one-sixth of the territory remained in Maori hands, with much of the most productive land leased, cheaply, to Pakeha farmers. Politically, Maori had been co-opted into the state and had at least a foothold within the seat of power. Co-option is a more benign policy than outright coercion, but it produced a comparable end result. Leaving conspiracy theory aside, 'by the end of the nineteenth century, Maori were undoubtedly a chapter heading in the rewriting of the history of their own land, but it was Pakeha who had editorial control' (Pearson 1990: 68).

The creation of aboriginal minorities

Aboriginal minorities are created out of the colonial processes through which metropolitan, national and provincial states establish territorial, political, economic and socio-cultural control over the indigenous peoples they encountered and subsequently 'settled'. Our case studies reveal a number of key differences in the types of encounters between indigenes and settlers shaping initial and subsequent contacts. Levels of conflict and co-operation were influenced by the respective numbers and military strength of colonisers and colonised; the size and topography of the colonies; the forms of aboriginal economic life and social organisation encountered by Europeans; and the set of colonial ideas and perceptions of 'the Other' shaping metropolitan policy and the views of local elites at the time of mass settlement. These factors, and many other contingencies, influenced the presence or otherwise of founding documents of co-recognition of native and colonial powers, and the unitary and federal political structures that developed to manage competing interests within newly created mass settler states. Nevertheless, overlying very important differences between our three societies are trends suggesting a consistent pattern of variations on a similar theme.

Microbes, muskets and men had fatal consequences. Aboriginal peoples were decimated by disease, starvation, war, forced migration and genocidal practices reducing their numbers to a mere fraction of the total estimated populations existing before European contact. Although the indigenes often adopted new technologies and used them to offer even greater resistance to intrusion, Europeans had more technological resources, and the new weapons of destruction were used against old and new enemies. Heightened 'tribal' skirmishes, small-scale raids and murders by private settlers, and, in the United States and New Zealand, full-scale battles against professional European soldiers (often with native allies), all took their toll (Diamond 1998: 374). Dispossession of land and territory was equally severe, through alienation, removal and seizure. As indigenous numbers and land bases dwindled, settler populations and land occupation swelled. Native peoples and their land were literally swamped by newcomers.

The evangelical incursion and the rapid dissemination of competing knowledge systems were a further vital factor in disrupting and transforming aboriginal peoples and their cultures. Native mythologies, kinship customs and socialisation practices that wove together a holistic fabric of ecological, economic and political relations were faced with varying levels of assault from the inrush of novel ideas matching the tide of strangers. Many indigenous peoples in North America and New Zealand had been nominally Christianised by the end of the nineteenth century. The presence of Europeans compelled Amerindians and Maori to re-examine their animistic sense of the cosmos and broaden their sense of humanness in their own and other worlds. Christianity proved, with adaptation, capable of meeting this need. The political result was often paradoxical. Syncretic beliefs frequently articulated and inspired millenarian political activity of strategic attack or withdrawal, but the very same conditions provided fertile ground for direct and indirect propagation of internal division and disruption that weakened the possibilities of solidaristic resistance. In other contexts, notably Australia, where the bridges between different sets of ideas were decidedly flimsier, the epistemological gulf between peoples was seized upon as a ready rationale for more direct and blatant coercion. In all settler societies the matching of religious ideals to racist hierarchies proved to be the most potent colonising force, supporting, at best, a recognition of common humanity in a fateful transition towards the inevitability of white superiority. At worst, combined sacred and pseudo-scientific beliefs explained away the most profane of acts.

Metaphysics were also combined with material advantage in the rapid intrusion of capitalism; resulting in severe damage to indigenous economies, the loss of strategic natural resources, and unfavourable distribution of surpluses from remaining or previously occupied aboriginal territories. The arrival of Europeans transformed many indigenous peoples into producers for, and customers in, world commodity markets (Cornell 1988a: 20). Both new roles had a major impact on the balance between peoples and their local ecologies, relations within previously non-cash trading indigenous economic systems, and the effects of new modes of aspiration and consumption on existing patterns of status and ranking. As Cornell notes of the North American fur trade, with his remarks having wider applicability to, for example, early Maori trading in other commodities.

> For (the Indians) the trade was decidedly ambiguous. It gave some groups unprecedented power and even, for a while, the means of survival in the face of European invasion. But it also transformed their environments, their cultures, and their lives, and linked them irrevocably to an evolving economic order that ultimately had no use for them. (Cornell 1988a: 19)

The phrase 'ultimately had no use', needs qualifying, given the ongoing demand for aboriginal labour in a wide range of economic activities in North America and the Antipodes. What Cornell is stressing is the critical shift in the balance of power from dependence of European capital on local indigenous economies and resources, towards a situation where aboriginal occupied land greatly outweighed their labour as a valued resource. Deprivation of a land base, depletion of numbers, and the formation of ethnic divisions of labour where enclaves of indigenes acted as a reserve pool of workers, often on a seasonal and casual basis, were common features of colonial invasion in all three of our case studies.

An imposed political and legal system acted as a further, vital feature of encapsulation. Here lies the unique political quality of aboriginal minorities. What began as a policy of land acquisition and 'peace making' gradually evolved into a distinctive federal-aboriginal relationship, or, in New Zealand's case, a special indigenous form of political representation within a unitary state. Dispossession is the hallmark of aboriginal minorities. For indigenous peoples, the nation-states they live within are stepfathers, not mother countries. Yet in its dealings with these minorities settler states came to act as though *they* were the hosts.

Tribe, ethnie or nations?

How do we describe and analyse the political process through which the peoples who were 'in place' at the point of European arrival and invasion were forced into new social and political formations by colonisation? Given the differences and similarities described above it seems pertinent to reconsider some conceptual questions raised in the last chapter, before drawing some conclusions together about initial aboriginal/settler contacts and resultant political change. The term 'peoples' is possibly uncontentious, but much ink has been spilt debating the merits of 'tribal', 'ethnic' and 'national' prefixes? And what of being 'in place'? As Perry notes, the 'place' that peoples were 'in' 'implies far more than the locality where they happened to be...at the time outsiders first encountered them' (Perry 1996: 8). The relationship between such peoples and their understanding of land, territory and belonging contained innumerable subtleties that eluded the 'outsiders', even if they had the desire to enter empathically the life world of those they had encountered. Some peoples stayed in the same place on at least a semi-permanent basis, and had conceptions of 'their' territory, that seemed to approximate to European beliefs. Others shifted continuously and expansively, but retained a sense of familiar or unfamiliar places and notions of who 'we' are in the scheme of things. This rich variety of meanings and practices posed problems for universalising, colonising states, although it proved ideal for policies of divide and rule.

One solution was the devising of uniform categories and unified systems of control and imposing them on political and cultural diversity. 'Aborigine', 'Indian', and 'Maori' arose out of the dynamics of imposition and acquisition, of categorisation and identification. Inelegantly, we might call this aboriginalisation. Such categories embraced a wide array of indigenous socio-political groups and communities, although the basis and form of communality shifted over time and place. Ultimately, the categories themselves became the basis for political group formation, and communal solidarities ebbed and flowed based on categories-cum-groups, although the conceptual tensions between these alternative bases of politicisation remained in place.

Despite their highly contested status, I think the terms 'tribe', 'ethnicity' and 'nation' can aid us in gaining some purchase on the slippery slope of conceptualising the formation of aboriginal minorities. The recent remarks of Calhoun (1997: 36–42) on the distinctions between kinship, ethnicity and nationality are a useful starting point. Calhoun argues each of these concepts is a dynamic feature of the making and remaking of social and political existence, not a static unit of organisation. Kinship (and descent) provides basic organising principles for experiencing immediate social, economic and political life and for inserting such lives into a broader understanding of one's own and other kin's place in the world. Such principles directly shape individual and group relations and they are embedded within understandings of wider, indirect, frameworks of categorical identity like clans and age sets.

One cannot specify neat population densities to accord with different levels of political organisation, but there are major shifts in the size and territory encompassed by nationalities and clans for example, despite both being categorical extensions of interpersonal relations. Nationality is a large categorical unit encompassing many groups and describing them without reference to internal differences. Consequently, national identity provides a layering of attachment above kinship and descent affiliation, and it is problematic whether these 'lower' allegiances will reinforce or be in tension with 'the nation'. Ideal-typically, Calhoun avers, displaying his preference for seeing 'nations' as modern phenomena, 'one is a member of a nation directly as an individual' (Calhoun 1997: 39). Kinship and descent are important in modern nations, and familial myths and metaphors are often drawn upon by nationalists to engender a sense of communality, but kinship and descent are not the stuff of modern nations as they are of clans.

Ethnicity occupies an intermediary position between kinship and nationality, becoming important when interaction occurs between multiple, proximate groups, specifically when such groups are not organised by the same kinship and cultural principles. Ethnicity is always interactive, becoming salient 'at the boundary between internal ways of organising group life and external attribution of character by others' (ibid.: 40). In short, as noted in the last chapter, ethnic groups define themselves by comparison with others.

Underlying Calhoun's approach is the key political question of how strangers are categorised and what actions and organisation their presence stimulates. Kin relations and categories are organised among known members. Such relations and categories may not operate purely face to face, although in small, isolated populations this is the case, but kinship principles provide the 'test' for inclusion of others in lineage and ancestry terms. Age and sex differences clearly operate as further reference points. Ethnic relations form on the basis of the known presence of strangers. Kin relations operate in groups that exist in complete isolation from others, ethnic relations never do, although ethnic identification may rest on the basis of believed past relations with strangers rather than the co-presence of 'us' and 'them' now.

If ethnic categories, groups or communities form *in relation to* strangers, their national counterparts *incorporate* strangers, in modern times, *en masse*. Nations are *abstract* communities (James 1996: 184), comprised mainly of strangers, embracing relations with ethnically mixed people one has never met, and to whom you are not related in kin and descent terms, despite possible nationalist rhetoric of belonging to the same 'family of the nation'.

Given these distinctions between kin, ethnic and national affiliation, is there a place for 'the tribe' in this scheme of things? Conceptual imprecision and contamination by Eurocentric colonial notions of 'primitive peoples' certainly beg caution. But if contestability were a guide to word usage the social analysts' thesaurus would be a book of blank pages. Crone (1986: 51), for example, suggests 'tribe' is best defined as 'a descent group which constitutes a political community'. In tribes, genealogical ascription provides a basis for political integration over and above a level required for communal production and the allocation of collective property rights. So tribes need to be distinguished from small, intermarrying groups having only a vague sense of unity and those relying on age organisation as an alternative basis to descent for political organisation. Her perspective places the tribe within a continuum that, arguably, could have the band at one extremity and chiefdoms at the other. Most groups along this continuum, organised primarily around kin, sex and age relations, lack an identifiable, specialised, political community (viz. the tribe).

By defining the tribe as a particular form of political organisation, the concept is given more precision than the much vaguer use of 'cultural' or 'ethnic' group. Neither shared culture, language, nor ethnicity necessarily signifies political unity, and ethnicity, although vitally concerned with descent, is not confined to this aspect of relations. Ethnicity, as a mechanism of inclusion and exclusion, seems more appropriately confined to relations *between* tribes, and encounters between tribes and non-tribespeople. Here, Anthony Smith's use of the term *ethnie* can be put to use to describe bounded, interactive units of affiliation found among some indigenous peoples prior to European settlement. Ethnie, for Smith (1986: 189), are networks of communication found throughout the world in the pre-modern era, that promote group clusters of common language and custom. Ethnie traditions, myths and sentiments might form the basis for eventual nation-making, most probably when pre-modern and modern worlds collide.

If there is some slippage between ethnie and 'nations', we can feel more assured tribes are not states, since their organising principles are fundamentally different. For states (unlike tribes) are organised around concepts like polity, class or bureaucracy, external and often not directly visible to people and requiring 'a great deal of cultural brainwashing' for (them) to appear as natural (Crone 1986: 66). In this they resemble the abstract communities of nations, but, as we have noted before, there is no automatic congruence between states as a form of political organisation, and nations as a particular sense of peoplehood.

There is little profit in seeking to discern 'representative' political units among the array of peoples who occupied pre-European contact territories, but some general trends seem to enjoy widespread support in a formidable literature. The levels of socio-political organisation found across the North American continent at the time of European contact encompassed a profusion of small (less than 50) family units, and larger clan-based villages and bands. Much less typical were tribes, and even rarer, multi-tribal confederations, leagues or 'nations' (Champagne 1989). These varied groups coexisted with neighbours with whom they might exchange or trade goods or persons, intermarry, and, in some instances, occasionally join in communal events like hunts and ceremonies. Peoples also feuded and fought, and formed and re-formed different levels of alliance in the process. What distinguished these groups was the level of political identity and integration beyond the immediacy of family and kin relations. Whether such groups had ranking systems, how hierarchical they were, and what propensity they showed to develop systems of governance allowing more long-standing alliances between sub-tribal and tribal societies, are key distinctions. Patterns of short-run or long-term fission and fusion, within and among different groups of people, predated the arrival of Europeans, as indigenes responded to environmental and technological changes and the contingencies of local and regional relations with others.

We can also extend much of the literature on the United States to Canada, not least because the borders between these states were artificially placed across the far less distinct boundaries of indigenous perceptions of territory. Most peoples in Canada also lived in relatively egalitarian, sub-tribal societies within which there was no entrenched authority or wealth hierarchy, nor any strict division between rulers and ruled (Boldt 1993: 119). In these settings formal political 'offices' were noticeably absent, and decision-making was a communal, collective endeavour. But chiefdoms also existed in Canada, and some 'tribe-like' societies, notably in the Pacific north-west, had more pronounced hierarchical arrangements between leaders and led.

The semi-nomadic hunting and gathering groups in Australia also display variation in size and level of organisation, and relations between neighbours and strangers, but these cover a shorter spectrum of sub-tribal, and, far more debatably, tribal, possibilities (Turner 1980). Political power and authority related to age and sex differences, with older men (and some women) having most influence in small-scale settings of face-to-face relations. If elders were prevalent, there was a noticeable lack of chiefdoms, or, indeed, any ranked societies exhibiting forms of corporate political control.

In contrast, pre-contact 'Maori' people were universally located within chiefly societies, but the size, density and degree of political corporateness of particular groups of people were constantly in flux. *Iwi* was the 'tribal' category within which groups identified with shared common descent to a known ancestor. *Hapu*, or a fragment or cluster of same, was the unit of population within which even smaller extended family groups (*whanau*) lived out their daily lives. In the eighteenth century, before mass colonisation, the *hapu* was the organisational context within which 'Maori' sought alliances of defence and offence and generally made policy towards others (Ballara 1998: 124).

Belich (1996: 85), reflecting on the dynamics of Maori political organisation, introduces a useful distinction between kin, neighbour and stranger zones having wider applicability to the distinctions between categories, groups and communities of persons discussed above. Kin zones, for Belich, denote permanent or regular assemblies of face-to-face interactions, neighbour zones embrace persons in close proximity, some of whom could be directly known, others indirectly categorised. The stranger zone defines everybody else within an imagined area. Extending the logic of his argument one can argue the arrival of

Europeans heightened or introduced entirely new ethnic imaginings of neighbours, while the eventual engulfment by invading mass settler states ultimately inserted tribal kin relations into a national and international world of strangers.

Nations without states?

Aboriginal minorities are distinctive because of the nature of their dispossession, the centrality of territorial control in this process, and the linking of these factors by particular socio-legal and political relations. All three processes had major influences on political organisation and identity because they promoted profound changes in the frequency and form of encounters with strangers, the level of resources indigenous peoples controlled, and the quality of power relationships among themselves and in dealings with others. European exploration and trading altered the relationships between the peoples 'in place' at the time of contact. Subsequent settlement and colonisation massively displaced such peoples and introduced new layers of categorisation and administration, affecting the way indigenes viewed 'us' and 'them'. As Cornell (1988a: 72) notes, political identity and organisation did not always change in tandem. Organisationally, indigenes were forced and/or chose to restructure their patterns of political behaviour. Conceptually, native peoples voluntarily or involuntarily reformulated their group identities.

Resistance to colonial expansion often led to increases in the scale of indigenous political units. Kin-based groups coalesced into tribes or confederations to fight wars (against or with colonisers); formed non-military regional coalitions to combat land sales; or combined into religious movements to protest or retreat from spiritual and material assaults. These forms of political reorganisation were extensions of historical patterns of coalition and division as well as innovations in the arena of contacts between themselves and Europeans. By the end of the nineteenth century in North America and the Antipodes indigenous peoples were still diverse and scattered, but they were now living in settler states that had created uniform or very broad categories to administer such peoples in vastly changed territorial spaces. The initial colonisation process left some pieces of the pre-contact indigenous jigsaw untouched, other pieces were left in place, but much reduced in size. Many pieces were lost, destroyed or flung far and wide. In the process the jigsaw was renamed and its pieces forced into new shapes.

As our case studies reveal, colonising settler states triggered the formation of new political communities by introducing systems of governance and surveillance through the imposition of new leadership structures and political arrangements, or by influencing complex sets of appropriations arising from settler/native interaction. Chiefs, real or imagined, were recognised. Band, village or 'tribal' councils were appointed, ignoring, complementing or unsettling traditional patterns of leadership. The incorporation of indigenous societies into colonial, bureaucratic systems of control lends weight to those who argue concepts like 'the tribe' and other forms of extra-local political institution arise out of prolonged subjection to state powers and the undermining of kin-based organisation (Fried 1975). But not all tribal organisation was the outcome of exposure to states, as many Polynesian and some North American chiefly societies reveal. The state both subverted 'tribal' organisation and created it in differing circumstances, with the political meaning of 'tribe' being used in different ways in different contexts: a process of revalorisation still operating today.

The introduction of state-generated political labels, institutions and places did not necessarily eradicate pre-contact names, *mores* and boundaries, it promoted new levels of political identity, organisation and settlement coexisting with past frames of reference. Kin, tribal, ethnic and national levels of meaning became available as interactions between strangers increased, although the relationship between the organisational and conceptual elements of political life remained complex and problematic. In part, this depended on the degree of displacement and marginalisation experienced by particular indigenous societies. For example, in the United States many peoples were forced onto reserves but often still within their own territories. In Canada, indigenes were more often scattered across territories, with several different bands occupying the same, frequently smaller, reserves. In Australia, reserves were even less common, but, as in North America, intermixing was prevalent in missions and residential schools, and in the fringe settlements outside townships. A reserve policy was not adopted in New Zealand, but *hapu* and *iwi* were still pushed back into the margins of their own or others' territory. At one end of a continuum of cultural and geographical persistence indigenes remained in isolated, familiar places, still protected by internal tyrannies of distance and ecological hardship, but increasingly influenced by knowledge of events elsewhere. At the other extreme, native peoples were forced into 'reserved' alien places, experiencing involuntary segregation and assimilation. Between, were many groups and individuals pushed back into the periphery of society, capitalism and the polity, but reflecting varying degrees of movement within and across the spectrum of possibilities.

The trend in all of these situations was towards increased contact and incorporation into 'the dominant culture', and reorganisation into larger-scale political units as the boundaries of experience and constraint widened. Kin-based relations were still vitally important, and quite possibly the most immediate signifier of who 'we' are, and to whose authority in ancestral and lineage terms we should defer. And neighbouring and regional relations were by far the most common horizon. But new measures of political status had been set beside the old, and imposed and/or accepted ascriptions of a different order were now in place. Beyond small-scale local kin relations, 'tribal' and 'ethnic' categories and groups were more evident. 'We' were now 'Indians', 'Maori' and 'Aborigine' as well as Assiniboine, Arawa or Aranda in relation to a settler 'them'. Indigenous people returned the 'compliment' of stereotyping, using their own general names for others. Both sides of the 'us' and 'them' equation created and recreated changing patterns of ethnic and racial labelling disguising the different degrees of differentiation within native and settler populations. The interesting question is how far these different categories had become conceptual frameworks for ethnic group affiliation, with the potential for forging communal political activity, potentially of a national character.

Oommen (1997: 97) has recently suggested that it is profitable to draw a distinction between national and ethnic groups when describing the outcome of colonisation for different sets of indigenous peoples. He believes the key distinguishing feature of group formation is the relationship between culture and territory. Ethnicity is a product of conquest and immigration. 'Ethnification' describes the process through which the link between territory and culture is stretched or severed by colonisation. In contrast, nations are territorially anchored cultural communities within which a national collectivity has established a moral claim over its homeland. Thus, indigenous peoples, for Oommen, have been transformed into either a 'minoritised' and marginalised collectivity in their own territories as national groups (for example, reserve 'first nations') or they have been 'ethnified' by dispossession and displacement.

This approach succeeds in distilling many essentials of colonisation, classical and internal, into a useful illustration of different comparative outcomes, but the binary contrast is ultimately too simplistic. All indigenous peoples experienced some degree of ethnification after colonisation, and this process was far from unknown in some regions before European contact. The emergence of 'national projects' was also not confined to indigenes remaining in their ancestral homelands, although one should acknowledge the notions of 'being in place' or 'displaced' did have a major influence on the shape and outcome of future rights claims. What needs stressing is the qualitatively different nature of these projects in pre-modern and modern times.

We do not need to venture into the labyrinth of debate about the origins of states and nations, to acknowledge the vast majority of meetings between indigenous peoples and settlers were between persons from stateless and state-organised societies. These encounters took place within a world rapidly becoming organised into nation-states. The formation of aboriginal minorities took place over a time period when their colonisers increasingly viewed *modern* nations existing in a world of states. Within this world the political project of nation-making takes place against the backcloth of statehood, even if a nation-state was not necessarily the ultimate goal of all nationalists. Perceptions of nationhood among the political actors in mass settler societies altered in step with the geopolitics of global empires in *both* the old and new worlds. The juxtaposition of 'nationhood' and the idea of the longevity of 'worlds' neatly illustrates the point.

Nation has the same linguistic roots as 'native'. In seventeenth-century Europe the term simply meant 'the people of some particular place or region, by the eighteenth the ideas of state and nation had become more frequently intertwined' (Perry 1996: 11). In the nineteenth century 'statist' conceptions of nations were paramount, but lexical and politically motivated usage was interwoven. Initially, colonisers often used the term 'nation' while denying any meaningful 'Western' political structure to the indigenes they encountered (ibid.). Later, new words replaced 'nation' in treaties and legal/political frameworks, 'tribe' and 'band' being common framing devices, or they significantly qualified the word 'nation'. Consider Supreme Court Justice Marshall's coining (in 1835) of the phrase 'domestic dependent *nations*' in the United States (my emphasis) to describe what he, and many indigenous peoples by the early to mid-nineteenth century, called groups of American Indians. What better illustration could one find of an abstract community in the making, whose statist origins were forged within the fires of modernist revolution, seeking to define the constitutional position of peoples no less fundamentally changed by the clash of pre-modern and modern forces. The definitional (and constitutional) problem under scrutiny being solved by qualifying the 'nation' status and nesting it within a 'state'. Significantly, as we have seen, other colonies of settlement that remained British, politically and legally incorporated indigenous peoples in rather different ways.

Aboriginality, to return to Beckett's point opening this chapter, is a rather potent artefact resonant with past and current socio-legal, political and cultural meanings. Socio-legally it inserted indigenous peoples into a history of national and international discourses and actions relating to the juridical claims that can be made on the basis of 'being in place' at the point of colonial contact. Politically, aboriginality eventually provided a platform for the pursuit of power, paradoxically, marking the entry and potential exit from minority status. Culturally, 'aboriginal' signified a material and symbolic construction of 'being' relating to this socio-legal and political positioning. But what of the 'majorities' whose interactive presence the artefact derives from? They also, ultimately, emerge from the same historical juncture, with their own prehistories. At the time of mass colonisation Britain was a multi-nation-state remaking itself while it was making 'other worlds' in various parts of its Empire. The British imperial diaspora in settler societies exemplified this process. So having looked at indigenous peoples without states, let us now consider whether settlers had states without nations?

3
States without Nations

By the turn of the nineteenth century local elites within the colonies of settlement had achieved ascendancy in statist terms. Politically, the process of colonisation had dispossessed indigenous peoples, leaving them, at best, as minority players in the state arena. Mass settlement of British migrants had cemented in place the governmental, judicial, militarist and educative institutions that produced and reproduced political rule, surveillance and, ultimately, at least for many settlers and their descendants, legitimate violence. But what were the borders of legitimacy, and how effectively could they be patrolled?

Ideally, for elites, statehood is reinforced by a patriotism finding its most solid foundation on national sentiment. States become linked to nations by a common thread of people, polity and territory. These foundations have to be constructed and continually refurbished. State-making for elites is about setting in place a polity, with its requisite institutional supports, that can successfully claim sovereignty over a bounded terrain. The task is the harmonising of politics and geography within these confines. Nation-making is the, potentially, complementary process of achieving a sense of belonging to the aggregate of people who occupy a territory – the establishment of an abstract national community. The potential is often unrealised. Patriotic and national loyalties may be divided, because the object of support is not the same. Loyalty to the state (patriotism) should not be analytically confused with support for 'the nation' (nationalism), although, empirically, separation of these sentiments is difficult. The elite endeavour to erect an autonomous, self-governing state, does not depend on the creation of a common peoplehood. In fact the reverse is often the case. The state makes the nation. Yet sovereignty is rarely uncontested and 'the people' are seldom homogeneous. *Patria* is politically fraught. *Natio* is ethnically divided. The 'aboriginal problem' confirmed these maxims, but what of the settlers, their descendants and other 'others'? Let us return to our case studies before reviewing this question in general.

The French fact

Ambivalence runs through the entire history of Quebec as a distinct people within a larger federation. The basis of this ambivalence resides within a political, cultural and linguistic duality arising out of the history of French–British settlement in the seventeenth and eighteenth centuries. Canada, in contrast to the Antipodes, was founded on a colonial history of competing colonisers. Colonies, as I noted earlier, are indirectly controlled either from the metropole through establishing a limited, strategic, collaborative infrastructure, or by extensive settlement swamping the indigenous populace in the process of establishing new states and nations. In British North America the limited settlement of the French met the massive colonisation pattern of the British (See 1986: 109). Out of this meeting arose what André Siegfried called 'a *modus vivendi* without cordiality'.

France, concerned with its own internal religious conflicts, political consolidation in Europe, and expansionary aims in the Caribbean, invested little capital and manpower in New France. 'Colonisation' was left to metropolitan-controlled French missionaries and merchants, or private fur traders. At the time of the Conquest (1759), the French were a numerical majority among the settlers, and many of the *habitants* were clustered in a compact territory along the Saint Lawrence river organised in feudal-like rural parishes. The character of Quebec was concentrated, after the Conquest, by its abandonment by the French metropole, the exodus of much of the French commercial and political upper classes, and the local entrenchment of the political control of the Catholic Church (See 1980: 118). Initially, the British Crown sought to introduce a draconian programme of forced assimilatory measures as set out in the Royal Proclamation of 1763, but the British military and colonial officials in Quebec adopted a more conciliatory line. The external threat from the American rebels, and the need to ensure the loyalty of the clerical elite, led to the British incorporating the French into a governing structure giving them a significant degree of legal and cultural autonomy. The Quebec Act (1774) countermanded the assimilatory stance of the Proclamation and established what was to prove a long tradition of a British, then Canadian, state strategy of devolution and accommodation of 'the French fact'. Quebec retained its own language, seigneurial land system, old civil law, religious freedom and the restoration of its boundaries to pre-Conquest dimensions, although it was not granted a separate political assembly and its leaders were selected through a British-imposed electoral system.

These concessions illustrate the maxim that colonisation is as much a policy of seduction as coercion. The British metropole was ever mindful of the continuing military threat from the south and its desire to protect and further its financial and trading interests. Hence the provision of a territorially defined dualism forming the basis for subsequent French Canadian political organisation and the advocacy of ethnic particularistic interests within the Canadian heartland.

The stratification system within Quebec was a vital ingredient in explaining the eventual shape of ethnic politics. Most of the *habitants* were rural farmers and artisans, politically controlled by small, competing clerical and professional elites. The Catholic hierarchy in Quebec, the cornerstone of a fledgling nation since the Quebec Act (See 1980: 119), was co-opted as a regional minority elite into the British-Canadian state. The French Canadian clerical elite adopted a strategy of maintaining their ethnic identity and sectional political supremacy at the expense of a broader, structured economic and political subordinance. *Canadiens* controlled religious, legal and medical services, Anglophones dominated commerce. Each group's elites intermingled with colonial authorities to control the Province.

The Quebec Act's restoration of the old colonial order sparked fierce resistance among the British settlers whose numbers had been swelled by the thousands of Loyalists who crossed into lower Canada as a result of the American victory. The arrival of these settlers and the boosting of a small, but powerful English commercial class, 'completed the conquest of New France. Canada was not to be French, but French and English' (Wade 1968: 281). The Loyalists, firmly committed to the British flag and Empire, some independence of church and state, and representative governance, resented a local, elitist political structure dominated by a foreign faith and language. They succeeded in passing a Constitution Act in 1791 dividing the colony into Upper and Lower Canada, each province having its own Governor General and elected assembly. A restricted property franchise ensured the political ascendancy of a powerful British oligarchy of landed and mercantile interests in a 'Family Compact' with the metropolitan-appointed colonial administration. In Lower Canada, where a large majority of the population was *Canadien*, the French presence controlled the provincial Assembly, but only a handful of Canadian French persons was elected to the executive and legislative councils. At this level, the Chateau Clique, most of whom were English-speaking, had a virtual monopoly on political power.

The oligarchic shape of governance in Upper and Lower Canada promoted political unrest, shaped as much by class as ethnic interests, and framed within different political agendas. In Upper Canada the conflict was over the democratisation and freeing up of frontier capitalism. Hostilities were sporadic, relatively bloodless and easily quelled by the state. In Lower Canada, the demands for greater political and economic equality were set within a populist, nationalistic framework that promoted more bloody encounters between protesters and the colonial state. The names of the 'rebels' speak volumes here. In Upper Canada they were Reformers, in Lower, *Patriotes*. The events of 1837–8, particularly the solitary victory over British troops at St Denis, and the subsequent death or exile of prominent *Patriotes*, became, literally, a monument to the birth of a Quebec nation. Another image of oppression was woven into a rich tapestry of French Canadian myths of origin and destiny.

In truth, the Lower 'rebellion' always embraced Anglophone sympathisers and was against Church as well as Crown, and the power of *Canadien* and British middle- and upper-class alliances. These factors loomed large in subsequent decades, particularly since Lord Durham's report (in 1839) on the rebellion stipulated assimilation into a unitary state as a remedy for the, now apocryphal, 'two nations warring in the bosom of a single state'. A union of 'the two Canadas' occurred in 1841, but it reflected a renewed coalition between French and British elites within a legislature displaying a dual linguistic and ethnic administration. Ultimately, this unwieldy arrangement collapsed under its own impracticality. The gulf between a political class coalition seeking to balance French and British interests, within a country whose demographic and economic profile revealed a marked Anglophone bias, became all too apparent.

Between 1815 and 1865 British North America received nearly as many emigrants from Britain as the entire American continent had received from the whole of Europe between 1500 and 1783. Most of them went to the United States, but what was to become Canada received sufficient British migrants, and enough of them stayed, to greatly outnumber a dwindling French population (Buckner 1997). The *Canadien* elite in Quebec was faced with an English counterpart whose economic control was disproportionate to their numbers. Beyond the province they confronted a country becoming swamped with British settlers of varying class complexions. Looking south, they saw many of their countrymen crossing into states espousing republicanism. Faced with this external threat a British monarchical tradition might, ironically, be a better bulwark against change for those who savoured the autocratic underpinnings of French society. Given this scenario, French-speaking elites 'chose' to maintain the status quo. Lower Canada voted narrowly for confederation[1] and the aptly named British North American Act created a new Canada while conserving an old Quebec. The province had its own government, education system, language and legal institutions. At the federal level French Canadian politicians occupied prominent positions in the main Canadian parties (Keating 1997: 172).

With confederation Canada cemented a cultural and linguistic duality, a pluralistic compact within which many of Canada's two largest and most powerful populations did not generally participate in the same educational, social and religious networks. A *de jure* hyphenated identity, if you will forgive the presentist phrase, was therefore officially sanctioned despite *de facto* resentments on both sides of the cultural fence.

The French Canadian population rapidly became isolated, cultural islands, within a sea of British and other migrants, with only Quebec, and to lesser extent, Acadia, having the critical mass to sustain 'the French fact'. Nevertheless, a Canadian ideology of two founding 'races' or 'nations' had emerged. This image, 'would not only obliterate the history, role and claims of aboriginal peoples, but also placate the Québécois and, for a time, forestall their own claims to national sovereignty (Stasiulis and Jhappan 1995: 110). But the use of the term *Québécois* here is a trifle premature. *La survivance* was an essentially defensive nationalism based more on myths of origin than destiny at this point and French-speaking Quebeckers continued to call themselves *Canadien français* (McRoberts 1984: 56).[2] The French Canadian elite saw Quebec as the homeland of the French in North America (not just Canada).

For the remainder of the nineteenth, and much of the twentieth, centuries, a pan-French *Canadien* national identity existed. It was fed by the fear of demographic swamping and British Canadian control. Nationalism was also fanned by the flames of anger at the time of the Louis Riel-led, Métis 'rebellions' in Manitoba and Saskatchewan, and the festering questions of linguistic and religious rights in the schools of New Brunswick, the North West provinces and Ontario. Canada's support for Britain's imperial adventures and participation in the Boer and First World Wars also stretched the compact between French and British elites (within Conservative and then Liberal Party circles) to near breaking-point. Ultimately, however, on the national and international front, French Canadian elite interests were as much a product of capitalism as ethnic particularism. In Quebec the reverse was true. Faith, farm and family were the trinity Catholic elites used to maintain their control, with language providing a persistent thread in a story stretching back to the *habitants* and forward to what was to become *Québécois*. Add in a descent pattern based on the demographics of a limited French immigration and vigorous natural increase and we have a recipe for ethnic nationalism, in this case, centred on the collective survival of a bounded, organic community faced with a continual external threat.

English Canada

In French Canada the nation created a state, in English (or British) Canada this equation is reversed. But what was *English* Canada? As Jeffrey Ayres (1995: 182) notes, 'the term "English Canada" does not suggest either an ethnic group or a sovereign nation-state, but rather a national community linked by the use of the English language and bolstered by certain symbols and myths essential to its collective identity'. Writing towards the end of the twentieth century, Ayres is careful to distance himself from any suggestion that English Canada is typified by an 'essential Britishness', but a century earlier, as he concedes, the contention is far more apposite. In this period the Canadian state and polity managed to fashion an ephemeral alliance between imperialism, nationalism and patriotism.

Building on a British emigrant infrastructure, initially flimsy, and eventually thoroughly reconstituted, many Canadians after Confederation developed a temporary assurance of a common origin and destiny belying the absence of an American-style foundation. Canadian myths, indeed, made a virtue of such a deficiency. After 1783 approximately 60 000 Loyalists moved north, and, as noted above, were instrumental in the partition of Upper and Lower Canada. Not all were English-speaking and most were native-born Americans, not British emigrants. The lengthy struggle against France and the brief war with America in 1812–14 undoubtedly bolstered imperial British loyalty among Anglophones, but this political allegiance did not remove a receptivity to American cultural influences (Buckner 1997: 15). Thus, if ambivalence persistently marked 'The French/English Fact' within Canada, it also characterised relations between the two northern Americas.

Innumerable Canadian schoolbooks in the nineteenth, and much of the twentieth, centuries, portrayed the Loyalist period as an important milestone on a road to self-government originating with Wolf successfully storming the Heights of Abraham in Montreal (Francis 1997: 56). More recently, historians have acknowledged the pivotal cultural and political impact of later British immigration. Between 1815 and 1837 almost half a million British migrants arrived in British North America, while settlers from the 'other America' were a mere handful. By 1861 the Francophone population had trebled by natural increase, the Anglophone population had swelled tenfold, largely through British emigration. This swamping transformed what was soon to become Canada. The aboriginal population, and *Canadiens* were scattered and compacted into respective minor and major ethnic nodes of resistance. Their languages and cultures were often retained, but their earlier stages of political and economic supremacy had been supplanted by the English vernacular and British institutions. The massive influx of migrants ensured British dominance in a post-Confederation state whose continued links with Crown and Empire were viewed, by most English and many French-speaking members of national elites, as providing a protective shield against an expansive America (Sturgis 1997: 97). The question was whether this elite view had penetrated the minds of the masses. As John A. Macdonald, one of the fathers of Confederation, is reputed to have said, 'We have made Canada; now we must make Canadians' (ibid.: 102). A process of Canadianisation was duly instituted, aided more by demography than conspiracy. Further British immigration recruiting schemes were initiated, with emphasis placed on remedying the imbalance between men and women. Upper- and middle-class women in particular, shared the vision of their male counterparts that Canada should become a better Britain (Bacchi 1983).

Education, religion and the media were all seen as important vehicles of popular nationalism, with English a vital prerequisite of vernacular culture. Canadians, like Americans, viewed the little red schoolhouse as a key vehicle for ethnic change, with the churches, invoking a Protestant 'social Christianity', adding a further link between state and nation (Sturgis 1997: 114). Whether in the pulpit or classroom, teachers were frequently British-born. The Canadian press often wore patriotic garb, and, eventually aided by the transatlantic cable, introduced the latest imperial images of empire into Canadian living-rooms. From the mid-nineteenth century the monarchy became an increasingly popular institution. Royal tours in 1860 and 1901 drew huge crowds in all the major cities, including Montreal and Quebec (Buckner 1997: 24). Victoria Day, initiated in Toronto in 1849, became a national institution by the end of the century, and Empire Day (introduced in 1899) became Canada's Fourth of July (Francis 1997: 65).

These selective signs of imitation and celebration buttress the argument that the nationalism of English-speaking Canada was attempting to construct a nation using a state template of British institutions, and a national identity was emerging based on a British ethnic core. But this weave of civil and ethnic nationalisms was not a simple emulative process. 'British emigrants and their native-born were becoming more British and yet more Canadian at the same time' (Buckner 1997: 36). For most Anglophones, English Canada was an expression of a Canadian nationality embracing a British nationality extending beyond the boundaries of their state. For their part, Francophones continued to view themselves as *Canadiens*, a nationality anchored firmly in a quasi-state, Quebec, within Canada.

Better British

There was no 'French Fact' in Australia. Political elites in the colonies and later in federated Australia were dominated by British, and, to a lesser extent, Irish immigrants until the First World War. Being native-born is hardly an infallible guide to local national feeling. In all the colonies of settlement many colonial-born continued to regard Britain as 'home' and many emigrants swiftly became committed to their new abodes. Some commentators can detect the stirring of an Australian nationalism in the early part of the nineteenth century, but there is general agreement that its last few decades were more propitious for those wanting to determine a more tangible sense of who Australians were, and wanted to be. Until 1880, when the native-born had become a majority, the infusion of, predominantly English, convicts (until the 1840s), and a continued stream of voluntary and assisted British migrants 'enveloped the growing core of colonial-born Australians, largely smothering an incipient nationalism' (Day 1996: 200). At every Census, in every colony throughout the nineteenth century, the English were the largest group of emigrants, usually outnumbering Scots and Irish migrants combined (Jupp 1991: 7). Nevertheless, Celtic emigrants formed a very substantial minority (almost half) of the Australian population during this period. The Scots, Irish, Welsh (and not forgetting the Cornish) displayed some regional concentration and language retention, but, as Jupp notes: 'Very little bound the Celtic immigrants together and religion kept them apart' (ibid.: 36). If there was a unifying theme in the debate among intellectuals and elites about the relative weight to attach to convict, emigrant and native-born traces, it was a tendency to regard the environment as more important than inheritance in moulding national character (White 1981: 27). This emphasis on the landscape, a feature common in Canada ('The Far North') and New Zealand ('The Bush'), captured a broader sense of being transplanted.

For most of the nineteenth century, White argues, most Australians saw themselves as part of a group of new, vigorous, politically advanced, predominantly Anglo-Saxon, emigrant societies. The United States was the archetype, particularly for the Catholic Irish in America and the Antipodes, who saw these new societies as freer, if not free, from British oppression. Conversely, the colonial middle class, particularly from the aptly named 'Home Counties' of south-east England, saw America as foreign, most notably in its politics. Independence was an inspiration for those seeking liberal reform. For elites, the Britishness of the other colonies of settlement was far safer and civilised. In short, there were two currents flowing through the stream of nineteenth-century thinking that had a bearing on national aspirations. One current emphasised 'the new society', taking America as its template; the other stressed a British-inspired continuity. The former fostered a social democratic, occasionally republican tradition, the latter, a conservative, Empire loyalist one (Pettman 1995: 66). This second tradition took centre-stage at the turn of the nineteenth century, and on through much of the twentieth, but the first was always waiting in the wings.

The Australian state (much like Canada, although without its longer colonial history), was formed within the Victorian world of Empire. A move towards unified statehood had as much to do with strategic advantage as the flowering of national sentiment, although the relative balance between political and cultural nationalism is still much debated. By the end of the nineteenth century provincial elites, in both senses of the phrase, were concerned about economic and military protection. Tariffs, defence and immigration were the key issues promoting federation in 1901. Australia was heavily dependent on British capital and trade, and 'everybody else's Far East was their near north' (Inglis 1996: 341). Britain offered protection and 'men, money and markets'. Just like the BNA that formed Canada, Australian federation was primarily a benchmark of state-making. Henry Lawson may have proclaimed Australia was 'a nation at last', but the words of Alfred Deakin, the first Premier, echoed those of his Canadian counterpart, John 'A': 'The federation was not a nation, but simply preludes the advent of a nation.'

There were cultural fissures in Australia, but they were not as wide or deep as in Canada. By 1901 more than 90 per cent of the population were Australian or British born, and most were urban dwellers. For the vast majority of this group, a marginalised, remote aboriginal minority could be, and was, ignored. What was espoused at federation was a multilayered identity. A majority of Australians identified with 'Protestant God, British King and Anglo-Australian Country' (White 1981: 112). They also saw themselves as Tasmanians, Queenslanders and so forth. This regionalism, the international situation, and the mechanisms of imperial socialisation militated against full-blown indigenous nationalism (Alomes 1988: 47). For most Australians these multiple identities created little angst.

The Irish situation, however, was more ambiguous. As Akenson (1993: 114) notes: 'The viewpoint, that the Irish were a distinct and dynamic element in Australian society, has to be juxtaposed to the undeniable statistical evidence that the Irish... were totally ordinary in most ways.' They had not formed the same urban ethnic enclaves as they had done in America, and compared with Canada's duality, at least spoke the same language. Despite discrimination, upward mobility, particularly for Protestant Irish, was far from impossible. Almost a quarter of Australians (in 1901), however, was Roman Catholic, most of them of Irish ancestry and working class. There were clear social lines between Catholic parish schools and exclusive Protestant private schools, although most Australians went to secular, state schools and there *were* rich Catholic educational establishments. Religious adherence provoked divisions across all strata, not least within the working class itself. But there was no neat congruence between radicalism, class and ethnicity. Many English, Scots and Welsh emigrants brought a distinct distaste for their so-called 'betters' with them, or their children very soon acquired it. But the Irish, largely clustered in the industrial labour force, most clearly worked and played apart from the more Anglophile middle classes, and were most distant from the decidedly British upper echelons. The higher the class, the higher the level of imperialist sentiment, is a somewhat simplified dictum, but not too erroneous. The ruling elites had the closest ties to Empire (ibid.: 55). Government House, Oxbridge, the Church of England, the legal and medical professions, all reflected an umbilical link with the mother country, with its lifeblood constantly renewed by international travel, telecommunications, and networks of marriage and acquaintanceship.

Loyalty to the Crown and Empire, as ever, was most graphically demonstrated by a willingness to shed patriotic blood. Australians, provincially then nationally, sent small contingents of troops to aid Britain's avenging of Gordon in India (in 1885) and to put down the Boxer rebellion in China (in 1900). Thousands went off to assist the

English Uitlander in the Boer War. Support for British imperial expansion was axiomatic for most politicians and much of the populace (Trainor 1994), but class and ethnic cleavages continued to complicate the process of national myth-making. Empire Day was instituted in 1905, but not without controversy. The British Empire League was strongly Protestant, mainly Conservative voting, and middle class. The Australian Natives' Association, Labour Party and union radicals, and the Irish working class, favoured an Australia Day. This became Catholic Church policy in New South Wales in 1911, so Catholic pupils saluted the Australian flag instead of the Union Jack at morning assembly (Alomes 1988: 54). These tensions filtered through to the First World War, particularly after the Easter Rising in 1916 personified Irish resentment of British authority – directly in one homeland, indirectly in another.

If the discernment of the embryo of Australian nationalism invoked constant reinvention, the birth was likewise chimerical. Unquestionably, however, the Gallipoli landings loom large in any Australian national iconography, with the subsequent Anzac legend cementing the process. The First World War experience brought together a series of recurrent, often contradictory, stereotypical themes: many with a masculine and military flavour (Lake 1992). Typically they ranged across the 'noble frontier', the male camaraderie of mateship, the egalitarian ethos, and the flowering of an environmentally produced 'superior stock', exemplified in heroism displayed on playing and battle fields. In 'The Great War', the 'crimson thread of kinship' was further strengthened, and stretched. Australians, at least those with the right ethnic credentials, were not British, they were 'Better British'. Such views were refracted through a dual Canadian lens, but they came into even clearer focus in New Zealand.

Greater British

Ernest Gellner remarked in the early 1980s: 'Most New Zealanders and most citizens of the United Kingdom are so continuous culturally that without a shadow of a doubt the two units would have never separated, had they been contiguous geographically. Distance made the effective sovereignty of New Zealand convenient and mandatory...' (Gellner 1983: 134–5). This rather glib contemporary linkage of statehood with the tyranny of distance has, not surprisingly, drawn local criticism (Williams 1997: 19). But there is at least a half-truth here that would have had even greater resonance a century earlier. In the 1880s the native-born first outnumbered British migrants, a New Zealand Natives'

Association was soon to be started (in 1890), and a unitary New Zealand polity had already evolved from its provincial beginnings in the 1850s. Federation with Australia was mooted in the 1880s and 1890s, but was never seriously contemplated, mainly because, to revive the Gellner thesis, of geographical barriers – 12 000 miles of ocean (Sinclair 1988). All these trends seem to reveal an, at least incipient, sense of New Zealandness, as the state progressed and a core of local-born grew in prominence. Such tendencies, Sinclair argues, were reinforced in the last decade of the nineteenth century as the country became more centralised. There was a marked spread of colony-wide institutions and associations. The Liberal–Labour coalition (voted in, in 1899) was the first national political party, and its brand of 'radical statism' was perceived as equally novel. A national education system was in place, without the depth of ethnic and class divisions that its Canadian and Australian provincial counterparts displayed. The professions, employers, unions and sports associations were all becoming national. These shifts from provincial to more expansive units of identity and control were indicative of what Williams (1997: 38) calls 'progressive nationalism'. By 1900, Sinclair (1986: 64) argues, it became possible to see oneself as a New Zealander. But both these writers acknowledge the persistence of a sense of *Britishness*. The exotic was still flowering alongside the indigenous.

As André Siegfried noted in 1904, in striking contrast to his Canadian comment, New Zealand 'may with justice be regarded as the English Colony which is most faithful to the mother-country' (cf. Gibbons 1981: 308). Each generation of New Zealanders may have felt less 'British' than its predecessor, but their society continued to nourish its roots from the same well of origins, often with state assistance. Assisted British immigration was at its highpoint in the 1870s, but economic depression and a rapid rise in natural increase, saw the percentage of native-born rise rapidly between 1886 and 1896 (from 51 to 62 per cent). But most of these New Zealanders were children. Hardly fertile ground for fervent nationalism. Migrants had to come under their own steam between 1888 and 1903 when New Zealand's economic times were hard, but despite the ebb and flow, the stream of migration until well after the Second World War was overwhelmingly British. Such migrants were not always welcome. The 'Homies', as they were sometimes called, were often resented as economic competitors. But the play on 'home' reveals an intimacy of attachment. Distance, as the flow of letters, telegraphs, and local press content reveals, was no inhibitor of contact. Isolation fostered a greater sense of the need to keep in touch.

Why were the bonds between New Zealand and Britain even tighter than Australian (and Canadian) links at the turn of the nineteenth century? New Zealand was more recently colonised, so the indigenisation of the settlers was less advanced. Given its size, geographically and demographically speaking, state-making was swift and expansive across the country. This did aid the nation-making process. More and more people experienced similar institutions. But these were often replicas or remoulded from British models, and the narrow stream of migration did not seek to leaven the process of emulation too much. Provincial, regional differences were prevalent, and in some areas remain so, but the path to a non-federal, political independence, despite the New Zealand wars, was, unlike its colonial counterparts, relatively uncontentious.

Regional and class differences existed but they were not as divisive. New Zealand had no convicts, apart from the ones that fled across the Tasman, and far fewer Catholic Irish (both populations being decidedly equivocal about the English). New Zealand had a disproportionately large number of Scots that, Belich, remarks wryly, 'were to New Zealand what the Irish were to Australia – the chief lieutenants of settlement' (Belich 1996: 315). The local Caledonian clique more than matched the elite performance of their North American and cross-Tasman cousins.

The lack of felons, and a supposedly more 'respectable' working class, became a mark of compensatory superiority against more powerful provincial rivals. As did the European perception of Maori. New Zealand, even more than Canada, used the United States, Australia and, most strikingly, South Africa, to sustain a myth of comparative advantage in 'race relations'. The myth was not so much in claiming relations were better, but in the use of the faulty logic inspiring a leap from 'better' to 'good'. Within this reasoning Maori were accorded the imagery of not-so-distant races of people on the Social Darwinian scales prevailing towards the end of the Victorian era. This legend enabled 'our' Maori to be cast, paternalistically, in the role of Aryans of the Eastern Seas conjoining with their Western counterparts (Sorrensson 1979). The complexity and intimacy of these relations provokes thoughts of some aspects of French/English dualities in Canada, particularly the Maori ambivalence about statehood and British patriotism in the First World War, but the degree and form of social, economic and political incorporation of the two 'minorities' were greatly different. Nonetheless, European New Zealanders (for they had not taken on the term Pakeha) formed a consolidated sense of themselves in relation to Maori as much as Britain. As Williams notes: 'This process of indigenisation of the settlers is marked by the evolution of the meaning of the term New Zealander which meant Maori in the early nineteenth century and white descendant of the settlers by the latter part of the century' (Williams 1997: 22). The 'Maori fact', in its own way, was as important as 'the French' in northern climes.

The Empire was an abstraction for the masses. Every New Zealand Premier from 1883 to 1912 supported the idea of imperial federation, but this hardly stirred the imaginations of the electorate (Sinclair 1986: 173). And the New Zealand polity's pursuit of its own, highly circumscribed, imperialist aims in the Pacific met a similar response. Royalty and rugby were what tightened national and imperial heartstrings. New Zealanders *en masse* flocked to see visiting 'royals', while taking intense pleasure in beating the British, particularly the Poms, at their own game. The masculinity and mateship of the playing field spilled over into the arenas of war in South Africa in both a military and sporting sense. Victories, at home and abroad, were trumpeted at the 1906–7 Exhibition, where, much like the other settler society commemorations preceding it,[3] an increasingly confident nation proclaimed its assumed greatness. Here New Zealand was depicted as a wealthy, healthy, social and political laboratory. A scenic Maoriland doubling as a Britain of the South. But, as in Australia, it was the First World War that seemed to be the watershed of New Zealand/British nation-making. By that point, many historians at least agree, the local-born saw themselves as New Zealanders and British, but they were 'the best British' living in a Better or Greater Britain (Belich 1996: 302).

The Great White Walls

Civic and ethnic national sentiments among the majorities in the colonies of settlement were diverse but, as we have seen, the maintenance of imperial ties with Britain, the reliance on a bedrock of British institutions, and the construction of a dual sense of belonging to homelands in the mind and in the making, provided a distinctive character for dominant groups in these societies. In one sense this duality seems to be outward-looking, for we have a national identity for many people of British ancestry not solely residing within the territorial boundaries of the state and nation. And being societies whose capitalist development depends on immigration, there is an expectation those boundaries will constantly be crossed. Here of course lay the rub. Even an international sense of 'us' was firmly bounded by an ethnic particularism conflicting with a pursuit of capital and labour which, rationally speaking, ought to know no bounds. This friction point, as we will see throughout this book, is perennial, but during the nineteenth century, the delicacy of the balance between economic and cultural forces was particularly acute. Notwithstanding their peculiarities of difference and distance, by the turn of the twentieth century, there was agreement in Australia, Canada and New Zealand that the preservation of a fledgling nationhood required state protection of ethnic borders. The case of Chinese migration neatly serves to illustrate the point.

Over the period from 1848 to 1888 more than two million Chinese spread across the globe. Indentured workers ('coolies'), free artisans and entrepreneurs, laboured and traded in economies as distant as South East Asia, the Caribbean and Latin America. They also sought their fortunes in the colonies of settlement. Chinese workers and traders could be found in California and Australia prior to the 1840s, but their numbers excited little more than curiosity. It was the discovery of gold in the mid-nineteenth century that sparked a chain of exclusionary events linking North West America with Eastern Australia and New Zealand. Chinese gold diggers arrived in California in increasing numbers in the 1850s. By 1861 they had become 9 per cent of the California state population, and at the height of the gold fever formed a quarter of the mining community (Markus 1979: 1). In Australia the lure of 'gold mountains' brought smaller numbers of Chinese, but by the 1860s they were a noted presence in Victoria and New South Wales, and in Queensland a few years later.[4] There were 4000 Chinese in British Columbia in 1860 and almost 3000 Chinese miners were searching for elusive nuggets in New Zealand a decade later.

In each setting there were diverse local conditions and variations in reception of these culturally and phenotypically distinctive communities, but the overall pattern of ethnic relations was tense, divisive and, sporadically, violent. This social climate provoked attempts at exclusion, ultimately successful in each of the settlements. Chinese immigration was restricted in Australia from 1855 to 1861 after regional Sinophobic agitation and local riots. Restrictions were briefly removed in 1867 when the gold boom had subsided and an economic downturn promoted a labour surplus. Controls were swiftly reinstated between 1877 and 1881 after further unrest on the later developed Queensland fields.

In California, Chinese immigration initially went unchecked. Despite considerable violence on the goldfields, West Coast pleas for limitations fell on deaf ears in Washington. The United States government, with sole authority over migration, sought to foster its expansionary external aims in China rather than placate what was seen as a peculiarly local

'Chinese problem' within its borders. Such calls were also greeted with mixed feelings among employers. An economic boom in California in the early 1860s saw thousands more Chinese workers recruited. By the early 1880s, 88 000 Chinese had become established in the United States, their communities forming 10 per cent of the Californian population (Choy et al., 1995: 19).

The Canadian West Coast never attracted such numbers, but a combination of national and regional economic interests provoked further growth despite local hostilities. Similar visions of uniting nations shore to shore were invoked in Canada in the early 1880s, and miles of Canadian Pacific Railway track were laid by 15 000 Chinese labourers (Knowles 1992: 48). But almost as the last spike was hammered home, the first federal anti-Chinese bill was passed in 1885.

A similar trend is evident in New Zealand. Between 1870 and 1881, just over 6000 Chinese entered the country (although half of them departed in the same period). They too were employed on the railways and in construction work, as well as working the goldfields. Here too, the ripples of anti-Oriental feeling and restriction in Australia and North America reached the shores of the most distant dominion. A Chinese Immigration Restriction Act introduced in 1881 followed a familiar pattern of ethnic and racial exclusion.

What caused this pattern, and was it primarily a question of ethnocentrism and racism? No single cause or parochial theory can adequately explain the rise, partial fall, and rise again, of anti-Chinese (indeed anti-Asiatic) sentiments and actions in North America and Australasia. Class and gender divisions were clearly important. Outbreaks of anti-Oriental sentiments and practices coincided with the recurrent economic booms and slumps of the mid-to-late nineteenth and early twentieth centuries. Economic competition between workers, and divisions between sections of capital and labour, were persistent features of hostilities seeming to follow ethnic lines. Some, mainly larger, employers clearly benefited from the importation of cheap foreign labour, while membership of anti-Chinese leagues that formed in each society had solid small-business support. Those trade unions most affected by the arrival of Chinese workers were the most vehemently opposed to Asian immigration. The consolidation of regional and national labour organisations, and the intermittent support from sections of the self-employed and employer classes, was instrumental in bringing about the entrenched post-1880 immigration restrictions in each of the above societies. The importance of economic factors, moreover, is also underlined by the persistence of a pattern of protest among native-born or long-settled groups against most migrants, including British immigrants, at times of economic recession, before and after the arrival of the Chinese in the nineteenth century. These factors were freely drawn upon by politicians eager to fan the flames of fear and antipathy to enhance their electoral advantage.

Chinese communities, by virtue of sojournment and, ironically, the immigration restrictions they confronted, were strikingly male.[5] This factor laced racial opprobrium with stereotypes of sexual promiscuity and moral degeneracy. The lack of family commitments also added a further negative ingredient to the mix of attitudes towards economic competition and transience. If the most desirable settler was the established, family man, then the sojourner was not the 'right sort' of migrant. Admittedly, many 'rough' attributes of the white, male lower orders would not find favour among the 'respectable' middle and upper classes of either sex, but physical dissimilarity proved the most virulent additive to class and gender differences. The Chinese were not only culturally strange. They also raised the spectre of racial intermixture. This phantom had already influenced the nature of aboriginal and slave relations in the colonies of settlement and implanted fine or coarser grained distinctions of cultural and physical distance between and within immigrant strata.

The Great Chain of Being furnished earlier generations with a rationale for racial supremacy and colonial dispossession. By the end of the nineteenth century Social Darwinism served the same ends. Ideological models of national/racial competition and survival underpinned relations of proximate or distant ignorance, fear and antipathy. Such models constructed an *image* of the Chinese that often had more impact than direct observation and interpersonal ethnic contact and conflicts (Ward 1978: 13). The image mainly explains why the threat of the 'Other' extended far beyond those directly involved with 'coloured aliens'. Built on a long-standing Western construction of 'Asia', the arrival of the Chinese in the 'New World' illustrates a potent, often localised potpourri, of fears and animosities about economic and sexual competition, and social and cultural avoidance. Within this brew the preservation of economic and racial advantage became inextricably mixed. The relatively small populations of Asiatics symbolised a far broader set of social changes. In Price's (1974: 260) words, the Chinese 'were the anvil on which the new young societies were slowly hammering out their national identity'. What was being forged was an imperfect armour of racial inviolability and a flawed shield against the, putatively, culturally and physically unassimilable.

The Great White Walls, patrolled with increasing, incremental vigilance in the decades either side of the end of the nineteenth century, were firmly in place in North America and Australasia by the 1920s. The Chinese, having suffered the ignominy of progressively stiffer head taxes and a stark disallowance of citizenship rights, were ultimately, with few exceptions, banned from entry. The Japanese, Indian and other 'Asians' were similarly restricted. In Australia, after federation, the Melanesians imported to work the Queensland canefields, were summarily sent back. Black persons, of course, were universally unwelcome. Even Eastern and Southern Europeans offended race/nation expectations. Canada, running short of British migrants, had encouraged Ukrainians, Russian Doukhobors, and other, mainly central and eastern Europeans to populate the prairies in their thousands. Their arrival raised 'a groundswell of hostility' (Knowles 1992: 74). A mere trickle of Dalmatians, from what was to become Yugoslavia, were called 'the Chinese of the North' in New Zealand, and treated accordingly (Trlin 1979). By the 1920s immigration administration in all of our case studies displayed a marked unanimity about the virtues of Anglo-conformity.

Despite these trends, the White Walls had shaky foundations. The pressures of world diplomacy, the liberal rhetoric of Empire, the advocacy of Christian principle and natural justice, and fluctuating market forces for labour and capital, produced noticeable cracks in the stonework. Nonetheless, these were often, literally, papered over with administrative legerdemain. 'Race' was often discreetly avoided in legislation. The widely used Natal formulaic 'dictation test', and Canada's 'direct passage doctrine', exemplified the successful circumvention of imperial sensibilities about British subjects. Things were little different in the land of the free. The 1924 United States Immigration Act euphemistically enshrined a definition of 'involuntary Inhabitants' of the nation sending out an all-too familiar message (Ringer and Lawless 1989: 185–6). Non-white need not apply.

Diverse diasporas

The term diaspora has come back into fashion with a rather more expansive meaning than its pedigree would suggest. Initially confined to groups experiencing involuntary migration and its aftermath, the concept now embraces voluntary movements and their, often planned, consequences: including the choice to build roots anew rather than return to the homeland. Diaporas can therefore, potentially, be victims or victimisers, sojourners or settlers. Not surprisingly, given this array of possibilities, there is wide scope for using this lens to view ethnic groups in the societies under examination. For example, the experience of

Afro-Caribbean slaves and their descendants, many immigrant groups, both British and French settlers, and aboriginal peoples have all been seen by some commentators to have diasporic qualities.[6]

This looser and selective definition process runs the danger of covering everything and nothing, but an insistence on the presence of certain key features rescues the situation. Most basically a diaspora has to be seen as emerging and enduring through a process of multidirectional migration. As Van Hear (1998: 6) notes, building on the innovative work of Cohen (1997), any group defined as diasporic has to meet three minimal criteria. The diaspora's population must be dispersed from a homeland to two or more other territories; its presence abroad must be reasonably enduring, although permanent exile is not a necessity; and there must be some kind of (continuing) exchange – economic, political or cultural – between homeland and hosts. In short, if diasporic, journeys are *multiple, transnational* and *recurrent*.

This definition, in my view, places many immigrant and aboriginal minorities, and 'the French fact', outside our diasporic purview. Diasporas do not come from elsewhere in the same way many migrants do. For some, temporary or permanent return may be contemplated and possibly achieved, but this is usually a two-way relationship between old and new abodes. Once assimilated into the latter, the former is not forgotten, kin, friendship and other ties may be enduring, but the ongoing interaction between multiple departure points and destinations is missing.

Equally, the scattering, the forced exile, the movement in and out of reservations, the dream of return to the homeland of 'first nations' has many of the hallmarks of classical and revisionist diaspora, but there are vital differences. Many aboriginal peoples are still 'in place' despite being displaced. They still remain in their territory, although materially dispossessed of it. This sense of rootedness in the land is of a different order to the sense of belonging diasporic peoples may retain. Francophones were also dispersed, in Canada and the United States, but the potential formation of a diaspora was truncated or still-born. Quebec became a homeland isolated within the French Empire. There was little subsequent interchange between Quebec, France and French territories. Admittedly, Quebec became a symbol of 'the French Fact' for Acadians or French Americans, but this is a diasporic tendency once, or twice removed, again without the recurrent movements between multiple nodal points to sustain the argument.

Notwithstanding these caveats, if used discriminately, the diaspora concept is an effective counterweight to the highly simplistic binary relationships implied by minority/majority and home/host models of ethnic relations and migrations. If distinguishing immigrant and aboriginal minorities highlights fundamental differences within a status of relative ethnic powerlessness, use of the diaspora concept enables us further to illuminate parallels and distinctions across the power spectrum. If cross-national movements are set against a framework of global linkages then our understanding of both analytical levels is enhanced. A return to the 'Chinese' and 'British' categories will reinforce these points.

The Chinese, mainly Cantonese, communities described above can be usefully described as labour and trading diasporas, whose fates often converged. Like the Lebanese, and Gujurati workers and traders, for example, these groups typify a dynamic responsiveness to the interweaving of the forced and volitional character of multidirectional migrations. Their communities were flexible and changing. Mobility was common in geographical and frequently in economic and social terms. Labourers often became traders, and the reverse was far from unknown. Labour diasporas were particularly powerless, but their trading equivalent often carved out innovative niches as pariah capitalists that afforded a modicum of economic sustainability: in some cases rather more than this.

The Chinese retained strong group ties of family, village and religion in their various new homelands, so the general sobriquet 'Overseas Chinese' (*huaqiao*) covers a variety of distinctive affiliations. They also sustained enduring myths of attachment to their regional Southern Chinese origins, well into the twentieth century. A national sense of cultural belonging was preserved by imaginings of birthplace and sharing the same 'flesh and bones' (Ong 1993: 751). The Chinese also had myths and memories of empire, and occupants of 'the Middle Kingdom' clearly saw themselves as superior beings.

Overseas, Chinese ethnocentrism was more than matched by a shared opprobrium as a racialised category in unhostlike settings. This had palpable, political repercussions. Economically, acumen and sheer hard work produced entrepreneurial 'middlemen', but one form of limited influence did not necessarily spill over into others. Despite the liveliness of internal politics within and between Chinatowns, few Chinese persons exerted an influence in local politics beyond their own communities. Generally speaking they kept their heads down, through fear of reprisal and a greater loyalty to profitability than their place of settlement. However, important political links with China were often retained. Diaspora Chinese provided vital support for the Sun Yat-sen led Nationalist

Movement and the 1911 revolution from which emerged the Republic of China (Cohen 1997: 89).

The comparative emergence and eventual regeneration of Chinese diaspora are tales of a particular transnational form of immigrant minority. The 'British' diaspora has a linked narrative, extending the concept into imperial and dominion forms, and creating or consolidating minorities in the process. The 'Chinese' diaspora sought to promote economic niches, and, through specialisation, forced and chosen, to achieve material success within confined spaces. They became a distinctive ethnic category, made up of various regional groups, through the twin forces of exclusion and inclusion. The 'British', another formative ethnic category, but with polynational origins, also scattered across the globe with an eye for profit. However, they expanded across territories, making states and seeking to build new nations in the process.

Australia, New Zealand and (Anglophone) Canada were 'a direct product of the massive British Isles diaspora of the eighteenth and, especially, the nineteenth century (Akenson 1995: 392). The English, Scots, Irish and, to a far more limited extent, the Welsh, had their own diasporas, but what we are discussing here is the melding of diverse regional and national origins into something called an Anglo-Celtic or British ethnic amalgam. Elites, mainly English, but with important Celtic infusions, stamped a British identity on multiple settings around the world. This identity was multifaceted and different elements were emphasised in particular contexts. Chief among them was the English language. The 'British' diaspora was English-speaking, not English. Anglicisation both preceded and followed multipolar movements. This vernacular had outpaced Gaelic retentions *within* Scotland, Wales and Ireland by the end of the seventeenth century, and the process continued unabated in the colonies. Language was a prime cultural marker, a badge of inclusion, effectively policing conditions of access and signalling the potential for assimilation. Possession of the English language did not ensure membership, but it facilitated entry to a global network of possibilities within the British, and subsequently, American empires (ibid.: 399). The pre-eminence of the English vernacular was bolstered by other institutional 'British' underpinnings. English and Welsh law, Scots, Irish and English educational institutions, the Anglican Church, and other Christian denominations, aspects of Westminster-style polities and civil services, and various professional, voluntary and recreational/sporting associations all added to a multinational mix of popular and high cultures (Cohen 1997: 75–6).

Combined, these ingredients comprised a style of manners and modes, which, despite the importance of gender and class filters, engendered a broader sense of belonging. A feeling of kith and kin was directly reproduced through chain migration, intermarriage and acquaintanceship. For those with the money and time, journeys across the Empire and back to the metropolis, refurbished memories of Home past and present. For those, the majority, lacking both commodities, ties were recreated through letters, media, patterns of economic consumption, and the sharing, often vicariously, of a common set of values and lifestyles. These social affiliations were underpinned by flows of finance, labour and trade. Both Chinese and British used multidirectional support systems to 'get on', 'get by', or 'get out'. But the British diaspora, unlike the Chinese, was a hegemonic endeavour.

In many parts of Asia and Africa an imperial British diaspora epitomised the ephemeral, limited impact of aristocratic imperious power: the Raj being the pinnacle of extended or emulative *hauteur*. Elements of this could be discerned among those with genteel, if not gentry, pretensions in mass settler colonies, although its aristocratic pretensions were rendered precarious by their own humbler origins and, more pertinently, a notable lack of deference from the 'lower orders'. Despite their increasingly native-born 'Creole' membership, they nonetheless considered themselves Britons abroad: a select, transoceanic group with diasporic qualities transcending local ethnic and regional boundaries.

Over the nineteenth and early twentieth centuries imperial, elite diasporas, gradually or swiftly, took on mass forms. They became dominion diasporas in both senses of the phrase, retaining or creating control over aboriginal and immigrant minorities, while maintaining a 'special' relationship with their own mother countries. In so doing, a 'British' culture came into being, exhibiting a blend of endogenous and introduced identities. Within this intermixture 'British' and 'colonial' identities were in flux. Multiple identities, conflicting and compatible, were nothing new. What was novel was a deeper sense of being 'British' beyond Britain.[7] This sense was strongest in upper-class circles, Protestant and mainly English, and weakest among Catholics of Irish origin. How widespread, beyond elites, that consciousness existed is difficult to say. The attachments of locality, region and nation, deferred and rebuilt anew, would vary across homes remembered and remade.

Unlike the Chinese diaspora, circumscribed in situations and legal statuses where the state stems the lifeblood of migrant replenishment, the British could depend on an intermittent, but steady, often state-supported, reinfusion of persons who did, or more to the point, might be believed to be, reminders of things past in the present. The 'kin-migrant' relationship, as McKinnon (1996) describes it in New Zealand, between the new 'British' and those who continue to arrive from various parts of Britain, was the ethnic core of colonies of settlements.

The meeting of generations born within or beyond 'the colonies cum dominions' is as much a tale of difference as solidarity. Kin relations, real or imagined, are rarely uncontentious. Incoming waves of migrants first created then consolidated the 'British' presence, while simultaneously promoting a greater awareness of nativistic distinction. Kin-migrants were 'one of us' but also an 'intimate other'. Out of this blend of cultural beginning and becoming it seems plausible to argue that, 'by the time of the First World War it is clear that something has developed in several New Worlds that did not exist in the Old World ... a commonality of culture and identity' (Akenson 1995: 397). Was this 'something', this Britishness, a *national* phenomenon, and, if so, did it stem from indigenous ethnic roots or state grafting of exotic forms of belonging?

States without nations?

Four major sources of state-nation building within British colonies of settlement were noted in Chapter 1 and have been illustrated above. First, there is the process of establishing the civic, institutional underpinnings of a national community and aligning them with an ethnic kernel of sentiments. This promotes integration of a new and renewed 'abstract community'. British civic institutions are set against imaginings of British descent and culture. Subsequently, myths of origin of 'homes past' and 'homes present' are created and recreated, and these are linked with myths of the shared destinies of colony and Empire. This process promotes a global sense of position as well as aiding the task of local settler unification. Finally, there will be processes of appropriation of cultural symbols from aboriginal peoples, 'national minorities' and other ethnic categories and groups. What is left out is equally important to what is adopted here. That which is taken, ignored or cast aside provides a sense of a national and transnational 'us' in relation to the 'Other' within and without. The first two themes embrace semi-gradualist derivation. Colonial elites reproduce the institutions of their metropole, through state-building, and seek to instill a sense of belonging to an abstract community – a people – based on native-born reimaginings and those of migrants arriving with similar cultural baggage and memory banks. Nation-building in this light is a process of remembering and emulation. Forgetting, however, as Renan pointed out, is just as vital for nation-making: especially when we consider the central role of myths of origin and destiny in creating an inclusive peoplehood out of the act of dispossession, and the secondary nature of any claimed exclusivity.

Australia, Canada and New Zealand are particularly interesting cases here, since they are juxtaposed between Old and New World prototypes – Britain and the United States. The former, or so the narrative goes, born out of the timeworn accretion of gradual change, the latter from the immediacy of revolutionary moment. Alone, Nairn argues (the British system) 'represented a slow, conventional growth... the product of deliberate invention... Because it was first, the English – later the British – experience remained distinct' (Nairn 1981: 18). Conversely, the United States, was the first *new* nation (Lipset 1963). The first to revolt against a European imperial power.

The deeper intricacies of ongoing debates about when the English-cum-British nation-state emerged, or whether the American Revolution should be so termed, need not concern us here.[8] What needs to be stressed is that neither the myths of gradualism nor revolution, in the English or American senses, could be drawn upon unambiguously by nation-makers in the other mass British settler colonies. Yet both the Uniteds, Kingdom and States, as points of reference, were intrinsic to the development of modernising settler and post-settler states. And the realm of Britishness in the Empire and America had repercussions for the sense of being British in Britain, given the process of identity formation in settler and metropolitan societies was occurring simultaneously.

The past for most British settlers was too short to form powerful local traditions and migrants tended to dwell more on their myths of destiny than local origin. Conquest and dispossession would serve as crucial founding moments for the French in Canada, and aboriginal peoples everywhere, but British settlers, particularly their elites, were more intent on capitalist development, acquiring the political autonomy to achieve this, while retaining the security and prestige of Empire. The scaling of the Heights of Abraham, the signing of the Treaty of Waitangi, the arrival of the First Fleet, were woven into stories of nation-making at a later, in some cases, much later, stage. The initial drive towards Canadian and Australian federal arrangements, and New Zealand's unitary system of governance, was primarily an exercise in state-making. This was achieved, at least as far as the majority was concerned, without revolution or civil war. There was no parallel to the vexed American taxation issue. There were indeed skirmishes along ethnic and class lines, but no full-scale hostilities. Demands for self-rule, to varying degrees in each society, were based on a blend of inherited British and borrowed

American rhetoric (Cole 1971: 167). As Kaufmann notes for Canada, there was a melding of American 'Whig' liberalism and British 'Tory' conservatism, based on a folk culture revolving around a pioneering New World lifestyle and a British set of myths, symbols and collective representations (Kaufmann 1997: 111–12). The former was more typical of the masses, the latter sat most easily with elites. This lifestyle and an ideology of liberty proved a potent mythological force for differentiating America from Britain, despite the clear linkages remaining between the first old and new nations. For Canadians, particularly those of Loyalist descent or persuasion, the American identity had to be rejected. Thus developed an insistence on Britishness while sustaining a fiction of not being American. The result, for Canadians, was a double dualism of American/British and Anglophone/Francophone tensions.

Nevertheless, between Confederation and the end of the First World War, the British pole of Anglo-Canadian identity dominated (ibid.: 123). Most Anglo-Canadians, and many *Canadiens*, were able to reconcile a patriotic attachment to Canada and Britain with comparatively little disquiet particularly when it came to assessing the constant fears of United States dominance. French Canadians had a tangible ethnic national core married to civic expediency. English-speaking Canadians identified with the Crown, the Empire and British civic traditions, while experiencing the more amorphous but still discernible ethnic patterning of a sense of Britishness: embodied in accents and vocabulary, a sense of place, sport and recreation, artistic endeavour and emblems of identity. Immigration and war both reinforced a local and international patriotism while provoking renewed tensions within the dualities.

This scenario, minus of course the French fact and the geographical proximity of America, had many echoes in Australia and New Zealand. From their beginnings the homogeneity of the migrant population in the Antipodes ensured some form of derived ethnic consciousness grew alongside the state. A sense of 'who we are' linked to a civic culture. In New Zealand the kin-migrant linkage was overwhelming, Britishness was assured, although the signs of indigenisation would still be perceptible within the native-born. Australia, with a larger territory and longer frontier, more definite (if far less than Canadian) regionalisms, and a more pronounced nonconformist Celtic influence, exhibited greater signs of endogenous nationalism, most notably in the 1880s and 1890s, when some Australians, Anglo and Celtic, particularly their intelligentsia, asked 'who we *really* are'. And yet, in both states, as in Canada, the stories of nationalism in their earlier stages were more akin to weaning than radical separation. Australian national identity 'remained weak and contradictory, and the adhesion to British civic and political traditions was offset by a republicanism played in a minor key' (Davidson 1997: 49). New Zealanders played basically the same tune with an even more muted American influence.

Questioning of 'who we are' inevitably entails asking 'who we are not'. Canadians were not Americans, New Zealanders were not Australian, and none of them were really British in the sense of being Brits. Civically speaking, we only have to look at the successful striving for political semi-autonomy and the failure of localized (Australia/New Zealand) and more grandiose schemes of imperial federation of the colonies of settlement to see the progeny of Empire were a trifle recalcitrant. A 'United States of the Empire' never eventuated (Eddy and Schreuder 1988: 44). The offspring had the numbers and the affluence to get some of their own way. Nevertheless, the apron strings were only partially untied. Unlike the Americans united in their own states by citizenship, the other siblings (or should that be cousins?) remained imperial subjects. They were transnationally British within a largely chosen state of economic and political semi-subjection.

Ethnically, the theme of maintaining Britishness meant exclusion of the non-British. Nation and state were tied to race, with masculine thread. The 'New Men' in what Kipling called 'the Younger Nations' epitomised a superior colonial breed of British. Aboriginal societies were ignored, relegated to prehistory or woven into romantic tales of civilisable Others. They were condemned to extinction if classed as irremediably inferior, or culturally doomed if capable of uplifting. Promoting a path to oblivion was the white man's vocation or burden. Assimilability was the litmus test of acceptance or rejection for all 'Other' immigrants. By the latter half of the nineteenth, and well into the twentieth centuries, a Darwinian-inspired mood of Anglo-Saxon racial superiority evoked the most telling indicator of Britishness. On this indicator, at least, there was like-mindedness across the Americas, Australasia and Britain itself. Irrespective of the incidence of innumerable exceptions, these were, and should remain, irrevocably white societies. Hence the construction of walls, reinforced by legal sophistry and popular practice, dividing us and them, other and alien. The settler state, however, did not build nations, 'pure' nor simple. The marriage between civic and ethnic identities was never an easy relationship. What was constructed and reconstructed was a set of pluralistic ethnic and national formations, fraught with internal and external ambiguity, held together by an, admittedly powerful, glue of Anglo-conformity. How lasting and impermeable this adhesive proved to be, will be explored in subsequent chapters.

4
Migrations

Nation-state making in settler societies was based on the state displacement, attraction and importation of populations and the attempt to forge national identities out of the resultant ethnic mix. Political movement was always intimately related to other forms of travelling. The latter half of the nineteenth century had been marked by mass population transfers in the still developing capitalist sectors of North America, Britain and Oceania, as, despite periods of recession, the drive for economic growth and its seemingly insatiable demand for labour, sustained an expansionary world-view. What also linked these societies in the early twentieth century, in elite and mass majority terms, was a vision of an increasingly exclusive ethnic and racial destiny and the use of putative physical and cultural signs of potential assimilability as a marker of entry to national membership of the state. An era of optimism, heralded in the jingoism of the Great War, was soon followed, however, by a period of insular uncertainty that dampened migratory movements. This interlude proved to be short-lived and events, as Castles and Miller recall, took an unanticipated turn:

> After 1914, war, xenophobia and economic stagnation caused a considerable decline in migration, and the large scale movements of the preceding period seemed to be the results of a unique and unrepeatable constellation. When rapid and sustained economic growth got under way after the Second World War, the new age of migration was to take the world by surprise. (Castles and Miller 1993: 65)

In the space of a few decades the comparative relationship between political and population movements, and subsequent assessments and policies of assimilation, was radically altered, if not necessarily fundamentally transformed. Castles and Miller are referring to international population movements, but we will also be concerned with internal migrations, particularly the journeys of aboriginal peoples. The ethnic political results of these relocations, in their varied geographic, residential, economic and socio-demographic guises, will be the focus of the next few chapters. In this one, I will sketch in the major parameters of internal and external migration, roughly between 1945 and the 1980s, in order to provide a descriptive backcloth for the more in-depth analysis to follow.

Waxing and waning powers

By the early twentieth century one can perceive a changing geopolitical and economic world order as the cards of political power were reshuffled and the imperial phase of an international division of labour was giving way to a new transnational pattern. Within this scenario the United States was consolidating its position as the classic exemplar of a society of diverse immigration whose phenomenal natural and technological resources made it a hegemon. In contrast, the United Kingdom's place in emigration and power terms was in relative decline. Meanwhile, our other settlement societies were moving rapidly from colonies to independent status, with much lower volumes of less heterogeneous peoples still contributing to a far from inconsequential prosperity and regional influence.

United States

Between 1820 and 1987 over fifty million people migrated to the USA, with three-fifths of that total arriving in the few decades from 1861 to 1920 (Borjas 1990). This latter period was punctuated by recessionary intervals, and it was soon followed by the depression in the 1930s, but overall it marked a phase of enormous expansion in industrialisation, investment and urbanisation. The high native birth rate and substantial internal migratory flows from rural areas to cities still could not meet the labour demands of the times. Black slave labour that had fuelled earlier capital accumulation, although now nominally 'free', remained entrapped within a racist 'Jim Crow' system in the southern states supplying much of the raw materials and foodstuffs for burgeoning urban industries. Sharecropping and gang labour for wages was a deeply impoverished kind of freedom, so thousands of black workers and their families moved north, meeting largely unskilled, labour shortages left by upwardly mobile white labour and the abatement of immigration during the First World War. Movement of non-white workers continued in subsequent decades, and was matched in the south-west by the start of an ongoing exodus of Mexican workers crossing the American border in search of a better life. Most migrants, however, continued to come from further afield (Dinnerstein et al. 1996).

With the curtailment of black slavery, and the gradual closing of the 'golden door' to Chinese and other Asian migrants, European immigration remained predominant. But whereas northern and western European workers dominated earlier migrations, their southern and eastern neighbours became the major sources of labour between 1860 and 1930. Italians, Greeks, Jews from Russia, Galicia and Romania, and Slavic peoples made up the bulk of a very diverse set of new European immigrants who flooded into America. Not all of these migrants stayed. More than a third of three million Italian migrants, for example, returned to their homelands, some remigrating to Australia and Canada, while Jews fleeing persecution in Eastern Europe contemplated a return to a new homeland in Israel after the Second World War. This diversifying of the origins of migrants reached a ceiling of toleration in the 1920s, as images of American national identity became even more imbued with a sense of white exclusivity. The move to restrict Chinese entry in the 1880s was the first overt sign of a desire on the part of the federal state to override the laissez-faire policies and regional state control (or lack of it) over immigration. 'The massive influx of foreigners in the first decade of the twentieth century, the newly exercised federal regulatory powers, and strong nativist agitation culminated in the early 1920s in broad legislation controlling both the numbers and the ethnicity of immigrants' (Freeman and Jupp 1992: 8). The series of laws enacted in Congress in the 1920s attempted to freeze the ethnic composition of the immigrant nation into an adjudged acceptable pattern of assimilability by establishing quotas of national origin, based initially on the census of 1890, and then 1920 (Green 1994: 42). This effectively favoured immigrants from northern and western Europe as these regions had dominated early flows to the United States. Economic depression and global wars, the overt military kind and the insidious 'Cold War' that followed it, successively combined with strict regulation, to slow large-scale immigration to the USA until the 1960s. The unskilled and semi-skilled needs of capital were met by the overall expansion of female paid labour and the increased infusion of primarily black and Mexican workers, the latter encouraged by temporary labour schemes (the 1940s' *Bracero* program) or the turning of blind eyes to illegal labour movements across the southern border. Skilled and professional labour demand was satisfied by the upward mobility of generations of offspring of earlier white, foreign-born arrivals who fuelled the American Dream. Thus, internal sources met a need previously reliant on external forces.

Nevertheless, economic considerations were tempered by other facets of American domestic and foreign policy. Seeing themselves in the Cold War era as the major defender of the Free World, American elites could not blatantly exclude so much of the globe, although the general tenor of USA immigration legislation remained restrictive. Hence, the McCarran-Walter Act (1952) reincorporated Asia and the Pacific into the national model, with small quotas allotted annually to each state in the region. Liberal sentiments were pushed further in 1965, when, in the heyday of civil rights, the Democratic administration stripped all signs of racial and national discrimination from immigration legislation. National origin quotas were removed from family reunification, refugee and labour demand provisions (Freeman and Jupp 1992: 9). This 'liberal credo of immigration reform' had far-reaching consequences, clearly unforeseen at the time (Dittgen 1997: 260–1), as immigration levels rose sharply, particularly in reunification and refugee categories, and Latin America and Asia swiftly overtook Europe as major source regions. Negative public and governmental reaction to such changes, and the backlash against growing numbers of illegal, mainly Hispanic workers and asylum seekers, ultimately pushed the immigration pendulum back towards restriction in the late 1980s. In the meantime, however, the national myth of entry and achievement 'only in America' was readily sustained.

Britain

Prior to the mid-twentieth century Britain was mainly a country of high levels of emigration and internal movements between the various nations in the British state. The vast majority of migrants to Britain since the early nineteenth century were of European origin (Miles 1993: 130). Most striking was the exodus of seasonal and permanent Irish workers, male and female, into the industrial heart of England, southern Wales and western Scotland. These, mainly unskilled and semi-skilled manual workers, shared the opprobrium of the religious and cultural stigma of a 'race' apart. Racist hostility was also encountered by the 120 000 Jewish refugees fleeing the pogroms of Russia between 1875 and 1914. German and, to a lesser extent, Italian migrants were also subject to anti-foreigner agitation that grew in intensity as war broke out.

All Irish workers, as British subjects, were free to travel into and across neighbouring British nations, and this position persisted, somewhat anomalously, even after what is now the Republic became independent in 1921. Jews soon became subjects, and many moved from wage- to self-employment, but the hostile reaction to their arrival, in tandem with anti-German hostility, led to the first steps in a spiralling legislative process of British immigration restriction that was to mark most of the twentieth century.[1] A severe labour shortage at the end of the Second World War was initially approached through short-term work permits and labour contracts, notably the European Voluntary Scheme, that brought 90 000, mainly male, alien workers from Poland, Italy and other European refugee camps to Britain (ibid.: 155–7). But the British, unlike most north-west European states, did not use 'guestworkers' extensively, and soon returned to their offshore subjects as a source of labour. Workers continued to flow across the Irish Sea, but 'surplus colonial manpower' started to appear as a possible solution to labour shortages.

This surplus, as we have seen in earlier chapters, was not a new commodity. Nor was population movement within the Empire and Commonwealth a recent phenomenon. What was novel were the size and political impact of the movement of non-white British subjects from peripheral regions into metropolitan Britain. The history of black and Asian people in Britain is centuries old (Fryer 1984). Thousands of slaves and ex-slaves, many of them children, were employed as servants in upper-class households in the eighteenth century. Small communities of black and Asian seamen were established in various British ports by the end of the nineteenth century, while London had always been a base for non-white students, businessmen and professionals. The two World Wars brought further Asian and black men and women into the United Kingdom on active service and as munitions workers, some of whom remained afterwards. But the most far-reaching migration, in political terms, of workers from former British colonies in the Indian subcontinent, the Caribbean and Africa, occurred after 1945.

One of the effects of the McCarran-Walter Act, was the tightening of immigration restrictions on Caribbean, particularly Jamaican labour, into the United States. The resultant ripples of this policy reached the shores of Britain (and Canada), where many employers were actively searching for workers. Transport services and hospitals in London, for example, recruited hundreds of West Indian staff. Foundries in the West Midlands, and Yorkshire and Lancashire mills, also drew thousands of Indian and Pakistani workers. By 1961 there were over half a million people of New Commonwealth origin in Britain, mainly employed in semi- and unskilled manual work viewed as unattractive and uncompetitive by the local white labour force. Some of the latter had packed their bags and departed for the now independent ex-dominions vigorously competing with one another for skilled workers and their families, of 'the right type'. The ironies of this transfer of populations between, euphemistically described elder and younger fragments of Empire, are inescapable when one considers how, since 1945, successive British governments spent considerable time and money facilitating the migration of UK residents to the 'Old Commonwealth' while, at the same time, increasingly resisting the entry of citizens from the 'New' (Paul 1997: xii). Racial criteria clearly lay at the heart of these age distinctions, since Barbados had been British since 1627, New Zealand from only 1840.

From the early 1960s, British subjecthood, citizenship and nationality were redefined in an attempt to embrace what was always a compartmentalised conception of global Britishness. In a nutshell, New Commonwealth immigration was seen as creating 'a race relations problem'. The 1962 Commonwealth Immigrants Act confirmed the transformation from universal British subject to 'coloured immigrant', while a further Act (in 1971) heightened the distinction between 'the truly British' and the rest. Ultimately, the aversion to the New eventually forced the exclusion of the Old. In turn, the failure of much of the favoured Commonwealth to attract enough British migrants, and their eventual loosening of immigration restrictions, added a further twist to this story.

Widening the gateways

'For Britain, non-white immigration occurred in the context of the obligations of a declining imperial power to former colonial territories. For Canada, non-white immigration was a trend within the context of a long-term program of national development' (Reitz 1988: 117). This contrast extends to all our case studies, but as we shall see, shifts in immigration policy were more often attributable to ad hoc pragmatism than lengthy foresight.

Canada

Canada followed the United States in shifting from a relatively open to more protectionist immigration policy in the first half of the twentieth century. At the turn of the century the main goal of immigration policy had been the acquisition of settlers to open up the west, but the Canadian state subsequently adopted a far more restrictive stance with a series of legislative and administrative immigration discriminatory amendments between 1906 and 1923. Yet the Canadian-style policy regime did not resemble the American quota system but developed within a more flexible set of arrangements much more attuned to short-run economic self-interest (Green 1994). When post-Second World War labour demand grew, the objectives of population growth and economic development were emphasised, but far greater weight was attached to current economic fluctuations (Hawkins 1972, 1989). This promoted a 'tap on, tap off' approach to immigration intake, far more concerned with attracting workers with skills in short supply locally than long-term population building. Canada was more cautious than Australia, for example, in respect of immigration levels, but it led the way in moving towards a non-discriminatory selection policy. A 'triumph of economics over discrimination' (Passaris 1984: 91) eventuated because labour market demands could only be met by drawing upon the manpower resources of previously shunned source countries. Since the Immigration Act of 1910, Canadian immigration legislation and procedures had reflected a distinct anti-Asiatic bias and a marked preference for migrants fitting an Anglocentric norm. That norm broadened by the early 1950s to accommodate French and other north-western European sources, as altruistic and economic considerations combined to promote changes in intakes. Humanitarian motives were clearly important in accepting displaced persons from Eastern Europe in the 1950s and 1960s, for example, and their arrival eased the way for subsequent continental European migrants, but these migrants were seen as a valuable source of labour, with many of them being indentured as farm workers or domestic servants.

In the 1960s the desire to improve Canada's international standing, particularly with non-white countries within the Commonwealth and United Nations, and to make immigration a more effective means of meeting labour market requirements, led to the dismantling of racially discriminatory legislation and the move to a more universalistic system of migrant assessment. The 1962 Act removed most country of origin and racial restrictions and the last vestiges of formal discrimination were eliminated in 1967 when a points system was introduced, for independent migrants and nominated relatives, with the emphasis mainly on skills and qualifications suitable to Canada's labour requirements. Subsequent adjustments to economic criteria in the 1970s and 1980s further widened the range of admissible migrants from less developed countries. At the same time the family reunification category was expanded and business migration, particularly from Asia, was encouraged through special provisions for the self-employed and investors or entrepreneurs. These legislative changes had a marked impact on the ethnic profile of new Canadians over a few decades. Immigration to Canada was still dominated by European migrants until the late 1960s, but United Kingdom and Irish migration was first of all supplanted by continental European migrants, who in turn were superseded as major immigration sources by migrants from Asia and the American region. By the end of the 1980s fewer migrants were arriving from the UK than Africa, and Asia was providing half of Canada's total intake (White and Samuel 1991: 73).

The United States has always proved a magnet for substantial numbers of Canadians but, for much of this century, sizeable numbers of Americans have also moved north. Since the mid-1970s migration from the United States has remained relatively stable at just under 10 per cent of the total number of arrivals, but the movement from Latin America and the Caribbean has grown substantially, largely through permanent family and humanitarian admissions. Canada has also made considerable use of temporary migrant workers since 1945. Like their European counterparts, and those of its neighbour, Canadian programmes recruit migrant labour from less developed countries within the Americas region to fill low-skilled and low-paid jobs shunned by local workers. Caribbean domestic service workers and seasonal farm labourers, as a major example, now largely fill the role once occupied by Eastern European refugees (Satzewich 1990).

Australia

Up to the immediate post-Second World War period the most striking aspect of Australian immigration patterns was an exclusive British stream of assisted migrants and a mere smattering of unassisted arrivals from other destinations. But since 1975 almost half of the immigrants to Australia have been unassisted non-Europeans (Freeman and Jupp 1992: 5). Wars and depression, as in the United States, promoted disruptions in immigration flows in the early part of the twentieth century, while the official initiation of a White Australia policy affirmed previous favoured sources of migrants. Comparatively speaking, however, Australia has placed the highest priority on immigration since the late 1940s, and experienced the greatest proportional population increase as a result. Moreover, the striking ethnic exclusivity of its pre-Second World War migration pattern gave little clue to the cultural heterogeneity of arrivals in subsequent decades. Between the end of the Second World War and the late 1980s about five million people from some 100 countries had come to Australia (BIR 1990: 32).

The foundations of Australian postwar immigration policy were laid in 1945 when population growth targets were firmly aligned with economic objectives of stimulating growth through expansion of the workforce and consumption base, plus the aim of securing the country's defence against the threat of invasion (Hawkins 1989: 32). Immigration figures ebbed and flowed in tandem with economic cycles, political whim and popular levels of toleration and resentment, but an expansive immigration population building policy was pursued until the mid-1970s. It was not until 1976, with the end of the long boom, consequent global restructuring and local labour market contraction that Australia posted its first net migration loss in thirty years.

The White Australia policy had a similar history to its Canadian counterpart, with explicitly anti-Asiatic sentiments formalised in the 1901 Immigration Restriction Act. Once again, though, economic expediency and unforeseen events partially thwarted discriminatory sentiments and practices. Plans (in 1945) to recruit ten British for every one 'foreign' migrant were soon frustrated by excess labour demand in the United Kingdom and inadequate shipping, forcing Australia to meet its high targets from alternative sources (Collins 1988: 22). Foremost amongst these were the displaced persons of Europe, 170 000 of whom settled in Australia between 1947 and 1952. As in Canada, the intake was also geared to Australia's labour requirements and similarly paved the way for greater acceptance of Eastern and, most notably, Southern European migrants. Although British immigrants were still preferred and more actively recruited it was gradually accepted during the 1950s, at least by interests driving the policy, that at least half of new Australian immigrants should come from outside the United Kingdom (Appleyard 1988: 98).

Non-European migration remained severely restricted, but the history of Australian immigration legislation eventually followed the Canadian experience of gradually opening discriminatory gateways, albeit at a more cautious rate and still within firm discretionary limits. Over the 1950s and 1960s a similar progression of legislative and administrative changes towards assessment of skills and qualifications gradually outweighed subjective evaluation of racial and national acceptability. The White Australia policy was formally discarded in 1973, with the new system of migrant classification and universally applied selection criteria being similar to that adopted by Canada in 1967. Because overall intakes were being severely reduced at the same time, the changes did not immediately lead to significant increases in migration from non-traditional source countries (Hawkins 1989: 94–106). Indeed, with Australia following Canada in retaliating against Britain's less welcoming attitude to migrants from the 'Old Commonwealth', New Zealanders were the only citizens who enjoyed unrestricted entry. Nevertheless, the

United Kingdom still remained Australia's most important individual source country, with British migrants making up a far more significant contribution to population building than for Canada. Kiwis moved rapidly up the league table of arrivals from the mid-1970s, but movements from elsewhere within the Pacific region have been small. Unlike New Zealand, Australia has not sought significant numbers of low-skilled temporary workers from the Pacific Islands in the postwar era, and there is a marked absence of settlement opportunities extended to indigenous Papua New Guineans, despite their island's history as a past Australian protectorate.

A points system was introduced in Australia in 1979, differing from the Canadian system in attaching more importance to the assessment of 'personal suitability' of new migrant workers and the relatives of those already working in Australia. Growth in family reunion migration has also been an important factor in producing rising levels of Asian migration, as has the business migration programme which was launched in 1978 and expanded in subsequent decades. Australian immigration, in common with its most northern American cousin, has therefore occurred in waves, with each successive decade since the 1940s seeing a further widening of source countries. And yet, the historical ties of British settlement had not become as attenuated as they had in Canada by the mid-1980s. Between 1945 and 1985, despite the notably increasing trend towards Non-English Speaking Background (NESB) immigrants, to use the local bureaucratic vernacular, almost half of 'new Australian' permanent arrivals were from the UK, Ireland, New Zealand, the USA, Canada and South Africa (Webber 1992: 167). The sun had long set on the British Empire, but there was still a trace of an after-glow in Oceania.

New Zealand

If the mid to late twentieth century has seen Australia becoming remarkably heterogeneous, but still remaining somewhat 'British' by immigrant intake, New Zealand broadly retained its reputation as the quintessential Britannia Pacifica, being far more cautious than Canada and Australia in respect of non-European immigration levels, and decidedly more tentative about moving towards a fully non-discriminatory policy. New Zealand's post-Second World War immigration policies tended to be ad hoc and closely geared to short-term labour market conditions (Farmer 1986: 486). Successive governments showed little sign of viewing immigration as part of a long-term economic or population development strategy. Favourable export markets and domestic policies of tariff protection ensured economic growth until the mid-1970s. Significant labour shortages were experienced then, particularly in expanding secondary industries, but these shortfalls, as we shall see below, were met in part by Maori rural–urban migration.

In sharp contrast to Australia and Canada, between 1977 and 1990 more people left New Zealand than arrived. Much of this pattern was attributable to emigration to Australia, with whom New Zealand effectively shared a common labour market since the fostering of economic ties under Closer Economic Relations (CER) agreements initiated in the 1960s. The flow of New Zealanders across the Tasman bears some resemblance to cross-border movements between Canada and the United States, but the movements of people going to Australia greatly outnumber those coming the other way.

With the exception of population movements from neighbouring Pacific Island societies, New Zealand's immigration intake remained predominantly British until the mid-1970s, with very low levels of non-British European immigration by comparison with the flows to Australia and Canada. Both of these countries had a third or more of their intakes between 1945 and 1976 coming from this source. New Zealand in contrast had 9 per cent. While this trend reflects the strong preference for British migrants, it must also be seen in the context of the comparatively low immigration targets and labour requirements of a much smaller society which ensured large-scale recruitment from continental Europe never became a necessity as it did in Australia and Canada. The growth in Asian migration has also been a more recent and limited phenomenon than in Canada and Australia, reflecting New Zealand's more hesitant and belated moves towards a non-discriminatory immigration policy.

Although an explicit White New Zealand policy was never adopted, the entry procedures introduced and modified between 1899 and 1920 effectively maintained a colour bar. People of British birth and descent were allowed unrestricted entry while others required permits, the issue of which was at the discretion of the minister and could thus be manipulated to exclude certain groups. This remained a cornerstone of immigration policy after the Second World War and was reaffirmed in the Immigration Act of 1964. As a result, New Zealand's immigration flows remained considerably more homogeneous than those of Canada and Australia. Given New Zealand's immigration targets were far lower, they could be met by assisted passage schemes from favoured sources without recourse to large-scale non-British immigration.

As in Australia, the acceptance of displaced persons from Europe was the first departure from Anglocentrism, although between 1947 and

1952 New Zealand accepted just 4600 refugees, selected largely on economic grounds. This was a very small intake, comparatively speaking, and did not pave the way for acceptance of large-scale immigration from Eastern Europe. In 1950 an assisted immigration scheme was negotiated with the Netherlands government, leading to a significant increase in Dutch migration and small numbers of assisted migrants were accepted from other Western European countries. Italian, Greek and Yugoslav migration was largely restricted to close relatives of their small New Zealand resident communities. The entry of Asians was also largely confined to family migrants, but under even more restrictive provisions.

The only significant non-European migration was from Pacific Islands with close historical and economic links to New Zealand. The Pacific provided a valuable source of unskilled labour for New Zealand's expanding secondary industries, and Pacific Island workers performed a similar role to the early wave of Southern Europeans in Australia and the parallel use of Caribbean guestworkers in Canada. Much Pacific Islands migration was of a temporary nature, with many entering as visitors and seeking work on arrival, often overstaying the duration of their permits. This situation was tolerated by the state and encouraged by employers as long as excess labour demand continued. The deterioration of economic conditions in the early 1970s, however, prompted a clampdown on Pacific Island overstayers involving dawn police raids and random street checks. But levels of migration remained high, due to growth in family reunion admissions and the varying citizenship rights of residents of some Pacific states whose intertwining colonial histories allowed them limited or free access to New Zealand.[2]

The Labour government elected in 1972 had included a non-discriminatory immigration policy in its election platform but this was only partially implemented. A major policy review (in 1974) recommended following the Canadian and Australian stance towards Britain's closing door policy on her ex-dominions, and ended the unrestricted right of entry for British migrants (Brawley 1993: 33–5). But New Zealand did not come fully into line with Canadian and Australian practice until the mid-1980s when another major review of immigration (in 1986), under the auspices of another newly elected Labour government, signalled the final move to a formally non-discriminatory immigration policy. Following in familiar footsteps, the post-1986 legislative climate included business migrant policies, aimed at comparable Southern and Eastern Asian markets. The encouragement of an entrepreneurial intake was part of a much broader pattern of male and female Asian labour recruitment, whose occupations, although skewed towards the highly qualified, covered the whole spectrum of skill levels. The figures for those with claimed Asian ethnicity climbed from 55 000 (in 1986 census) to 99 000 five years later, most of this attributable to immigration (McKinnon 1996: 50). So, much like in Vancouver and Melbourne, a Chinese person encountered in Auckland by this time was more likely to be a recent arrival from Hong Kong or Taiwan, than part of the old Cantonese diaspora.

Finally (in 1991), New Zealand introduced a points system modelled on Canadian and Australian lines. A continued emphasis on marketable skills and qualifications, English proficiency, and miserly post-migrant assistance in comparison with many cross-Tasman and Canadian states, begged caution, but New Zealand seemed to have opened its gateways to a degree comparable to that adopted earlier by its North American and Pacific 'cousins'.

Refugees and asylum seekers

If the bulk of population movements in the twentieth century is still attributable to the state-assisted and unassisted passage of migrant workers and the relatives of past and present generations of such persons, refugees, displaced persons and asylum seekers form an increasingly important facet of a widening global picture of transnational settlement. Broad geopolitical considerations relating to the growth of international bodies like the United Nations and its umbrella organisations, and more specific foreign policy relations, have influenced the flow of people seeking refuge from persecution, wars and natural disasters.[3] Such movements further exemplify the difficulties of seeking to separate non-economic from economic causes, and free from unfree conceptions of migrant volition. These distinctions are conceptually problematic, bureaucratically fraught and highly susceptible to elite and popular prejudices. Ethnocentricity and economics have often been as important as altruism in shaping the transfer of those seeking refuge, particularly when their attributes have been perceived as somewhat distant from the 'host' population.

The availability of sponsorship, assistance with accommodation, employment and other aspects of resettlement, also play a significant role in determining the number and type of refugees in the broadest senses who are accepted. Not surprisingly, given its history of state decentralisation, voluntary assistance has been the hallmark of United States refugee settlement policies, although after the Cuban inflow in

1960 national state funding and programmes expanded to meet what was seen as an exceptional form of immigration. British settlement policies too, despite more extensive welfare state protection for citizens and permanent residents, rely heavily on local and national voluntary bodies. There is much debate about the adequacy of Australian and Canadian settlement policies, and there are important differences, particularly in Canada, in respective regional state and province levels of provision, but many commentators see them as comparing more than favourably with comparable programmes in the United States and Britain (see, for example, Jupp 1992: 138). In New Zealand, however, the reliance on a small and underfunded voluntary sector exercises a severe constraint on the number of refugees who can be adequately resettled.

Notwithstanding these contingencies, over two million refugees acquired permanent residence in the USA between 1946 and the late 1980s, with Cuban and Vietnamese settlers making up almost half of this figure. Until 1980, when American legislation was brought into line with United Nations conventions, virtually any person leaving what was deemed a communist regime was defined as a refugee (Castles and Miller 1993: 85). Britain's acceptance of European Voluntary Workers in the 1940s, as noted earlier, had some elements of refugee status, but this case neatly illustrates the blurring of economic and political definition. The British government never waged the Cold War with the vigour of the United States, so anti-communist refugee policy was more conservative and reactive (Cohen 1994: 76). The Hungarian and Czech uprisings against the Soviet bloc saw 15 000 and 5000 dissidents respectively, settling in Britain in the 1950s and 1960s. More recently, small quotas of Chilean and Vietnamese persons have entered the UK, under refugee programmes or as the result of processing 'spontaneous' asylum seekers (ibid.). Overall, despite Britain's much-vaunted history of giving refuge to dissenters, it has not been a prominent European safe haven in recent years.[4]

Up to the 1970s, Australian, Canadian and New Zealand refugee settlement eventuated from largely ad hoc responses to specific crises, particularly those occurring in Europe. In each case New Zealand's intake was proportionately far lower than those of Canada and Australia. This may suggest greater humanitarianism on the part of the latter countries but it also reflects a higher demand for immigrants, while New Zealand's more cautious stance was in keeping with the overall tenor of its immigration policy. In the 1970s and 1980s the range of source countries for refugees broadened considerably as a result of conflicts in Asia, Africa, Latin America and the Middle East. The first significant movement of non-European refugees came with the expulsion of Asians from Uganda in 1972. This impacted mostly on Britain, but the ripples of Amin's policy reached far-flung regions of the unravelling Empire. Having abandoned its discriminatory immigration policy, Canada responded far more generously than New Zealand and more particularly Australia, which was still bound by the White Australia philosophy.

A sterner test of the non-discriminatory stances of all three countries came with the Indochinese refugee crisis from 1975 onwards. The initial response from Australia and New Zealand was hesitant, with foreign policy and domestic political concerns taking priority over humanitarian considerations. A change of government (to Labour) in 1975 and pressure from the United Nations Convention on Refugees (UNHCR) and the Association of South East Asian Nations (ASEAN), brought about a marked change in Australian policy, while New Zealand remained tentative until the escalation of the crisis in 1978–9 (Binzeggar 1980: 59–63; Collins 1988: 63–4). By 1985, when the peak of the second wave had passed, Canada and Australia were both amongst the top five receiving nations for Indochinese refugees fleeing the killing fields, with Australia receiving the greatest proportion relative to its own population.

The 1980s saw refugee flows becoming increasingly diverse with important movements from Eastern Europe and the Middle East. All three countries admitted refugees from Iraq and Iran, and Australia and Canada also took many Lebanese. Conflicts in Latin America, particularly in El Salvador and Guatemala, have been of more significance to Canada's intake, although Australia has received large numbers from El Salvador in recent years. Canada has also been the most responsive to refugee situations in Africa, having recently admitted significant numbers from Somalia and Ethiopia while Australia and New Zealand have responded more cautiously.

New Zealand's overall refugee intake remains significantly lower than those of Canada and Australia, as a proportion of both population and total immigration flows. In 1987 New Zealand established an annual global quota of 800 refugees which has not increased, nor indeed been filled every year, despite the subsequent adoption of a more open immigration policy.

Aboriginal migrations

The rural to urban shift of American blacks and the movement of Irish workers into England and Scotland reveal migrant flows within states paralleled those between them in facilitating economic growth and national expansion. At a very general level these movements exemplify the continuities of colonialism and the repercussions they have on patterns of negative categorisation and structured inequality. Yet just as the slave and non-slave backgrounds of black and Irish workers introduce very different historical and contemporary features into an analysis of their situations, the unique characteristics of aboriginal peoples add a further important variation to a common theme of work, mobility and stratification.

We have already seen in Chapter 2 how aboriginal land was ultimately more important than labour in settler societies. In North America, for example, Europeans in what were to become the United States and Canada, were dependent on Indians for the production of furs, while, for a much shorter period, Maori food production and labour were vital to the initial phase of New Zealand colonisation. Some Indians were enslaved in the American colonies, and some Australian Aborigines encountered a different, but equally pernicious form of servitude. None of these situations led to the integration of aboriginal peoples into the economic structure of emergent settler states as individual paid workers *en masse*. Instead, to varying degrees across our case studies, with considerable regional variation, the indigenes were pushed back into the geographical margins of their societies and forced into administrative structures more designed to facilitate land expropriation than labour exploitation. Aboriginal minorities were mainly confined to regions remote from white settlement, or were forced or chose to keep to themselves in areas more proximate to Europeans, engaging in wage labour on a casual and/or seasonal basis. During the twentieth century increasing numbers of aboriginal people came in from the margins in a geographical and economic sense and this was to have wide-ranging political effects.

United States

The legacy of land relocation and dispossession, as Cornell (1988a: 129) notes, was underdevelopment. His remark, although addressed to the United States, is readily exportable. Aboriginal minorities in general faced the problem of a mismatch between expanding population numbers and limited land and resource bases. In remote areas with traditional subsistence ways of life largely intact, Indians in North America were able to reproduce themselves without waged work, although the discovery of mineral wealth and the harnessing of hydro-electric power saw many previously isolated communities opened up to forces long experienced by aboriginal people resident in more temperate and populated zones.

In these and other regions a coexistence of capitalist and pre-capitalist forms of production fostered a precarious survival, although modest wealth, as farmers on the prairies for example, was not unknown (Dickinson and Wotherspoon 1992). Indians found work on nearby farms, in construction gangs and 'frontier' towns.

The two World Wars saw many aboriginal people leaving the reservations to join the war effort, as part of the armed forces or as workers in defence industries. Many returned to the reservations, for good or temporarily, but others remained, encouraging kin to join them. Urban migration in the 1950s and 1960s was further stimulated by economic conditions affecting white, black and Indian rural wage workers and farmers in general. Mechanisation and changes in the scale of agricultural production drove thousands off the land and depopulated small towns, destroying casual employment opportunities and underfinanced Indian farms in the process. Market forces impelled most of these movements, but government policies also spurred the accelerating process. Contact with the world beyond the reservation was seen as a pathway to civilisation, with entry into education and paid work key markers of progress in this direction. Off-reservation American and Canadian boarding and residential schools, introduced in the nineteenth century, continued to influence migration in the twentieth century (Miller 1996). These vocationally oriented institutions loosened the attachment to home reservations and encouraged students to travel further afield. Other Bureau of Indian Affairs (BIA) and Department of Indian Affairs (DIA) programmes were aimed even more directly at relocation. Job placement, further training, and housing grants for example, deliberately facilitated Indian urban employment in order to cut state expenditure and encourage assimilation. Seesawing support for on-reserve federal and tribally controlled services compounded the situation.

This combination of economic and policy forces produced an accelerating urban migratory flow over a remarkably short time span. At the start of the twentieth century most Native Americans lived on reservations, and by its midpoint only 56 000 Indians (16 per cent of total population) were classified as urban based by the 1950 US Census. However, by 1970, a further 300 000 had moved cityward, and in another decade urban numbers had more than doubled again. By 1980 over half (53 per cent) of the Indian population were categorised as city dwellers (Cornell 1988a: 132). These bald national figures disguise considerable regional variation, and complex patterns of outward and return reservation journeys, but in the space of a few decades the magnitude of United States urban migration was dramatic.

Canada

Regional and transitory patterns are also vital to an understanding of Canadian post-Second World War aboriginal movement. Comparisons, however, are greatly complicated by different administrative categorisations of the Canadian aboriginal population and shifting statistical measures of urban residence within and across national censuses. The northern Inuit population was still overwhelmingly rural in the 1980s, with Métis being the most likely to be resident in cities (Norris 1990: 40). Nonetheless, at a very general level, there are many similarities with the United States situation, although the overall rate of urban migration of Canadian Indians has been less striking and more recently experienced.

The decades between 1880 and 1930 have been described as the historical zenith of Canadian aboriginal employment as the country-wide shortage of labour offered widespread opportunities for waged work (Satzewich and Wotherspoon 1993: 48). The Depression marked a collapse of Indian labour, but demand in and after the Second World War saw an upwards swing in employment possibilities, both locally and in nearby towns. The shift in the Canadian economic infrastructure towards new staples, pulp and paper, oil and natural gas, for example, with accompanying transport and communication improvements, facilitated mobility from remote regions to urban centres. Racist exclusion and the competition from returning war veterans and new immigrants, however, countered the rise in labour activity. Nevertheless, the drift to the city continued, albeit often in a transitory way. The mechanisation of labour in agriculture and mineral development and deteriorating conditions on reserves forced aboriginal populations to seek a better life elsewhere. Cities, however uninviting for many, seemed to offer the only hope. As in the United States, the Canadian federal government was also highly instrumental in accelerating the movement of Indian people off reserves. From the 1960s millions of dollars were spent on job training and relocation for aboriginal people as the state and state-aided private sector programmes endeavoured to shift Indians into 'concrete reserves' (Grant 1983). Some aboriginal men, and often more educated women, did find work, but many, as Grant's phrase suggests, swapped one welfare ghetto for another.

The mix of inducement and enforcement promoted an inevitable result. In the prairie provinces, for example, accounting for approximately 40 per cent of all registered Indians in Canada, less than 10 per cent lived off reserves prior to 1960. By the mid-1970s between a fifth and a third were living in the cities of Alberta, Manitoba and Saskatchewan

(Buckley 1992: 93). The poorer districts of British Columbian, Ontarian and Quebec cities experienced a similar process of in-migration of aboriginal people. Nationally, 85 per cent of registered Indians lived on reserve in 1966, by 1981 almost a third (32 per cent) of women and over a quarter (28 per cent) men in this category were living off their reserve, mostly in the city (Norris 1990).

Australia

If the demographic presence of aboriginal people in North America varies greatly across regions, the distinctions between and within so-called 'settled' and 'remote' Australia are even more striking. In the heavily urbanised south-east of Australia the aboriginal population has been less than 1 per cent since 1901, while in the mainly remote Northern Territories, aboriginal people were in the majority up to the 1950s, and still constitute approximately a third of the region's population (Armitage 1995: 29). Even within this pattern, neither the socio-cultural and residential styles of life nor economic conditions of aboriginal people is homogeneous. Aborigines reside in rural outstations and aboriginal towns on or near reserves and missions artificially formed through the European presence. Others live in fringe camps near non-aboriginal townships or in the less salubrious areas of Australian cities. Aborigines have moved, in irregular fashion, into and around towns for over a century, but here too, the urban transition has hastened in recent decades.[5] Even in the Northern Territories, where 90 per cent of Aboriginals lived in rural areas in 1961, a third of the population was living in 'urban areas' by 1981, although this category includes small country towns.

In common with North America, the relationship between geographic location and a move into paid work is a recurring theme in the Australian literature on the aboriginal economy. For example, Darwin provided employment for northern aboriginal labouring and domestic workers after the First World War, many living in dreadfully insanitary conditions in special compounds on the fringe of the town (Broome 1982: 121). Most workers in the Territory, however, were employed in the cattle industry until, ironically, the eventual award of equal pay with white workers in the 1960s saw pastoralist shifts to European labour and a resultant slump in aboriginal employment. With few exceptions the advent of mining in the north did little to alleviate the situation of aboriginal stockmen. Mechanisation, inadequate training and employer hostility combined to ensure Aborigines were a reserve labour force for the most unskilled and lowly paid jobs. A comparable situation existed in settled Australia, with aboriginal unemployment commonly reaching figures of 50 per cent or higher (Altman and Nieuwenhuysen 1979). Nevertheless, relatively better urban living conditions promoted aboriginal migration in the early 1970s, although this slowed as urban communities later felt the effects of a deteriorating Australian economy. Persistent return migration from city to country, spurred by what was called the 'Outstations movement' in the 1970s, also needs stressing.

This complex migratory framework illustrates a culturally varied set of goals and values within urban and rural aboriginal domains, as well as revealing the ambivalence shown by successive governments towards aboriginal labour. The attitude of administrators and employers, developed earliest in Victoria and New South Wales, that persons of mixed descent were fitted for capitalism, eventually became a nation-wide policy for all aborigines in the 1950s. Yet this stance only partly echoed the moves in North America to 'encourage' aboriginal people into paid work, and, as we shall see, greatly contrasted with the New Zealand experience. Generally speaking, as Markus notes: 'The economic development that would see the Australian population double between 1945 and 1981 bypassed the areas where most aborigines lived and no serious consideration was given to meeting labour shortages by training aborigines for work in the areas of highest demand, the manufacturing and construction industries' (Markus 1994: 163–4).

New Zealand

If the Native American move to US cities is characterised as dramatic we run into problems of hyperbole in describing the rapidity and magnitude of the Maori rural to urban transition. A familiar pattern of improved mortality rates, high levels of population growth, rapid urbanisation and occupational change were the hallmarks of a new Maori migration. In 1936 the census revealed less than a fifth (17 per cent) of the Maori population was urban based, with many of them living in small towns. Four decades later (1976) less than a quarter (24 per cent) were living in rural areas, although the resilience of the numbers residing in townships (20 per cent) and the often high level of contact retained with ancestral areas needs to be noted. What sparked this move from rural, casual labour force to urban proletariat? As I have noted elsewhere, the Maori exodus is best explained by:

> Acute Maori overpopulation in relation to limited natural resources; high rural unemployment; the economic marginality of many Maori-owned farms that were smaller, less efficient, and hence less productive than many which were European owned; the generally slow rate of

regional development in those parts of New Zealand most heavily populated by Maori; the lure of better employment and income opportunities and therefore of greater economic security in the city, and the more intangible benefits of urban life styles. (Pearson 1990: 113)

This array of contributory causes highlights again how the economic conditions and state policies of the 1930s and 1940s impacted on aboriginal minorities across our case studies. Before the Second World War Maori were, with some regional exceptions, peripheral to capitalist production. At best they were seen by the state and employers as a marginal, mainly rural, labour force; at worst they were viewed as an unproductive drain on state resources. After the war, with the diversification of agriculture and the move towards an expanded industrial/manufacturing sector, particularly in North Island cities where Maori were most heavily concentrated, Maori migrants became a valuable source of labour at a time of economic expansion. The Maori war effort and the arrival of a more sympathetic government administration combined to remove some of the stigma of aboriginal status. This climate of opinion raised Maori aspirations. New horizons were opened up by war service at home and abroad, improvements in education, and better communications.

The state under the first Labour government that came to power in the late 1930s grew substantially in size as welfare provisions were increased and the public sector expanded. This created white-collar jobs for many men and an increasing number of women. Maori acquired few of these, but they filled the, old and new, blue-collar secondary sector slots vacated or unwanted by Pakeha workers. Aboriginal numbers swelled in the meat and forestry processing works in small towns and the assembly plants and factories of, particularly, South Auckland. With the onset of Maori urbanisation, the newly constituted Department of Maori Affairs (previously Native Affairs) assisted with job placement and family relocation. In short, a comparatively familiar combination of post-Second World War international and local capitalist expansion, and state policies designed to expedite assimilation and migration, provided the climate for Maori urbanisation. The material and cultural changes within the rural heartland of the tribes created the conditions for that climate to prove overwhelmingly irresistible (ibid.: 114).

Coming in from the margins

Since the end of the Second World War global population movements have grown in volume and changed their character, affirming Castles and Miller's (1993) image of 'a new age of migration' mentioned in the opening lines of this chapter. Up to the mid-1970s, as these authors relate, three main types of international labour migration have promoted the formation of ethnic minorities in advanced industrial societies, including settler societies (ibid.: 66). First, permanent migration to North America and Australasia, at first from Europe and later, mainly from Asia and Latin America. Secondly, the movements of manual 'guestworkers' into Western Europe, and rural blacks and Mexican Americans into northern US industrial cities, which have their parallels in Canada and New Zealand. Thirdly, the migration of mainly unskilled and semi-skilled 'colonial workers' to former colonial metropoli. Here too, there are resemblances, between Caribbean and South Asian moves to the UK and inter-island Pacific crossings. And, of course, we should add the continued travels of the British diaspora to and from the increasingly independent semi-periphery into the old colonial centre.

Ethnically diverse moves of people from peripheral to core regions are a major theme within this overall picture, but they reflect different sources and destinations of the journeys across and within national and global borders. The blend and balance between liberal and restrictive policies have also varied over time and space. The United States and Britain have followed divergent paths, partly reflecting their respective ascendancy and fall in geopolitical dominance over the twentieth century. As America grew in prominence as a self-proclaimed defender of international freedom it had to discard its cloak of racial exclusivity, although it remained clothed in the protective garb of not granting automatic rights of political and legal membership to all new arrivals. Britain, on the other hand, erected new barriers against its subjects, some of whom had arrived in the 'mother country' to find their legal parentage as members of Empire and Commonwealth offered little protection against racial discrimination. Others soon discovered their historical subjecthood did not even guarantee entry. Thus, as Britain was hastily slamming the doors on 'coloured immigrants' in the 1960s, the United States, albeit somewhat unwittingly, was opening them to previously unwelcome visitors. Most attention in the UK centred on the international movement of far-flung 'colonial workers' into the metropolis, but migration from internal or adjacent margins was equally pervasive in the USA. The coming in of African, Mexican and, to a lesser degree, Native American minorities from rural hinterlands into the cities were a major feature of American population movements this century. Such movements within, influenced policy on migration from without, as racial exclusion became a major civil rights issue.

If Britain and the United States reflect different migratory trends, Australia, Canada and New Zealand have followed steadily converging paths, especially with immigration flows. Since the Second World War, all three countries have introduced extensive changes in immigration legislation that have transformed their ethnic character. British migrants continued to be an important source of permanent settlers in Australia and New Zealand, although less so in Canada. Each country, in turn, moved to liberalise their immigration policies and open their gateways to a wider spectrum of source countries. This trend was partly attributable to the relative unavailability of British migrants as Britain's home demand for labour increased in the postwar boom. With supply from the traditional source drying up, our three societies were forced to adopt, within their own time frames and domestic political and historical contingencies, comparable gradualist policies of accepting immigrants more and more culturally and phenotypically distant from their traditional majority populations.

In contrast to Western European states, in settler societies, the immigration of migrant labour coincided with the internal migration of aboriginal minorities. The decades after the Second World War witnessed major shifts from rural hinterlands to urban settings of indigenous peoples. Land rather than labour eventually proved to be the more valuable resource of aboriginal populations for European states in earlier periods of settlement, and the removal of territory and displacement of peoples had profound effects on the lifestyles and political economies of the indigenes. The loss of land and capitalist expansion often impelled a move into labour. Up to a point, the conditions within the indigenous borders of settler societies paralleled those in less developed global hinterlands. This promoted, to widely varying degrees (contrast Australia and New Zealand), the increased insertion of aboriginal peoples into local, and then national labour markets, albeit within highly transitory and particularly impoverished patterns of employment and unemployment. The political ramifications, however, of being aboriginal minorities, as we shall see, promoted very different agendas to their immigrant counterparts. Nonetheless, both types of migrations produced highly complex patterns of spatial and labour market segmentation, with ethnic and racial differentiation always complicated by class and gender distinctions. Postwar internal and external migrations within and to post-settler societies formed racialised and gendered fractions, primarily, but not solely, within the working classes, at the same time as 'remnants of Empire' migrants created a similar phenomenon in Britain and other parts of Europe.

At one end of the occupational scale we speak of the 'brain drain' of well-educated people selling their labour to the highest bidder on the world market. Destinations and volumes differ, but our settler societies have been both the recipient and suppliers of such people over the years. In the early decades of post-Second World War expansion, more qualified migrants were invariably British, later other Europeans, but increasingly in recent years such persons hail from more diverse sources, and Asian origins are common. Permanent settlement is still prevalent, but professional transience is a growing phenomenon. If the skilled and qualified have often been in demand, far more numerous and frequent are the movements of the less fortunate. Migrations at this other end of the scale still represent despair and hope, but in a very different arena of limited choices and opportunities. The experience of the nexus of racism and sex discrimination is even more commonplace among those who enter the lower ranks of the stratification order.

Ethnic and racial minorities, immigrant and aboriginal, frequently exhibit higher rates of female labour participation than women in majority groups (Stasiulis and Yuval-Davis 1995: 15) There is a wide diversity of employment patterns related to class, ethnic, household and lifecycle factors, for example, defying generalisation within, let alone across, our case studies. Historically and currently, however, the role of 'migrant' and 'indigenous' women in settler societies, reflecting in part the broader cast of male hegemony, has tended to be over-narrowly perceived by policy makers and in popular parlance. Female migrants were, and often still are, seen as maintaining and reproducing the families of male migrants or indigenes, possibly supplementing their partners' incomes, or acting as unpaid labour in ethnic or native small businesses. This masculinist bias has fostered a view of dependency promoting gender inequalities in immigration policies (Fincher et al. 1994), as well as sustaining similar or even more negative representations of aboriginal families as has characterised debates about 'black' families in the United States and Britain (Pettman 1992: 65).

The effects of migration and labour market segmentation are most graphically displayed in the cities. Local debate often dwells on the formation of 'urban ghettoes', but few, if any, of the neighbourhoods within Canadian, Australian and New Zealand cities are reminiscent of those found in Los Angeles or New York. Nevertheless, the Canadian 'string of pearls' clustered along the US border, particularly Vancouver, Montreal and Toronto, and the highly urbanised 'Boomerang Coast' stretching from Adelaide to Brisbane, are now home to millions of new migrants. Some of these cities, like Toronto and Sydney, have become highly cosmopolitan global conurbations, containing diverse ethnic communities whose numbers rival the size of urban centres in their countries of origin. Other, smaller cities still have their own distinctive ethnic character. Auckland, for example, is only rivalled by Honolulu as the largest Polynesian city in the world.

Whilst economic imperatives loom large in the motivations of policy-makers and migrants alike, social, cultural and ideological factors are ever present. There is no simple divide between labour and non-labour migration, as even a superficial examination of the 'non-economic' characteristics of immigration categories of family reunification, refugees and asylum seekers, or aboriginal urbanisation, reveals. These migrations, plus the consolidation and demographic normalisation of previous generations of migrants, have typified the 1970s and 1980s. Further changes and continuities were promoted by the multiplicity of factors making up what Cornell and Hartmann (1998: 153–94) have called 'construction sites' for ethnic political identity and practice. This chapter has sketched in some of the descriptive parameters of these arenas, together with a selective glance at the migrations that created and reproduced them. In the next two chapters we will take a more in-depth look at the new platforms for politicisation of aboriginal and immigrant minorities that, in tandem with international trends, sparked new forms of state management of ethnic conflict within and beyond the locations highlighted above.

5
Management, Accommodation and Resistance

In the space of a few decades new migrations transformed societies whose demographics had become sufficiently indigenous and diverse by the mid to late twentieth century to warrant the phrase post-settler. Diversity was hardly a novelty, yet the pace and breadth of migrations post-Second World War were particularly striking in light of the period of border control preceding them. Did these movements promote new forms of state management of ethnic diversity, or were they the result of changes in governance? Was an apparent shift away from assimilatory aboriginal and immigration policies towards a greater recognition of cultural and political pluralism the cause or the effect of ethnic heterogeneity? This chapter seeks to problematise the posing of either/or questions, and the provision of answers demands us moving, if briefly, beyond the relations between representatives of states and ethnic groups within specific territorial borders. Ethnic politics in post-settler societies was much influenced by social movements that emerged out of changing international geopolitical and economic orders. Such movements encompassed quests for the establishment or enhancement of internal and external political and social legitimacy, and economic and environmental sustainability. Let us trace the most prominent brush strokes on a large and cluttered canvas before examining more in-depth portraits of our case studies.

Politics, ideology and the world order

What is it about the modern world system that has produced increasing numbers of ethnic-based political movements over the past few decades? Joane Nagel's (1998a) recent response to this question is to identify linked political and ideological factors. On the one hand she examines the international system of ideas simultaneously upholding and challenging the configuration of world states, while on the other she looks at the political competition within and between states for control of resources and self-rule. Global state alignments are therefore juxtaposed with national ethnic and regional arrangements.

Out of this analysis emerges a model of three waves of post-Second World War ethnic nationalism. The first wave, arriving soon after hostilities ended, saw the decolonisation of large areas of, mainly, Africa and Asia, controlled by European states. Their successors inherited diverse ethnic populations who remain entrapped within the borders formed by arbitrary lines drawn on colonial maps. The striving of sub-populations in these countries, in the 1960s and 1970s, to free themselves from neocolonial constraints, formed part of the second wave that washed across much of the globe. Finally, the third wave, which will not concern us here, arrived in the late 1980s with the overthrow of East European communist states and demands for self-rule among Soviet republics.

These 'hiccups in hegemony', as Nagel styles them, occurred as the major powers shifted their grasp on ideas, resources and areas, reorganising the international system in the process. Such international realignments had important local effects. 'The same principles that fashioned out of European colonialisms many Third World independent states, became the platform upon which challenges to those states boundaries were mounted' (ibid.: 349). Simultaneously, and greatly influenced by Third World contests, elites in ex-coloniser and ex-dominion states faced renewed questioning of their legitimacy. Chief among them was conflict about statist and nationalist conceptions of public authority and the limits of their jurisdictional domains – in a word, sovereignty – and the distribution of rights and resources within these political territories.

Understandings of sovereignty and rights are often re-examined during or after major wars or social upheavals, with the winners defining or cementing a new international order (Barkin and Cronin 1994: 114). The First and Second World Wars attest to the strength of this maxim. After the 'war to end all wars', Woodrow Wilson's League of Nations was designed as a supranational compromise 'for eliminating the very causes for war itself' (ibid.: 120). In Wilson's diagnosis, the lack of fit between nations and states and the existence of autocratic governments was the cancer in the world body politic. His principles of self-determination, democracy and international justice underpinned a belief that states should represent a defined national people and governments should be accountable to 'the nation'. Consequently, at the Versailles conference, 'representatives from dozens of dispossessed nations were allowed to press their claims before the assembled powers' (ibid.: 121).

This stance led to an increase in 'nations', and, as Britain had feared, the erosion of empires, but the Second World War revealed the dangers of nationalism out of control. The United Nations Charter, for example, reflected the fear of a recurrence of fascist expansion fuelled by xenophobia and racism. Self-determination was reaffirmed in the document, but it was now understood as the individual rights of people within unified states, not nations. The pendulum had swung back from national to state sovereignty. This vision still shaped a perception of the increasing illegitimacy of colonial empires but the emphasis on retaining existing state borders and non-interference in domestic affairs reaffirmed the legitimacy of rulers not peoples. Hence the tacit acceptance of what often proved to be highly repressive regimes, particularly in newly emergent Third World states.

This oscillation reflected a tension between shifting and contradictory conceptions of sovereignty and self-determination continuing to flourish during the Cold War and its aftermath. Indeed, the tension remains firmly planted today. The compelling impetus of ethnic nationalism and rights claims using these constructs perhaps should not surprise us. For, as Nagel notes, self-determination, sovereignty and representative government were, and are, seemingly unassailable general principles upon which to build democratic modern states. Their ill-defined nature merely adds to their potency in shaping both the relations between emergent and long-established states and the struggles within these settings. Thus, the power of such ideas within a global world system of political competition assist in explaining the unravelling of empires, the greater assertiveness of newly independent Third World states, and the increase in ethnic conflict within First World contexts. Quite simply, they furnished legitimacy for both governing elites and those forces opposing them. They not only sanctified existing borders and administrations, 'these same principles of state-building (also) provide(d) an equally sturdy platform from which to launch an attack on the integrity of modern states' (Nagel 1998a: 350). The most vivid example was the outburst of rights claims erupting in the United States just when ethnic and national conflicts were triggered in Africa, Asia and South America.

The Civil Rights catalyst

The American Civil Rights movement spanning the 1950s to the 1970s was a catalyst for other struggles within and beyond the United States.

At the core of a political process, never homogeneous or monolithic, was a struggle for the delegitimation of a racial creed and the dismantling of the lawful basis of America's black/white duality (Ringer and Lawless 1989: 157–8). The fight for desegregation was also a confrontation between two sovereignties, state and federal. Both battles were waged as much in the court room as the streets. The history of civil rights adjudication in the 1950s, the strategic bridge between a southern black middle class and white liberals, and the use of non-violent direct action through the organisational base of black churches, were important precursors for the urban riots of the 1960s (Tarrow 1995: 129–30). The fuse Martin Luther King lit in the South had explosive effects in the North and West of the United States, while the anti-colonial movements in other continents provided a rhetoric and model for American black nationalism in the 1970s. Black Power promoted Red Power (Nagel 1997). Native American politics were entangled with black issues, but there was a multiplicity of aspirations and goals within the hundreds of protest groups active in these movements. There was common cause in seeking greater access to the institutions and wealth enjoyed by other sectors of society and the removal of the stigma and discrimination experienced by all 'peoples of colour'. Yet there was a vital difference between Native Americans fighting for equal acceptance as individual citizens, and their struggle to regain their land base and greater recognition as distinct administrations and peoples outside and within the state. Red Power was reacting against the, all too aptly named, 'termination' policies of the 1950s and early 1960s,[1] designed completely to restructure US-Indian relations to the point where aboriginal peoples would be forced onto an equal footing with all other Americans.

Immigration issues were also part of the rights ferment. A coalition of civil rights, migrant and labour groups, and religious organisations fought to eradicate the national origins' quotas from United States immigration legislation and end the exploitation of Mexican contract labour (Bach 1992: 152). Links back to the United Nations are also revealed with humanitarian concerns for the treatment of migrants fleeing political oppression. Changes in refugee and migrant labour policy, as we saw in the last chapter, reopened and widened the gateways of entry to greater diversity. This prompted new and renewed political philosophies and strategies.

The Civil Rights movement provided 'a master frame' for the expansion of principles already embedded in the civic traditions of the American state (Tarrow 1995: 129). 'Rights' became a touchstone to put beside 'self-determination' in a proliferation of other movements spreading far beyond the boundaries of ethnicity and the shores of the United States. The national rights of women, gay men and lesbians, animals and the unborn, were also international movements that coalesced or collided with the student, working-class and New Left struggles for 'autonomy' in Western Europe. Anti-Vietnam War, peace, environmental and anti-apartheid campaigns similarly linked local and global issues. However, the Civil Rights era was not simply a catalyst for a 'climate of rights', it also proved to be a watershed for organisational innovation in the guise of non-violent direct action (ibid.: 129–31). This strategy proved particularly effective with the advancement of electronic media. Developing new repertoires of assertion, political activists drew upon a dramaturgical style feeding television's insatiable appetite for newsworthy imagery. The symbolic power of sit-ins, blockades, marches and freedom drives, almost matched the effect of cities burning, especially since the portrayal of violent suppression of non-violent protest elicited public sympathy.

A new economic order and the role of the state

If the ideological, political and symbolic strands of national and international rights claims need emphasising, one should not forget the changing economic milieux in which they were placed. In the space of four decades economic trends took a roller-coaster ride. A period of buoyant reconstruction in the 1950s was followed by remarkable growth in the 1960s and early 1970s. But 'stagflation', crisis and uncertainty characterised economies as they careered downwards into the 1980s. The postwar economic boom was the high point of the so-called Fordist era. Fordism was more than a model of mass production, it was a mode of social and state organisation marking the political and ideological conjunctures discussed above. This 'first neo-colonial period', as Hoogvelt defines it, heralded the expansion of the welfare state in core states and confirmed the ascendancy of a social democratic consensus (Hoogvelt 1997: 46). As profits began to fall, attempts were made to export Fordism beyond the core, particularly into the newly industrialising 'Tigerish' economies of Singapore, Hong Kong, Taiwan and Korea. Still, this was only a transitional phase in the shift towards post-Fordism, and it did not redress the huge discrepancies between a still resource-rich 'North' and a 'South' sliding into 'debt-peonage' (ibid.: 112–13).

Post-Fordism, like its predecessor, describes a style of production, administration and set of discourses. 'Niche' supplanted 'Mass' in the economic lexicon and diversity replaced similarity in political parlance.

Most pertinent to our discussion was the merging of economic rationalist doctrines and social and political policies. From the end of the 1970s, the belief that cutting and modifying the role of the public sector would enhance private sector growth became widely accepted. The need for states to be free from the fetters of welfare provision was the new mantra. Interestingly, this maxim fuelled a neo-liberal consensus among state elites seemingly independent of whether their polities were officially conservative or not. The result was a substantial reduction in public sector employment and a widespread restructuring of the welfare state. Both trends were affected by, and impacted upon, the tenor and practice of ethnic politics, greatly influencing forms of state management and the accommodative and resistive strategies of minorities. The 1980s firmly established a global climate of rights and self-determination, mainly due to the contagious, catalytic effect of the civil rights and other movements preceding this period. Momentum was halted but a subsequent economic and political backlash did not displace the aims of these movements. Aspirations of self and collective freedom had been raised to new levels within majority and minority circles. A dynamic process of innovativeness and retrenchment needs to be outlined in which ethnic group interests and attainments were neither neatly packaged nor internally consistent. Briefly comparing the twists and turns of state policies and minority activism in our case studies will not capture all the nuances of political interaction, but they will provide contexts within which we can see specific effects of the general trends described above.

A multicultural forerunner

A broad-brushed portrait of Canada in the 1930s reveals a regional clustering of French influence based primarily in Quebec, a diverse 'allophone'[2] population displaying varying degrees of assimilation into the French and English-speaking major categories, and an overriding British Canadian ethnic core dominating positions of economic and political power. Despite the resilience of this core, by the Second World War Canada was already a far more ethnically diverse society than either Australia or New Zealand. This, in part, explains why Canada was the forerunner among our three societies to move away from overtly assimilative ideologies and public policy frameworks.

During the Second World War, the Canadian state established a federal Citizenship Branch with a linked national Advisory Committee to encourage a united war effort within the British and non-French foreign-born population, and devise procedures for dealing with those groups classed as 'enemy aliens'. These initiatives have been seen as the precursors of what came to be called multicultural policies (Hawkins 1989: 218). Assimilation, however, was still the hallmark of a state reluctant to host groups who diverged from the Anglocentric, and, to a far lesser extent, Francocentric norms. The temporary merging of Indian Affairs into a newly created Department of Citizenship and Immigration (in 1950) showed native persons and newcomers alike were expected to merge into a monocultural public culture. Even the postwar Diefenbaker government, which contained a premier and cabinet ministers with surnames revealing their non-Anglo-Francophone backgrounds, was strongly committed to the idea of One Canada within the British Commonwealth. Yet their presence illustrated the heterogeneity of earlier migrations and was prescient of later diversity.

The 1960s was a pivotal decade. The dismantling of Canada's 'whites only' immigration policy, as we saw in the last chapter, added many new tiles into the national ethnic mosaic. The decade also marked a stage when immigrant and aboriginal minorities, echoing similar movements in the United States, became even more assertive in their demands for greater cultural and linguistic recognition. Such demands coincided with elite attempts to construct a distinctive Canadian identity in the light of waning British influence and the too-close-for-comfort presence of their powerful neighbour. Nonetheless, for these elites, the greatest perceived threat to Anglophone hegemony and Canadian unity came from Quebec.

We will be taking a closer look at Quebec nationalism in Chapter 7. What is noteworthy here, is how the gradual transformation of a regional and cultural identity was, in the main, peacefully contrived. The 'Quiet Revolution' as it came to be called, saw the state replace the church as a focus for national sentiment, using language as a consistent boundary marker. From the provincial election of Lesage in 1960, through the Bourassa administrations of the early to mid-1970s, linguistic policy buttressed a programme of regional state nationalization. Public and French command replaced private and English control in many sectors (Juteau 1992). Gallicised educational regimes narrowed the qualification gap between Anglophone and Francophone, altered the profile of occupational and social mobility, and enlarged the support base for a separatist, *indépendantiste* movement that culminated in the victory of the Parti Québecois in 1976. Support for secession ebbed and flowed in concert with the attempts by successive federal governments to appease the increasing numbers of Quebeckers whose worldview had shifted from 'we the *Canadiens*' to a more circumscribed '*maîtres chez nous*' (masters of our own house).

Pierre Trudeau did not share this view. For the Liberal Premier of Canada, whose reign stretched, almost unbroken, from 1968 to 1984, 'bilingualism unites people, dualism divides them'. In 1963 Lester Pearson's administration had established a Royal Commission on Bilingualism and Biculturalism to examine the crisis between 'the two founding races'. The Commission's mandate saw other ethnicities as a side issue and aboriginal people fell outside their purview. The 'Bi and Bi' Report, and the interstate flurry of Commission activity preceding it, acted as a focus for political activism from the 'other ethnic groups', especially those of Eastern and Central European descent who arrived at the turn of the century. Many of them resided in the 'prairie provinces', and these regions, and others beyond the Montreal–Toronto axis, predictably added a further dimension into the heated debate about Canada's future.

The Bi and Bi Report strongly recommended the introduction of a federal bilingual policy. The Commission also saw Quebec as a unique focus for French culture, justifying a special set of powers for a 'distinct society' (Oliver 1993: 326). Trudeau supported the first idea, but vigorously opposed the second. His passionate defence of the Official Languages Act (in 1969) raised the political temperature still further. The Act, designed to achieve equal parity between two official languages, heralded the end of a unilingual public service and set in place a programme of French language services designed to foster a nationwide accommodation between the two major linguistic groups. From now on all Canadians would have bilingual labels on their ketchup bottles.

The release of a White Paper on Indian Policy (also appearing in 1969) added to the furore. The Paper, echoing American moves noted above, proposed abolishing reserves, removing the special status of Indians, and integrating them into Canadian society as individual citizens, thus threatening to enforce an assimilation always underpinning aboriginal policy. These initiatives bolstered a range of increasingly vocal ethnic movements resulting in new governmental efforts to placate them. Chief among them was Trudeau's strategy of supporting multiculturalism within a framework of bilingualism. This combination was aimed at a multiplicity of issues bubbling away at the same time. In one stroke Trudeau sought to identify a distinct Canadian identity, defuse the threat of United States-style race riots and shore up Ontario's political strength in the light of Quebec and other provincial pressures. Trudeau's policies shifted the emphasis away from earlier 'expressive' multicultural formulations, with their cosmetic folklorist flavour, towards a civic model of a 'just, equal and plural society for all Canadians'. The move met with widely differing responses. In some provinces, Ontario, Alberta and Saskatchewan, for example, new multicultural programmes flourished parallel to national developments, creating or expanding existing ethnic associations strongly supportive of the ideology. However, the Quebec state was decidedly wary about a perceived threat to its distinctiveness, while aboriginal peoples were equally cautious about an idea and political framework promising to undermine their claims for a special collective relationship with the state. These fears were realised with the enactment of the Charter of Human Rights and Freedoms in 1982. The Charter, although accommodating diversity through its recognition of 'multicultural groups', women and other disadvantaged groups, and aboriginal people, was shaped within Trudeau's vision of individual rights and formally equal provinces within one nation. Quebec was not consulted nor consented to the Charter, and self-government for First Nations was not contemplated.

Meanwhile, the already polyglot landscapes of Toronto, Montreal and Vancouver, were becoming even more cosmopolitan. The life chances of these new migrants were as diverse as their origins, but many of them experienced discrimination in education, housing, and the ill-effects of a receding labour market. They did not reflect the size or strength of black and 'ethnic' constituencies in the United States, but in many regions their voting power could not be ignored. The problems of what were now called 'visible minorities' attracted parliamentary attention, and some provinces, notably Ontario, only had to glance southwards to see the results of rising racial tensions and unemployment. Pressure for reform, from public opinion and ethnic lobby groups at the federal and provincial level, resulted in a further refurbishment of multiculturalism to match the prevalent social and economic climate, particularly with the bolstering of employment equity legislation.

In the mid to late 1980s, the incumbent Mulroney-led Liberal government, with one eye on the free market models now in vogue and the other on burgeoning Asian economies, proclaimed multiculturalism should now be viewed as a resource with marketable value (Elliott and Fleras 1990: 67). A repositioning having the added potential advantage of containing electoral unease about increased Asian investment and business migration. The old themes of cultural heritage, national unity and social justice were not to be discarded but reshaped to fit new economic exigencies. With the introduction of a national Multiculturalism Act (in 1988) consistent with the Charter, the federal state placed on a *de jure* footing what had existed in reality since 1971. Renourishing the roots of multiculturalism in the 1940s, the federal agency charged, albeit fleetingly, with carrying out the Act, was called the Department of Multiculturalism and Citizenship.

The Multiculturalism Act highlighted a progression from the superficial attention to cultural preservation marking the multiculturalism of the 1970s, through the shift to racial discrimination and civil rights legislation in the mid-1980s, towards a broadening of a constitutional concern with ethnic diversity in the early 1990s. Immigration trends and the climate of individual rights claims spawning the Charter had sparked many of these reforms, but the Canadian state continued to face the problem of Quebec's, seemingly irresistible, drive towards greater independence – an issue around which persistent provincial rivalries still revolved. Aboriginal peoples, moreover, had their own versions of autonomy.

In the 1960s a proliferation of band, tribal council and pan-Indian organisations, some dating back to the late nineteenth century, but most of recent origin, had sought greater equality and freedom from their dependency on a sprawling Indian administration and spiralling welfare programmes. At first the main goal was to gain greater control over an imposed structure of 'welfare colonialism' by lobbying for a more culturally appropriate form of service delivery administered by aboriginal persons (Cassidy 1994: 175). Nevertheless, the land issue was always in the background, and this took a litigious turn in the mid-1970s. A series of landmark claim cases,[3] sparked by provincial and federal development ambitions threatening remaining aboriginal territory in northern Canada, were the prelude to an ongoing land rights movement. Such cases, although far from decisive or fully supportive of Native Canadian interests, enhanced a recognition of aboriginal title to land and resources. They also served to bring the plight of, often distant, peoples to the attention of urban Canadians. Increasing episodes of, mainly non-violent, 'ethnodramas' (Dyck 1992) further pricked the public conscience.

In part inspired by worldwide rights movements, neighbouring Native American activism, and Quebec's Quiet revolutionaries, a newly 'professionalised' Native Indian leadership sought further degrees of what they increasingly called self-determination for the 'Fourth World'. These phrases covered a variety of meanings and sectional interests within and across the boundaries of Status, Non-Status, Métis and Inuit categories historically created by the Canadian state. The spectrum of 'determination' ranged from visions of independent statehood to more control over the delivery of local provincial services, but all demands embraced the idea of a unique aboriginal status.

By the 1980s a collectivist rhetoric of 'distinct societies' and 'first nations' characterising ethnonational and regional discourses (Jenson 1993) rested uneasily against the more individualistic rights claims of 'Charter Canadians', including the multiculturalist lobby (Cairns 1992). This tension overlayed the often bitter debates surrounding the patriation[4] of the constitution with the Charter of Rights, culminating in the Constitution Act of 1982. The Act, as with the Charter, agreed on federal reform without Quebec or the First Nation's blessing. Their omission, and the ambiguity of understandings within the Act and among its signatories, made any thought of a lasting consensus illusory. As events proved in the 1990s, the Act and the Charter were simply the precursors for a series of, largely abortive, attempts to achieve what Russell (1993) has called 'mega constitutional solutions' to recurrent national, regional and ethnic eruptions, often enwrapped within national multicultural iconography. Some, if far from all, of the same fault lines and tremors were present in Oceania, as we shall see if we turn, first, to the Australian context.

The emergence of Australian multiculturalism

In 1945 only one in ten Australians was born elsewhere and spoke a language other than English. In the space of a few decades, however, the size and heterogeneity of immigration grew apace and the newcomers changed far more than the linguistic climate. As with Canada, mass immigration and the resultant growing diversity of immigrant minorities forced the Australian state to devise new social policies and symbols of national identity. Assimilation remained the *sine qua non* of immigration policy in the 1940s and 1950s, despite a shift from British to successive Eastern and Southern European waves of arrivals. These immigrants were given some initial assistance, were treated, legally speaking, as future citizens, and were expected to acquire the linguistic and cultural trappings of 'the Australian Way of Life' (Castles et al. 1988: 113). Yet the cultural baggage diasporic Jews and Italians, for example, arrived with, was not readily discarded. A variety of factors conspired to forestall assimilatory goals.

In Melbourne and Sydney in particular, 'ethnic' neighbourhoods emerged reflecting the reinvention of old lifestyles as migrants sought to reconstruct time-honoured images and practices within a world of new experiences. Such communities were not only chosen expressions of cultural renewal but also indicators of imposed economic and social disadvantage. New 'white', non-British migrants were differentially incorporated into local residential, education and labour markets, distorted by ethnocentric and racist practices. Non-whites experienced more of the same, but were also denied naturalisation. So a cumulative pattern of ethnic and racial stratification was ecologically imprinted on urban social maps.

It soon became obvious, at least to those directly concerned with migrant settlement policy, that assimilationist state policies had failed to produce an Australian equivalent of the American melting pot, even if the recipe Down Under had fewer ingredients to blend into the final dish: 'by 1959 the minister for immigration was talking of "integration" rather than "assimilation"' (Markus 1994: 160). Welfare grants designed to help community agencies, English language acquisition and qualification recognition were introduced. Naturalisation procedures were also eased. Such moves were a response to visible evidence of disadvantage and a sign of a shift in philosophy towards a grudging acceptance that non-British migrants might enrich Australian cultural life and benefit the economy.

This conclusion was far from evident with respect to aboriginal relations, although, here too, signs of, in this case centuries old racial inequality, were becoming more apparent. Except in those remote areas still relatively untouched by white settlement, aboriginal persons had been successively segregated and 'protected' from contact with the majority population in tightly controlled institutionalised conditions (Beckett 1988: 7–8). As a result very few people in the cities where most Australians lived had any day-to-day contact with aboriginal persons. Out of sight clearly meant out of mind, although the old saw about 'a dying race' was becoming rapidly redundant as aboriginal numbers increased. This resilience provoked reassessments among policy-makers about the possibilities of assimilation, although when they finally viewed it as appropriate in the 1930s, they deemed 'half-caste' individuals had the greatest propensity for civilising. Tragically, this assumption often entailed the indignities of further forced movement and residence.

Such processes reflected a dual contradiction. As Beckett (1988) points out, assimilation policies used the goal of eventual entry into the Australian 'mainstream' as a justification for forcibly segregating aborigines on settlements. At the same time, they offered the goal of eventual citizenship as a justification for curtailing their civil rights. These ironies did not go unchallenged. Aboriginal Advancement Associations and Leagues were formed between the world wars, mainly aboriginally led, and they grew in numbers, as did white sympathisers, in the 1940s. Though the assimilatory policies pursued by the Labor administration in the 1950s were less coercive, provincial state practices remained highly variable. Nationally, full legal and political citizenship remained an elusive prize, although some Aborigines gained the right to vote in federal elections, particularly if they had been in the defence forces. A federal council of Leagues formed in 1964 pushed for a referendum to support constitutional changes allowing the federal government to override provincial state barriers to aboriginal civil rights.[5] In 1967 the referendum got overwhelming approval. Control of more material resources was another matter. Local variations of black power saw the aboriginalisation of previously white-dominated reformist associations. The clenched fist and freedom rides in the Deep North of New South Wales became part of a growing swell of politicisation about cultural revival, anti-racism and autonomy. Still, control over land remained the consistent unifying theme in a multi-stranded movement. Highly publicised struggles over mining and pastoral rights in remote regions brought the politics of embarrassment into 'settled' Australia.[6] Other events occupied the political heartland. A newly invented national aboriginal flag flew in full televisual view of the Australian nation when activists erected a tent embassy (in 1972) in front of the Canberra Parliament building. The tent entered the mythology of the fight for civil liberties and land rights, its makeshift structure symbolising aboriginal living conditions and their flimsy hold on democracy.

If immigrant inequalities were becoming more visible, the aboriginal enclaves outside country towns and in city slum areas provided an even more telling indictment of the White Australia policy. In 1972, the newly elected Whitlam-led Labor government wanted to put its stamp on a programme of social reforms designed to reflect a new, home-grown Australian vision of nationhood, a greater degree of social equity, and an enhanced reputation in the eyes of a more assertive local and international lobby for ethnic rights. Grassby, the Minister of Immigration until 1974, took the Canadian idea of multiculturalism and refashioned it into his vision of an Australian 'family of the nation'. As a first step the Australian Labor Party (ALP) abolished the White Australia policy and introduced a series of reforms designed to meet the special needs of the mainly unskilled and semi-skilled migrants who had entered the country in the previous two decades. Unlike the Canadian model, emphasis was not placed on devising a culturally pluralistic template but on the provision of universal economic and social rights for all workers (Castles 1992: 555), some of whom, if NESB migrants or their descendants, would require additional services best provided by state-employed persons drawn from their own communities.

Although 'immigrant' and 'aboriginal' policies continued to be compartmentalised, the restructuring of the Department of Aboriginal Affairs and recruitment of aboriginal persons within it, reveal parallels in the general move to 'self-determination' in the Whitlam era. These strategies led to the creation of migrant and aboriginal representative bodies and the consolidation of representatives of the rights movements within national and local state bureaucracies. This institutional framework provided an ideal platform for the Fraser-led Liberal administration elected in 1975. What distinguished the Whitlam and Fraser administrations were their modes of welfare delivery, a system of state-subsidised 'ethnic community' self-help supplanting central state-funded provision. Fraser's regime co-opted the 'leaders' of these 'communities' into circumscribed arenas of power brokerage while it dismantled the welfare agencies, particularly migrant services put into place by its Labor predecessors. This strategy had clear philosophical and administrative echoes in the increasing shift towards self-management in aboriginal affairs. The immigrant and aboriginal minority models emerging by the late 1970s were designed to kill several political and economic birds with one carefully aimed stone. The state, as Castles says, 'was concerned simultaneously with developing the ideological legitimation for an ethnically diverse society, cutting government expenditure and enhancing social control over minorities' (Castles 1992: 188).

Multiculturalism remained contentious. Much like the Canadian situation, debate centred on whether the idea reflected a potentially radical move towards the redress of ethnic inequalities, or whether it cynically disguised them. Most sceptical were those sections of the aboriginal lobby who saw the model as irrelevant because of its immigrant focus, or, worse still, a conservative ploy to sideline their special demands. Neither stance gelled with opinion poll results showing increasing numbers of Anglo-Australians thought immigrants and Aborigines were getting far more than they deserved. Despite these competing currents, and in contrast to Canada, a period of bipartisan governmental consensus emerged in the late 1970s and early 1980s about the importance of the 'ethnic vote' and the general efficacy of multiculturalism. At the federal level, and in New South Wales and Victoria, the idea remained buoyant. The ALP introduced it. The Liberals had maintained it, and when Labor returned in 1983, the Hawke administration (after some hesitation and initial cutbacks) pushed the notion further.

Several interrelated factors soon threatened this consensus. Migrant adaptations to Australian society in general and the workplace in particular had been the dual central planks of multicultural policy since the 1960s. Two decades later there were signs that the next generation of New Australians, children of the migrant workers who arrived after the Second World War, were successfully adjusting, if not being absorbed completely, into their society of birth. Young Greek and Italian-Australians, for example, with new 'hyphenated identities' were educationally achieving and now competing with Anglo-Australians for higher skilled jobs. These mobility trends cemented positive images of cultural adaptation and partly deflected the claims of those critics of multiculturalism who still pointed to deep-seated forms of ethnic stratification (Collins 1984).

Such arguments still had some purchase however, given a deepening recession, a monetarist-inspired restructuring of the economy, and significant changes in immigration flows. Ironically, while some second-generation Southern European migrants were 'getting on', many of their parents were thrown out of work as the declining manufacturing and construction industries they were clustered in were particularly hard-hit by the economic downturn. Their chances of re-employment were not improved by the arrival of Middle East and Indo-Chinese migrants and refugees entering the lower reaches of a depressed labour market. At the other end of the scale, again echoing Canadian trends, the government's encouragement of capital inflows and entrepreneurial skills brought 'business migrants' from South East Asia. The diversity of these movements reveals the imprecision of 'Asian' and 'immigrant' labels, but this fact hardly touched the growing swell of discontent focused on 'overseas' (make that Asian) investment, and moral panics about asylum seekers. Multiculturalism was on the back foot. Notable landmarks of discontent included the furore over a prominent historian, Geoffrey Blainey's, highly publicised overtures (in 1984) about the 'Asianization of Australia' (Blainey 1984). Yet even this issue was overshadowed by the acrimony of the popular and academic discussion surrounding the Bicentenary in 1988, an event that publicised aboriginal concerns about policies that seemed to relegate them to being just another ethnic minority.

Doubts about national disunity were, not surprisingly, well to the fore in the Fitzgerald Report (CAAIP 1988) on immigration appearing in the bicentennial year, but it recommended a refashioning rather than retreat from multiculturalism. The multicultural ethos now espoused the virtues of 'a productive culture' that would solve Australia's economic and social ills. New policy initiatives, including the implementation of a national languages policy, underlined this reaffirmation contained within the National Agenda for a Multicultural Australia (OMA 1989). The Agenda set a new three-pronged strategy into place. The first two dimensions echoed earlier 1970s' multicultural models by re-emphasising the importance of cultural identity and social justice, but with a marked stress on the rights and obligations of all Australians rather than special provision for 'ethnic' groups. Areas of ethnic disadvantage were highlighted but the central message was social harmony, civic duty and equality. The third plank of reform, economic efficiency, was born in the 1980s and had matured considerably as the decade closed. The state now viewed multiculturalism, as in Canada, as an asset designed to meet global challenges in trade and technology in general, and the Asian market in particular. Despite continuities traceable in the fluctuating multicultural discourses since its inception, the late 1980s' model presented a more than subtle shift away from ethnic particularism towards the cultural, social and economic rights of all citizens in a democratic state (Castles 1992: 559).

The state saw all citizens, of course, as economically productive individuals in a sovereign Australia. Not surprisingly, this vision was greeted with muted enthusiasm by many aboriginal people. Aboriginal and immigrant policy had always displayed a marked bureaucratic separation at all levels of government in Australia. There had been major changes in representation and forms of state control since the establishment of the Department of Aboriginal Affairs and National Aboriginal Consultative Committee in the Whitlam era. The more regionally sensitive National Aboriginal Conference and land councils in the Hawke-led Labor administration marked a shift away from national top-down strategies, while the self-management philosophies of the Aboriginal and Torres Strait Islander Commission (ATSIC), introduced in 1989, seemed to be a further move towards 'self-determination'. Even the idea of a national Treaty akin to New Zealand's Waitangi, which surfaced in the late 1970s, remained on the agenda. Yet, in many ways, the Australian aboriginal population remained entrapped within their own set of provincial and federal state designated institutions, despite the major shift in emphasis towards greater degrees of political autonomy.

Since the 1940s, in Beckett's words: 'Australia may be said to have transformed its indigenous population from virtually passive colonial subjects, situated inside the state but outside the nation, to a political constituency consisting of citizens who are simultaneously a minority' (Beckett 1988: 17). This statement, including the allusion to minority, is sociologically apt, but Australian aboriginal groups vigorously resisted any suggestion to treat them merely as individual citizens. Like their Canadian counterparts, they saw themselves as a distinct people with unique claims who deserved the status 'citizens plus'. This tension between aboriginal and 'immigrant' conceptions of 'cultural' possibilities manifested itself in parallel but also different form in the New Zealand setting.

New Zealand biculturalism

In postwar Australia multiculturalism swiftly moved to centre-stage in response to dramatic changes in immigration patterns, while aboriginal affairs had to wait to be cast in a major role. By way of contrast, in New Zealand multiculturalism has always been part of the chorus. In the 1960s it exhibited some cosmetic promise, and more recently shows signs of a comeback, but biculturalism soon moved into the spotlight. The assimilationist flavour of New Zealand's immigration policies matched those of Australia in the 1940s but, unlike her neighbour, this stance remained firmly in vogue until the late 1980s. Even more striking, as we have seen, was the early integration of Maori into the mainstream of New Zealand society. 'Integration', indeed, was the word used in the influential Hunn Report (1960) that the, then, National Government, used as a benchmark for seeking to address increasingly publicised inequalities between Maori and Pakeha.

Hunn's use of the term, while criticised by some Maori for being a euphemism for continued assimilation, placed greater weight on cultural autonomy than previous regimes. This theme grew in strength in the climate of human rights legislation marking the 1970s. In 1976 a task force on education (*New Zealand at the Turning Point*), clearly with an eye on Australian and Canadian usage, adopted the phrase 'distributive multiculturalism' to voice its ideas on repairing the disparities between Maori (and Pacific Islander) levels of educational achievement and those of other New Zealanders. The Race Relations Commission's *Race Against Time* report (released in 1982) retained the term. The report equated multiculturalism with a universal philosophy of 'separate but equal' cultures, but it contained a prescient sub-theme speaking of the need to establish a framework addressing past wrongs as well as present injustices.

Treasury, the controlling arm of the state executive, gave multiculturalism its most prominent stamp of approval in the early 1980s. In 1984, with the Orwellian note adding more than a dash of irony, a newly elected Labour Government introduced 'New Right' economic policies with a vigour surpassing even the Thatcherite and Reaganite administrations overseas. Multiculturalism was hardly a major feature of the ensuing massive state restructuring, but the noises about cultural diversity laced with economic management and efficiency were very reminiscent of Canadian and Australian states who had not, as yet, waved the neo-liberal banner with quite the same enthusiasm. These sentiments promoted new directions in immigration policy, culminating, as we saw in the previous chapter, with a new 1987 Immigration Act. The Act not only brought New Zealand belatedly into line with Canadian and Australian policies, but also alluded to a similar goal of enriching 'the multi-cultural social fabric' of the nation (Burke 1986: 10). This aspiration signalled a move away from ethnic exclusivity and led to a significant rise in Asian immigration, although it stopped well short of acknowledging a unique status, let alone a modicum of collective autonomy, for Maori. Biculturalism rather than multiculturalism seemed to offer greater political leverage here.

We can also trace the competing discourses surrounding biculturalism back to at least the 1960s, but they gained an ascendancy over multiculturalism by the mid-1980s. Why did this happen? Much of the explanation is historical. Cutting short a reiterated story, despite all too familiar indices of social disadvantage Maori were a much more sizeable and relatively powerful political force in New Zealand than their counterparts in Australia and Canada. They also had closer links with the state and polity, particularly Labour administrations.

The Maori parliamentary seats, for example, although reflecting colonial co-optation, nonetheless provided a centralised focus for pan-tribal political mobilisation. The religio-prophetic Ratana movement that emerged in the 1920s was even more influential in providing a nationwide platform for Maori issues. Unlike previous movements espousing regional and ascribed elite interests, Ratana aimed his sermons at the mass of Maori persons who shared commoner and working-class roots, and a minority status. This stance led to a rapprochement with the newly established Labour Party, who swept into office in the late 1930s, aided by Ratana candidates who dominated the Maori seats for the next four decades. During the Second World War the Maori Battalion and the Maori War Effort Organization provided further impetus for Maori politics, with many leaders in these organisations finding positions in the middle and lower rungs of Maori Affairs and other government departments after being demobbed (Pearson 1990: 193).

Rapid postwar Maori urbanisation saw the proliferation of political, religious and voluntary associations. Further pan-Maori organisations – the

Maori Women's Welfare League, formed in the 1950s, and the Maori Council established by the National Government in 1962 – became parallel representative bodies to the Maori parliamentarians. Equally, if not more influential in shaping state policy, were Maori movements forming beyond and against the state. Interwoven with feminist, labour, peace, Green and anti-apartheid movements, local Maori politics became fully immersed in international political waters. In 1975 a national land march, 30 000 strong, highlighted a decade of visible and vocal protest actions highlighting conflicts over land and fishery ownership, the revival of Maori culture and the assertion of rights under the Treaty of Waitangi. Most of these themes, as we have seen, were common to aboriginal politics elsewhere, but the Treaty was a uniquely New Zealand event that became the focus for multi-stranded myths of origin and destiny.

Whatever the Treaty meant to its signatories, the 1840s documents (the plural is deliberate given different versions in Maori and English) acted as a platform for the intensification of ethnopolitics, being a potent symbol of debate over sovereignty, citizenship and self-determination. Given the highly charged political atmosphere of the 1970s, a smouldering issue just required a spark. Fuel was supplied by the Waitangi Tribunal established by the Third Labour Government (in 1975), and the Fourth Labour Government tossed a match in (in 1984) when they enlarged the Tribunal's powers. Thus, the Labour administration mixed a curious brew of neo-liberal economic policy and old style social commitment (Kelsey 1990). Both elements took the electorate by surprise, with the Tribunal proving to be a box worthy of Pandora.

The symbolic and political importance of the Tribunal far outweighed its restrictive legal powers. Even the 1984 version, which could now examine Maori land claims back to 1840, was strictly an advisory body. What the Tribunal provided was a new spiritual and ideological Treaty-driven locus for Maori and iwi politics, and a quasi-judicial forum for claims of reparation that encouraged a litigious stance against the state. The Treaty also served, as we shall see in more detail in Chapter 7, as a 'bicultural' symbol of nationhood finding favour among both Maori and Pakeha intelligentsia seeking an 'indigenous' Pacific identity. Thus, in contrast to Canadian and Australian attempts to draw on multicultural signifiers for reshaping 'the nation', in New Zealand biculturalism took over that role.

In the 1980s, the government began to incorporate bicultural values into Maori policy. Bilingualism played an important role within biculturalism as the dual naming of government departments, the ceremonial use of Maori protocol, and the addition of Aotearoa to New Zealand as an increasingly customary practice, revealed. Members of school boards, university councils and civil servants now had to ponder on whether their departmental practices and goals met with the principles of the Treaty now formally enshrined in their charters, as Maori increasingly challenged them to deliver appropriate 'bicultural' services. A shift towards self-administration in social welfare and criminal justice programmes, the growth of Maori-controlled preschool language classes, the spread of *iwi* and pan-tribal business cooperatives, and the decentralisation of the Department of Maori Affairs to *iwi* and regional bodies, were all signs of a groundswell of bicultural initiatives. Such trends coincided with a series of court decisions cementing a greater recognition of land, forestry and fishery rights.

Not surprisingly, given Canadian experience for example, the enhancement of rights in one sector inevitably provoked resistance or increased demands in others. Majority group reaction to bicultural initiatives was very mixed. An attitude survey conducted by the Royal Commission on Social Policy in late 1987 revealed a major disjuncture between a qualified support for meeting symbolic obligations and a marked lack of sympathy for hard-bitten material redress. Maori opinion, although much more solidly behind the enhancement of Maori rights and the honouring of the Treaty, was far from unanimous about how they might achieve this. What was interesting were the categories used by the Commission to construct its statistics. They ordered responses under the rubrics 'European', 'Maori' and 'Other'. The use of 'European' confirmed 'Pakeha' was still a contested concept in official parlance, and the use of the term 'Other' spoke volumes about current ethnic power imbalances. With the stroke of a pen, tabulators had swept all non-Maori/European persons into residual oblivion (Pearson 1990: 236–8).

The treatment of new arrivals also signified their political position. Compared with the level of multicultural support and organisation, for and among 'ethnics' in New South Wales and Ontario, most recent (non-European) migrants in New Zealand were still poorly resourced and weakly politicised. A national federation of ethnic councils was formed in 1989, followed by a council of refugee groups, both modelled on their Australian predecessors. These umbrella organisations formed in the wake of earlier formed official and informal Pacific Island bodies. Yet none of these developments undermined an overarching Maori/ non-Maori duality. At the end of the 1980s what threatened biculturalism was the growing tension between state-directed conceptions of 'partnership' and devolution, and a variety of Maori and iwi attempts to pursue their own meanings of *tino rangatiratanga* (self-determination). Most of these meanings were still reflective of accommodatory stances designed to extract maximum gains from reformism, but echoing Australian and Canadian experience, many versions of the New Zealand sovereignty game were being played. Within some of these games recodifications of Treaty texts pointed to rather more resistive degrees of self-governance.

From assimilation to self-management

Having described the main themes of state policy and minority activism in our case studies we can return to the questions posed at the beginning of this chapter. We can also flesh out several points made about the dynamics of inclusionary and exclusionary ethnic politics made earlier in the text. So why were policies of assimilation, firmly entrenched in the 1950s, replaced by pluralistic 'cultural' models and neologisms by the 1980s? Did the state choose to jump or was it pushed in this direction?

Dominant elites, and the states they constructed to serve their purposes, were always constrained by external forces and internal divisions. Minorities, moreover, proved consistently adept at adapting within the confines of relative powerlessness. Those confines were the territorial boundaries of Western states, whose supremacy still rested on military and economic power within the mid-twentieth century world order. Yet their legitimacy increasingly rested on a rights-based ethos within geopolitical alliances and international law and practice. Modernisation, with its attendant forms of production, technology, living patterns and values *did* promote a degree of homogeneity in mass aspirations for material improvement and political participation. But it defied those commentators, including state elites, who predicted the end of 'traditional' collective allegiances and ascriptive identities. Paradoxically, modernisation reinvigorated ethnic solidarities and state policies virtually compelled political activism. In a climate of rising economic and political expectations, ethnicity proved to be a highly salient mechanism for competing for material and symbolic advantage.

Recalling Mann's (1984) earlier noted epigram, the modern state is infrastructurally strong but despotically weak. Although forced surveillance and direct coercion are still recurrent themes in ethnic politics, so too are public outcries following such actions. Far better then to rule by informed or manufactured consent than blatant tyranny. Consequently, further co-option and increased devolution have been the major weapons of state authority over ethnic minorities in recent times. These strategies both create and sustain the very forces states endeavour to control or eradicate. The linked necessity (for states) to define, categorically and territorially, the limits of representation and containment, also promote new boundaries of accommodation and resistance.

The broad trend in our case studies over the period traversed in this chapter is one of convergence, although comparable points on a journey should not blind us to the elusiveness of an exact destination. From the 1940s to the late 1980s, allowing for local contrasts in timing, sociodemographic composition and nomenclature, we can see a shift in state immigrant and aboriginal policy from assimilative, through integrative to cultural and social pluralistic models. Assimilative migrant strategies were designed to facilitate forced and/or voluntary acculturation of populations, ideally, little different from one another. From the majority population's perspective, 'they' are supposed to become like 'us' through, for example, language acquisition, occupational and residential mobility, naturalisation and citizenship, and possibly, intermarriage. Cultural maintenance, if tolerated, is essentially a private matter for minorities expected to conform to majority norms in public. For the economic and geopolitical reasons outlined previously, the threshold of migrant acceptability in cultural and, less so, phenotypical terms, was pushed gradually outwards. The acculturation of new migrants continued, but it was always a partial process governed by internal choices and external constraints.

The 'construction sites' of ethnic and racial identity, to reintroduce Cornell and Hartmann's (1998) useful concept, reflect many intertwined processes. Restricted market opportunities coupled with ethnocentric and racist practices produce group segmentation, stratification and limited social and spatial mobility. Shared opprobrium and limited life chances strengthen ethnic group boundaries constructed by imposed circumstance. Ethnic identity and association, however, are not simply reactions to external stimuli. Overseas migrants and transient indigenes, for example, bring their own ways of seeing and doing with them to new places. They may choose to live and work together even if they are not compelled to do so. Even in situations where threat or constraint is absent, the size, generational composition, and flow of new arrivals, for example, will still influence the communality of ethnic groups. Usually, of course, ethnic (and racial) identities and institutions arise, remain, or disappear through the dynamic interplay of forces from without and within. They result, as Nagel concludes, from 'internal and external opinions and processes, as well as the individual's self-identification and outsiders' ethnic designations' (Nagel 1998b: 240).

Political opportunity is a key circumstance influencing this interplay (Esman 1994: 215). How open is the state to the toleration, let alone encouragement, of cultural retention or revival? As we saw above, governments shifted ground to integrative policies when visible signs of ethnic and racial inequalities, and indicators of cultural resilience, revealed the failure of assimilation. In the late 1960s and early 1970s, particularly in Australia and Canada, greater emphasis was placed on achieving equal opportunity regardless of ethnic affiliation. Subsequently, migrant and aboriginal services were increasingly delivered by state bureaucracies whose lower levels at least were 'ethnicised' and 'indigenised'. Much of this change came from migrant and aboriginal associations, and their sympathisers, pressing for resources in a welfarist period when state elites and polities felt they could afford, perhaps mildly celebrate, some degree of ethnic diversity.

The symbolic must be placed alongside the material in assessing the reasons for this move. As Breton perceptively argues (in the Canadian case, but with general applicability), shifts towards more pluralistic conceptions of the nation and state were designed to redefine and manage 'the allocation of public status among various ethno-cultural groups and thus regulate inter-group competition for public recognition' (Breton 1988: 39). Having established a new structure of political opportunity, expectations are raised and new demands are created. Innovative forms of state intervention – policies, programmes, agencies centred on 'culture' – promoted fresh waves of 'ethnic' organisation, often using symbols and practices introduced by other political game players at home and abroad, including the state itself.

Successive governments continued to approach Weaver's (1985) earlier noted problem of 'representivity' by categorisation and co-optation. Official 'immigrant' and 'indigenous' categories create, reinforce or reconstruct ethnic group boundaries in a continual process of culture-building and renovation. The designation of particular sub-populations as targets for economic resourcing and/or political recognition not only cements or revives existing group identities and organisation; it 'can also increase identification and mobilization among ethnic groups not officially recognized, and thus promote new ethnic formation' (Nagel 1998b: 245).

The 1960s' and 1970s' international climate of resource competition, crystallised in the United States imagery of civil unrest, proved fertile ground for the propagation of old and new identities by aboriginal and immigrant 'cultural entrepreneurs'. Typically drawn from expanding professional and intelligentsia classes, although often deriving their legitimacy from more 'traditional' leaders, these entrepreneurs were highly skilled in turning categories of 'culture' into communities of 'interest' (Cornell 1996: 277), both leaders and followers choosing from a wide array of local, regional and national identities, depending on the perceived strategic utility and symbolic appropriateness of the issue or audience. Many issues falling under multi- and bicultural labels were about access to resources, status, and non-discriminatory treatment in public affairs. In this sense they were about reforming the rights of selves, collective but more commonly individual, without altering the structure of states and their territorial legitimacy. Yet, as our case studies show, the shift from assimilation to multi- and biculturalisms had most difficulty facing the unfinished business of decolonisation embracing rather more radical self-determinative aims.

Settler states had decimated, dispersed or 'encouraged' aboriginal persons to assimilate in the hope they would vanish *in toto*, or through a process of gradual hybridisation become transmogrified into a more acceptable civilised amalgam. Acculturation, to widely varying degrees, had occurred. Many aboriginal languages and lifestyles had vanished. But by the mid-twentieth century there were visible signs of resurgence. Whereas elites in Britain might regret the eclipse of their Empire, they had some control over the discarding or departure of their colonies, but the post-settler successors to the British diaspora could not divest themselves of the peoples who remained distinct entities in the very states that colonised them.

After the Second World War, Australia, Canada and New Zealand, in typical semi-peripheral fashion, sought to balance their long-term relations with Britain and the United States with plans to raise their own profiles in international fora increasingly influenced by the Third World periphery. Presenting themselves as thoroughly modern social democracies, with varying, but generally progressive welfare histories, post-settler polities had some strategic purchase for enhancing their own independent status in a self-determinative era. But they were still faced with the dilemma of being colonialists in a post-colonial world. The delicacy of this situation is summed up in the welfare-colonial couplet, briefly touched on in the Canadian discussion above.

Robert Paine (1977) coined 'welfare colonialism' to describe the postwar contradictions of state/aboriginal relations in Northern Canada. The phrase seems best suited to some aspects of the reservation and settlement-based systems of Australia and North America, although as a metaphor for the ironies of new systems of control it has more general applicability, extending to New Zealand. In this wider sense, Paine's concept neatly captures the contradictions in regimes he described as 'solicitous rather than exploitive, and liberal rather than repressive' (Paine 1977: 3). As Beckett notes, building on Paine, juxtaposing 'welfare' and 'colonialism' highlights the character of state policies and practices that treat their subjects 'at one moment as citizens, but at another as indigenous peoples' (Beckett n.d.: 4). In their attempts to solve what they defined as the 'Indian', 'Aborigine' or 'Maori' problem, states were forced to confront both the (welfare) rights and (colonial) self-determinative claims aboriginal minorities made. On the one hand, energised by the civil and other rights movements, indigenes fought for greater equality as citizens. On the other hand, influenced by Third World liberation models, they struggled for the return and/or reconstitution of control over their own lands, resources and destinies. Using the weapons of guilt and embarrassment aboriginal minorities gained a remarkable prominence and degree of sympathy belying their small numbers and relative powerlessness.

The logic of welfare colonialism was intrinsically contradictory. For aboriginal minorities, any expansion of their citizenship rights brought them ever closer to the state as individual subjects, yet the pursuit of self-determination as a people demanded some form of collective autonomy in or beyond the administrative apparatus. State elites faced equally conflicting alternatives. On the one hand, they were caught between the demands of capital and aboriginal assertions of greater or sole rights over the assets within their territories. On the other hand, they were beset by burgeoning national debt and fiscal deficits clashing with a rising welfare bill for aboriginal persons disproportionately under- or unemployed. The result, in one direction, was an increasing shift to 'self-management' and the further indigenising of service delivery. In part, echoing migrant 'ethnic' policies, aboriginal elites and administrative structures would administer their own welfare, although the state would still oversee and control its funding. But, in another direction, these manoeuvres did not halt the momentum of decolonisation since aboriginal minority goals went far beyond those pursued by their immigrant counterparts, and they gained their legitimacy and strength from a different source.

The incremental march of resource and self-governance claims through the law courts and treaty tribunals highlights how aboriginal minorities did not ground their claims to self-determination in liberal social-contractual theories of citizenship: 'but in a body of law that explicitly legitimates their original sovereignty, that is friendly to their claim of being a distinct people, and that acknowledges that they were incorporated into the modern state through colonial processes' (Werther 1992: 43) – hence the link to the United Nations, cognate international bodies, and worldwide decolonisation movements. The vital difference being, however, that for much of the period discussed in this chapter, the UN saw the self-determination claims of aboriginal 'nations' as undermining the territorial integrity of states. Here lies a further contradiction we will return to in later chapters. Aboriginal minorities can access an international jurisprudence and politics that move them beyond the rights claims of immigrant minorities, but the very tools and state locations confirming this limit their potential, in *realpolitik* terms, for 'real' self-determination, not least because of the changing mood and temper of non-aboriginal dominated electorates. Nevertheless, by combining citizenship claims with unique self-determinative strategies, in a local and global climate in which majorities were susceptible to new national imaginings, aboriginal minorities could force state elites to add sovereignty issues into the mélange of new 'isms' describing the pluralism of the 1990s.

Conclusion

In this chapter we have described and explained how and why the overtly assimilationist stance towards aboriginal and immigrant minorities, typical of earlier phases of settlement and post-settlement, was discarded. Overtly, of course, is an important qualifier since minorities continue to get drawn into the 'dominant culture' and the inexorable clutches of the polity and economy. By accident or design, the very act of fighting for resources and/or independence takes one into the heart of the state and civil society being accommodated or resisted. Since the 1970s, various forms of pluralistic ideologies and administrative frameworks have arisen out of the dynamic interplay between states seeking to manage increasing socio-cultural diversity and ethnic movements exploiting new opportunities for status attainment, resource control and, possibly, self-governance. Multicultural and bicultural discourses loosely describe situations where immigration flows are no longer so strictly controlled by majority group perceptions of the inviolability of their own ethnic cores. Likewise, aboriginal populations states once ignored or expected to merge into the society built around them, have reasserted strong claims for some form of political and economic autonomy. In addition, in Canada, Quebec continues vigorously to pursue its ethnoregional interests. Recent changes, in part, have arisen because global decolonisation processes have not only affected aboriginal peoples and the waves of newcomers who have moved between various 'worlds', but also the successors of the settler populations that respectively dispossessed and resisted them. Out of the quests for new multiple identities and independencies emerge new models of freedom and restraint. These 'culturalisms' have cross-national continuities, but their current forms were forged in the fires of their specific histories and contexts. Let us examine this contention more closely in the next chapter.

6
Multi-Culturalisms

So are we all multiculturalists now? In the opening chapter I touched on Nathan Glazer's (1997) American rhetorical flourish to introduce a word with wide currency in numerous societies, post-settler and otherwise. A wealth of academic studies lends weight to the portability of the term across continents, yet ubiquity hardly squares with conceptual agreement or political consensus, and one needs to be cautious about confusing the pervasive use of a slogan with less common attempts to devise multicultural states and nations. Multiculturalism is a highly contested and chameleon-like neologism whose colours change to suit the complexion of local conditions. As the insertion of a hyphen in this chapter heading shows, we have many 'culturalisms'. These range from deceptively simple binaries to the theoretically boundless limits of 'multi' diversity, with frames of meaning shifting across space and time within and across nation-state borders. Faced with such confusion it is tempting to jettison the word and start afresh, but alternatives invariably beg just as many questions. What we will do here is to concentrate on key recurrent themes and distinguish them analytically, even if, in practice, they are consistently entangled.

First we can refer to multi-culturalisms in a demographic and descriptive sense. At this level, recalling the migratory trends and evident increased diversity outlined earlier (Chapter 4), multi-culturalism is an empirical fact, almost a banality. In assessing the reactions to diversity, however, we go to a second level where statements about 'what is' become questions of 'what should be'. Entering the normative realm of multicultural and bicultural ideologies and discourses, one assesses the beliefs and utterances framing the perspectives of, for example, parliamentarians, state officials or those active within aboriginal and immigrant minority political associations? Finally, at a third level, are the policies and practices these types of actors adopted under 'cultural' rubrics.

In the last chapter we saw how processes of categorisation and identification constructed and reconstructed various 'isms', and these, in turn, shaped and reshaped sets of institutions using the same vocabulary. Is this because similar causes had analogous effects promoting comparable consequences? In very general, time-specific, terms we might sustain this logical sequence. All these 'isms' are post-mid-1960s attempts to grapple with the ramifications of recent ethnic movements, political and demographic. But a closer, contextualised look at what is being agreed upon or fought over reveals the historical parameters of ethnic politics are still prominent in shaping current trends. More detailed scrutiny of contemporary multi-culturalisms in our post-settler locales, this time set against recent American and British multicultural experience, reinforces this argument.

Post-Civil Rights USA

American multiculturalism is 'an aftershock of the black-power radicalism of the sixties' (Lind 1995: 13). Recent immigration, particularly from Mexico, Central America and Asia was also an important factor, as were older republican traditions. Yet despite much ado about 'culture', this 'ism' is primarily about 'race'. Reaffirming a long-standing liberal faith, the 1964 Civil Rights Act explicitly referred to individual citizens, but subsequent legislation and programmes implemented affirmative action which promoted the categorisation of collective rights groups. Higham suggests, between 1910 and the 1950s, a new modernising intellectual class, much influenced by the social sciences and a literary intelligentsia, sought to introduce social democratic reforms designed to make the American Creed more responsive to the needs of ethnic minorities and the underprivileged (Higham 1998: 213–18). American liberalism had always eschewed the collective redistributive tenor of, for example, British and Scandinavian modern welfare states. The New Deal was firmly based on principles of personal insurance and voluntary contribution rather than extensive national state intervention. Nevertheless, twentieth-century 'progressive republicanism', as Heller (1997) styles it, moved towards a form of 'national liberalism' that, although falling well short of European-style welfarism, nonetheless strengthened state control over immigration, urban policing and more standardised public school education. The civil rights momentum that grafted collective rights onto liberal legacies partly transformed these innovations, initially designed to strengthen assimilation to the American way of life. Struggles from below combined with the important reforming strand above, to produce a new climate of reform designed to redress particular grievances that had always cast a lie to the universality of American rights. 1960s-style affirmative action programmes moved from insurance to 'undisguised redistribution' through 'explicit remedial recognition of the debilitating effects of race' (ibid.: 35). Race became a positive salient indicator for state hiring, contracting, educational access and finance. The post-civil rights era promoted racial categories for monitoring anti-discrimination measures, distributing government resources, and shaping electoral and educational recognition. Jobs and votes were apportioned on the basis of racially designated population shares.

Four major categories of hyphenated Americans emerged as the key beneficiaries of state recognition and representation. Two of them, American Blacks and American Indians, are persistent features of a historical landscape of slavery and dispossession. The others are more recent constructions stemming, in the main, from post-1960s immigration legislation and civil rights reforms. During this period, migrants from Latin America were arriving in increasing numbers, while the 'old Asian' communities were joined by newcomers from varied Eastern origins. By the early 1990s about 80 per cent of United States immigrants stemmed from these sources. Both migrant streams reflected differentiated social class and legal statuses, with sharp contrasts between, for example, illegal, unskilled Mexican and Dominican workers and sponsored Asian professionals. What these persons shared was their visibility, given the concentrated regional and residential areas they clustered in, and the recent high profile given to immigration and its impact. In particular, the changing demography, politics and immigration legislation of California provided a leitmotif within a theme of uncertainty about the links between immigration, multiculturalism and national identity.[1]

Out of this array of newcomers, new categories of 'Asian' and 'Hispanic' (or 'Latino') were fabricated. Such groupings, although fashioned far more swiftly, had some points of commonality with Black and aboriginal minorities. All these groupings had experienced a process of state categorisation and ethnogenesis promoting a series of recodings of a general identity overlaying various layers of internal differentiation. Hispanics had a common language, most of them shared a similar low-class position, and Mexicans at least, shared a colonialist legacy of the American south-west. Yet their official designation as a discrete racial category owes more to political positioning than physical/cultural commonality, given the plurality of Latin American status and racial classification (Kibria 1998: 956)

The Asian-American movement is an even more conspicuous example of how racialisation, in a climate of state-created political opportunity, fosters what Lopez and Espiritu (1990: 219) call 'panethnic' interest groups. Panethnicity describes the development of solidarities of identity and organisation among ethnic subgroups clustered together by outsider stereotyping and administration. Panethnicity helped state elites and bureaucracies by managing representivity, and it aided minority elites by maximising numbers and resources for mobilisation. The process is inherently unstable and susceptible to strategic manipulation by both sets of elites, since the categories disguise myriad internal factions. The Asian American leadership, in particular, had to transcend the distinctions between the pre-1960s 'Asian' population and the increasingly heterogeneous foreign-born newcomers that followed them. Inspired by the civil rights spirit of the transvaluation of culture and phenotype, it was not only Black that became beautiful. Other communities of fate and character, as Heller describes them, were formed or enhanced by modelling themselves on the African American experience (Heller 1997: 34). 'Asian American' is strictly a post-civil rights phenomenon. Asian features, physical, economic and social, once devalued, were now transformed into a means of political empowerment. Builders of the Asian American movement constructed racial unity out of ethnic and national diversity and in the process retranslated a history of success into one of victimisation.

Education was a key, third, vehicle for change in the shift from individual affirmative action to a more extensive recognition of multiple, constituent cultures. The 'schoolroom', as we saw earlier, was at the colonial forefront of assimilation, and its early to mid-twentieth-century equivalent continued to teach the civic American Creed. But by the 1960s, at least in polyglot conurbations, the 'great equaliser' had become a pivotal driving force for Third World-inspired decolonial movements. Ethnic and racial studies programmes proliferated in universities and colleges. Empowering new 'culturalist' leaders and instilling an exclusivity of group pride, they intermingled a politics of position and recognition. Such initiatives drew support, often qualified, from the 'Rainbow Coalition' of rights claimant groups that broadened the base of the Black and Red civil rights movement. A fashionable emphasis on 'hybridity' highlighted the intersection of multiple identities and sources of inequality and critiqued what was seen as a hegemonic 'Western' and 'American' common culture. Ironically, however, multiculturalists often replaced a national symbol of fabricated unity with an image of myriad bounded 'cultures'. Other commentators went further, suggesting border crossing was not only unrealisable, but politically questionable. By the late 1980s, some black intellectuals were talking of 'two nations', black and white, still separate, unequal and decidedly hostile.

If multicultural academies were important, the public school system became equally influential in promoting the 'ism'. Strenuous lobbying by ethnic interest groups overturned bilingual education provisions introduced (in the late 1960s) to help English language acquisition among new migrants, replacing them with native-language education in all school subjects in areas with substantial 'ethnic' populations. Not surprisingly, California and New York, with the highest levels of immigration and diversity in the nation, were in the forefront of multicultural education. Their public school curricula reflected the move against monoculturalism and the fostering of cultures of ethnic endowment seeking reform, recognition and respect for minorities (Higham 1998: 218).

The response to these changes, by what we might caricature as 'traditional' liberal opinion, was predictable: neatly captured in Schlesinger's (1992) book title, *The Disuniting of America*. For Schlesinger, the essence of America is its classic immigrant tradition of a merging of cultures by a common acceptance of a European civic culture and the English language. Cultural pluralism and ethnic diversity are inbuilt qualities of nationhood but a universalist set of civic institutions held them together. Multiculturalists' 'obsession with difference', Schlesinger argues, threatens this 'idea of an overarching American nationality' (ibid.: 74). The threat may be there, but the outcome remains indistinct. Where *e pluribus unum* extolled an assimilationist vision of unity out of diversity, American multiculturalisms portray a future in which any form of national framing is achieved *within* plurality. The 'ism' à la mode, claims a public status for ethnic and racial collective distinction challenging the supposedly now colour-blind communality of American civic ideals.

The British management of 'race'

'Whereas the United States would have multiculturalism even without immigration, western Europe has multiculturalism as a result of immigration' (Joppke 1998: 36). Multiculturalisms in Britain, the Netherlands and Scandinavia, for example, are the result of the very recent arrival of ethnically and racially distinct migrant workers. In Britain (and the

Netherlands to a lesser degree) most of these workers are not 'foreigners' in a legal sense, but are the legacies of a global 'dominion of generic British civilization' (Favell 1998a: 102).

As we saw in Chapter 4, the British state responded to the arrival of their Empire subjects by eventually imposing the most restrictive immigration controls in Western Europe, and altering the centuries-old basis of British nationality. Initially, there was disagreement between Labour and Conservative Party political leaders about the ethics and efficacy of slamming the door in the faces of Commonwealth 'family', but a consensus emerged between the centre right and left, in and across rival parliamentary parties. Public policy and public attitudes were neatly congruent on the need for immigration control, but this harmony of interest was clearly missing in other areas of 'race relations' where state policies were out of kilter with majority public opinion.

In Favell's convincing account, broad agreement among policy-makers had been reached by the 1980s about a distinctive pattern of British 'race' institutions. These contained a paradoxical blend of a racist external migration regime and a more enlightened internal 'race relations' policy stemming from the 1960s. Faced with the prospect of recurrent waves of arrivals from a fragmenting Empire, and American-style urban unrest, the state cobbled together a programme of ethnic management and control. The resulting policies and their underlying rationale had broad appeal to traditional British liberal ideas across the political spectrum. Britain's 'race problem', it was argued, was not about rights or equal opportunity *per se*, but was ultimately a question of public order. Ergo, keeping the lid on immigration and eliminating racial discrimination was the prescription for inter-racial harmony. Consequently, firm distinctions were drawn between new immigrants and settled, permanent 'ethnic minorities'. The former, excepting close relatives of those already settled, would be kept out or strictly controlled. The latter would retain full political and legal citizenship, and improving their life chances and reducing racial hostility would enhance their social membership privileges.

Global events and local contingencies reaffirmed these central tenets. Between 1962 and 1981 the evolution of British immigration and nationality legislation reflects a 'dynastic shift' from subjectship to national citizenship (Joppke 1995: 35). From the initial prospect of unlimited numbers of West Indian workers and their families, through recurrent moral panics about 'Asians' from Kenya, Uganda (and, potentially, Hong Kong) following earlier arrivals, British 'pragmatism' culminated in the 1981 Nationality Act. This further turning of the screw on overseas dependencies, saw the overthrow of a thousand-year convention of granting automatic citizenship for children born in Britain of non-British parents. With this Act distinctions were drawn between cultural, national and legal meanings of 'Britishness', with only those with direct genealogical connections and residency being granted 'full' membership of the state.

If the state could re-jig the legal boundaries of the state, internal barriers to national acceptance were less easily dealt with. The 'long hot summer' of 1967, punctuated by 'race riots', clashes between pro- and anti-racist factions, and incidents of police brutality, showed racial tensions remained, despite closed immigration doors. This fostered a climate of race relations legislation, policies and practices designed, despite the influence of American civil rights and affirmative action policies, to avoid what was seen as the excesses of United States plurality. To be sure, Roy Jenkins, the Labour Party Home Office Secretary in the mid-1960s, set the tone for a 'liberal hour' of racial integration with his call for cultural diversity and equal opportunity within an atmosphere of mutual tolerance. Yet it was Enoch Powell's infamous airing (in 1968) of the dire prospect of being invaded by unassimilable hordes that finally cemented Tory/Labour agreement that 'integration' had to be pursued within mutually defended borders.

The 1970s saw the establishment of a race relations 'industry' based on a national Race Relations Act and Commission for Racial Equality, and local Race Relations Councils set up (in 1976) to provide social welfare and monitor racial discrimination. The devolving of responsibility for these tasks to local government, coupled with a national state preoccupation with 'they will not pass', continued throughout the Thatcherite era of Tory rule: Thatcher's allusion to 'swamping' in 1978 being reminiscent of Powell's rhetoric a decade earlier. Immigration controls were exempt from race relations legislation, so public policy retained what seemed to be an inbuilt inconsistency towards external and internal relations between 'races' (Spencer 1994: 319). Yet resisting introducing further diversity into what was seen as an already potent racial mix was perfectly logical in the eyes of those who invented the theory. The test, of course, was whether settled minorities were achieving upward mobility and becoming more accepted in society. There were plenty of counter-factual indicators.

The Scarman Report (1981) on racial disadvantage, which resulted from further flashpoints of racial tension in south London, pointed the finger at urban deprivation and inequitable life chances rather than institutionalised racism. Some local councils were prompted to introduce modest programmes of affirmative action, but indicators of inequality, particularly low educational achievement among Afro-Caribbean youth, persisted. These trends resulted in the Swann Report in 1985. The Report is commonly seen as marking the official shift to multiculturalism in Britain, with its stress on 'diversity within unity' and an acknowledgement of different modes of attachment to 'being British'. So, as in America, education became a key site for multicultural policy. The Swann Report led to the establishment of more independent voluntary-aided schools for different 'cultures', for greater flexibility in modes of dress, cuisine and curricula within 'multiracial' schools, and the hiring of more Asian and black teachers. Tensions remained between those (particularly on the left and in black associations) who viewed multiculturalism as a 'cultural' sop deflecting attention away from the 'real' issues of racism, class disadvantage and powerlessness, and those on the far right who saw it as a cover for militant sedition. But, as Vertovec (1996: 51) notes, in a survey of multicultural initiatives in British cities, there is no single view, strategy or mode of political incorporation under this rubric. What we have is a plethora of associations, units and councils in the realm of local and national minority representation. In London, and other areas with sizeable Asian and black populations, increasing numbers of senior administrators and councillors drawn from these minorities, bear testimony to multiculturalism as a vehicle for the creation and consolidation of local and regional ethnic political associations. Parliamentary constituencies in these same areas can also exert some local electoral pressure. All major parties have an eye on the 'ethnic vote', as the rise in minority electoral candidates, and Labour's formation of black sections in some local party organisations, reveals. But there are few signs of American-style ethnic politics: Town Hall has not become Tammany Hall.

Some events, like the Rushdie affair in 1989, spark national (and international) recognition of the limits of majority tolerance and bring multicultural issues into the mainstream of British politics. Such incidents also create, if often ephemerally, a greater sense of unity among minorities, in this case British Muslims. The uproar over the *fatwah* (a death threat) to Rushdie rippled through cities, particularly Bradford, with significant Muslim communities, and brought into focus the limits of British antiracist and multicultural legislation and programmes. The refusal to award Muslims the kind of official 'racial' recognition granted to 'Blacks', 'Asians' and Jews reinforced the boundaries of cultural inclusion. Yet, as Favell concludes, British centrist political elites have been remarkably successful in steering a hazardous political course between the dangers of majority intolerance and minority separatism. Mainstream politicians involved in the Rushdie issue were able to distance themselves from media hysteria. They effectively defused the situation by sympathising with 'moderate' Muslims while extolling the virtues of Britain's multiracial framework. The Rushdie case, therefore, is an exception illustrating the rule, that, in sharp contrast to the United States, over the past three decades 'race' has become a comparatively minor national theme in British politics (Favell 1998a: 127–8).

Canadian multiculturalism: constitutional experiments

Given the complex array of local problems of cohesion and identity, Canadian multiculturalism reflects the perceived need of the federal polity and state to develop a formally stated inclusionary ideology and political framework appearing in several different interlinked guises. We might view it, altruistically, in a restricted sense as a set of policies and programmes initially designed to ease the movement of new migrants into Canada. These initiatives provide the symbolic, legal and, to a degree, material support for them to find a space to preserve some of their own social mores while adopting the conventions of 'the majority' of Canadians. More generally, we can also perceive multiculturalism as an innovative framework of ideas and institutions marking the final replacement of a British elite ethnic core with a pluralistic representation of origins and destinies. This plural model not only refurbishes the ethnic mosaic imagery designed to distance Canada from its American neighbour. It also serves to provide newly arrived and long-settled migrants with a more inclusive and equitable place within a multinational state with a decidedly polyethnic character.

Inevitably, the politics of Canadian duality was a prominent fibre in a loosely knitted ethnonational garment, and here the altruism becomes diluted if not completely abandoned. From its inception in the early 1970s, Anglophone elites and federalist Francophones used multiculturalism as a device to appease or subvert the sovereignty claims of separatist inclined Québécois. As a construct designed to solve the recurrent problem of preserving a federal structure within which they could maintain or contain Quebec, multiculturalism consistently embraced: 'The same three mythic protagonists: the British (sometimes and not exactly synonymously identified as the Anglophones or Anglo-Celts), the French (sometimes and again not synonymously described as Canadiens, Francophones and Québécois), and the "other ethnic groups"' (Harney 1988: 65).

Of course, Harney should have added aboriginal peoples to this loosely defined trio. The 'First Nations' now occupy the state arena as much stronger and influential political game players. Here too, multiculturalism has been used as a dissembling device designed to convert aboriginal minorities to 'ethnic' status, or, even if some form of political autonomy is achieved, to contain it *within* a multicultural Canada. Thus the state 'management' potential of multiculturalism is given prominence, although to counterpose cynicism with altruism oversimplifies the motives and movements of the interest groups using multiculturalism in multiple ways.

By entangling multiculturalism with the politics of bilingualism and aboriginal rights Canadian elites adopted a far more ambitious management strategy resulting in further intergroup competition for material and symbolic resources. Having adopted a national ideology of plural consensus (in the 1970s) as an attempt to disarm or reconcile Quebec, the Canadian state inadvertently enhanced the politicisation of immigrant minorities by establishing a climate of rights within which they were relegated to minor players. As new immigrants with new needs arrived in Canada, the state modified the multicultural strategy, albeit modestly, given the limited level of funding and legal protection of multicultural rights. Hence the shift to anti-racism and affirmative action programmes in education and employment. As 'ethnic' political constituencies became more influential, particularly in Ontario and the Western Provinces, the multicultural movement was reinforced by politicians and bureaucrats, some of whom represented 'ethnic communities', who viewed multiculturalism as 'a medium of exchange... and way of controlling new ethnic and immigrant voting blocs' (ibid.: 65).

This medium was an influential currency in a geopolitical climate where Canada sought to retain its image as a bastion of social democratic innovation and reposition itself in new global economic markets. Thus Harney's 'other ethnic groups' remained on the political agenda when the Canadian state embarked on a series of intricate accommodations with its more powerful linguistic, regional and, as it proved, aboriginal constituents. These adaptations culminated in constitutional attempts to redesign a form of Canadian consociation. What had historically been a framework devised to achieve a form of peaceful coexistence between the major language groups and regional divisions, was transformed into a far more challenging model of eclectic political interests.

A brief comparison between the late 1960s assumptions of the Bi and Bi Commission that triggered the birth of multiculturalism, and the themes of the abortive Meech Lake Accord and Charlottetown

Agreement of the early 1990s, illustrates the continuities and changes in ethnic politics over the past three decades.

As Oliver notes:

> The crucial insight of the B & B Commission was that a stable base for French-English cooperation cannot be achieved just by increasing French minority rights in Canada as a whole (seen as a single community) but also must involve the exercise of a set of powers, adequate for community development, by a community jurisdiction (Quebec) in which the countrywide minority (Francophone) is a majority. (Oliver 1993: 326)

Only English and French Canada, the Commission argued, had distinct societies, the latter in Quebec. Other ethnic communities had their own languages and customs, a sense of place and identity, but these should be 'nested' within the overarching French/English duality. Such societies were deemed to be open, their entry based on civic rights, not ethnic or racial ascription. So the Commission rejected the idea that Ukrainian Canadians, for example, were or should be second-class citizens, but they should not be conceived as separate social orders. The position of aboriginal peoples was beyond their mandate, but the Commission briefly alluded to the need to encourage and support their 'integration' and cultural survival within their model.

A variety of factors subsequently undermined this image of equal partnership between the two majorities, with aboriginal and immigrant 'others' located within it. Trudeau's vision would not countenance a 'distinct' Quebec. The 'other' ethnic groups became sufficiently mobilised, ironically partly based on the Commission hearings, to question a partnership of only two. A conclusion more than endorsed by aboriginal peoples who, pursuing greater autonomy, balked at further variations on a well-worn assimilation theme. The increased strength of regionalism, from the Atlantic, the North, and particularly Western Canada, also cut across the duality. As did the emergence of 'Charter Canadians', whose conception of a multiplicity of individual and group rights clashed with earlier evocations of two, linguistic, 'Charter' groups. Finally, of course, we have Quebec's initial repudiation of Trudeau's provincial bilingualism and multiculturalism and its subsequent drive towards secession.

A mere two decades after the Bi and Bi Report, the meetings at Meech Lake and Charlottetown highlight the move away from a simple model of majority founding partners. What the respective Accord and

Agreement sought to do was to weld together a new national framework – a 'community of communities' as Oliver (ibid.: 321) describes it. All the intricacies of these events need not concern us here;[2] what is illuminating is how the terms of debate at these discussions capture the major shifts in the Canadian ethnic political mood since the 1960s.

The Accord, seeking to find eventual agreement for notions abortively conceived at Meech, attempted to define what made Quebec a 'distinct society'. This phrase clearly has echoes of the Bi and Bi Report, but by now the relationship between Quebec and the Rest of Canada had clearly supplanted the Commission's Anglophone/Francophone binary. The Accord granted all provinces more autonomy,[3] and communities of aboriginal persons, now acknowledged as founding nations, were perceived as a third level of government in Canada with 'inherent rights' of self-rule. Existing minority rights legislation protected the interests of 'other' Charter groups, it was argued. As for the 'citizens from many lands', the Accord repeated the Charter's original position: namely that interpretation of the agreement should be 'consistent with the preservation of the multicultural heritage of Canadians'. The icing on this multilayered constitutional cake was a 'Canada Clause' enwrapping all these facets into a statement on fundamental Canadian values.

The Accord, building on the Charter, the Multiculturalism Act and Meech, scaled the heights of ethnically and nationally diverse ambition. With hindsight, its subsequent rejection by national referendum was inevitable, not simply because Canadians were suffering from economic recession, disillusionment with their polity and a bad attack of Constitution fatigue, but because the community of communities model reproduced a hierarchy of rights groups, albeit differently ordered from the equal partnership formula. The new prototype was also flawed by the attempt to encompass a range of 'communities' whose form and degree of communality varied considerably.

Canadian multiculturalism remained controversial throughout the 1990s. Its detractors claimed it had gone too far, its supporters not far enough, along the roads towards greater individual and collective rights and recognition, and a national image of plural consensus. Immigration figures continued to be a source of public anxiety and alarm, prompting a partial closing of 'floodgates, so to speak... to put in state-of-the art pay-turnstiles' (Foster 1998: 16). The polity could not placate the more hard-line Québécois and First Nation independence movements, and any semblance of bipartisan political agreement was removed when the Reform Party and the Bloc Québécois, neither enamoured with multiculturalism, became the official opposition to the reigning Liberal government. Thus, Canadian multiculturalism, as Fleras notes, remains 'double-edged in impact and implications' (Fleras 1998: 72). On the one hand, multicultural policies and practices have provided viable sites of struggle for ethnic and other minorities. On the other hand, official multiculturalism, Quebec and aboriginal peoples aside, has been a force for de-radicalising ethnic movements by legitimising state-approved differences as integral to society. This tension between containment and empowerment comes close to being a universal multicultural element, but Canada, as the first, official 'multicultural state', remains the front runner in seeking to control it by experimenting with constitutional, consociational arrangements.

Australian multiculturalism: retrenchment and reconciliation

The National Agenda laid down in the late 1980s by the Australian Labor Party set the tone for multiculturalism in the following decade, but its principles were often at variance with practices, and they did not receive bipartisan parliamentary support. The idea, which was introduced in the mid-1970s as a tributary response to changing immigration patterns and a recognition of the ineffectiveness of blatant assimilation, had moved into the mainstream. Yet, as in Canada, there was friction between state and polity recognition of cultural difference and a perceived need among elites for the endorsement of universalism. There was also chafing between social policies of equality and economic stratagems of efficiency. No longer confined to 'ethnic groups', the Agenda sought to define a format about the links between cultural and national identity, social justice and economic advancement for all Australians. Multiculturalism was not a model of cultural pluralism or minority rights, but a statement of citizen rights and obligations. In Castles' terms:

> Multiculturalism was defined as a system of rights and freedoms, combined with such obligations as commitment to the nation, a duty to accept the Constitution and the rule of law, and the acceptance of basic principles such as tolerance and equality, English as the national language and equality of the sexes. (Castles 1997: 15)

The rhetoric implied Australians had the right to be different and this recognition should not impede opportunity. The state had an obligation to redress disadvantage and combat discrimination, but citizens, in turn, should display a commitment to a core of institutions and values lying beyond their ethnic inheritance. The onus, therefore, was still on the terms of acceptance and assistance for recent generations of migrants within the Australian nation and state. A revised oath of citizenship, introduced in 1993, endorsed this sentiment, pledging new citizens to the rights, liberties and laws of 'Australia and its people' rather than the British monarchy (Jupp 1997: 36).

A National Multicultural Advisory Council document, *The Next Steps* (NMAC 1995), spelled out the policy obligations of the state and its citizens in more detail, and also assessed how successful government departments' social justice strategies had been. The Report acknowledged that, despite two decades of progressive policy reform, NESB and indigenous minorities remained disproportionately politically and economically disadvantaged. In 1989 all federal departments and agencies had been required to introduce Access and Equity strategies, but, much like state community relations and anti-racism initiatives, they were poorly funded and monitored. Evidence from a national inquiry (HREOC 1991) confirmed the high incidence of racist attacks, particularly against aboriginal people and some Asian migrants.[4] Nevertheless, despite this data, and the Keating-led ALP backing of *New Steps*, the Office of Multicultural Affairs, a central monitoring agency, was abolished (in 1996). Overall, the past decade has seen a gradual decline in migrant on-arrival services, with a switch, for many classes of new immigrants, to 'user-pays' for English classes and the introduction of waiting periods for eligibility to welfare services (Castles et al. 1998: 104–5). Thus, the fine policy words of social justice were capped by a thick veneer of economic rationalism guiding practices of overall retrenchment.

This clash between words and deeds with respect to immigrant provision was overlaid by the recurring problem of how to encompass aboriginal minorities within multiculturalism. If the latter was meant to be an overarching vision of social justice and cultural recognition, the inclusion of aboriginal peoples needed to be negotiated. In December 1992, Paul Keating, the Australian Premier, launched the impending International Year for the World's Indigenous Peoples in Redfern, a Sydney inner-city area with a sizeable aboriginal population. His controversial speech linked multiculturalism to aboriginal rights through its allusion to the need for non-aboriginal Australians to confront the issues raised in a 'socially just new multicultural society'. Keating stressed the necessity of seeking reconciliation, acknowledgement and 'a measure of justice' for Australia's indigenes in light of the Mabo case. The latter was a pivotal High Court decision made earlier in the year (1992) overturning the continued applicability of *terra nullius*.

The verdict stemmed from the claim of a Torres Strait Islander, Eddie Mabo, that the state had never extinguished his native title. Consequently, his individual and group proprietary land rights on Murray Island had been retained. A firm majority of judges (six to one) agreed with him. Their ruling prompted jubilation and moral panic in equal measure. Both responses proved excessive. Far from 'giving back the country' as some critics claimed, the Mabo judges reaffirmed the sovereignty of the Australian state under international law and the ultimate right of the Crown to extinguish native title without permission or compensation. Thus, the Mabo decision did not 'revoke action historically premised upon it' (Wolfe 1994: 122). Aboriginal peoples, moreover, had to prove an unbroken 'traditional connection' to land to claim native title. This undoubtedly benefited those aboriginal people who still resided in their 'traditional' areas by enhancing the possibility of consolidating or enlarging their land, and therefore their economic, base. A substantial majority of aboriginal persons could not make native title claims however, including those in Keating's audience in Sydney, who had been removed or moved off their land. Yet by recognising indigenous relations to land as having a legitimate relation to common law that survives the British seizure of sovereignty, and by publicly acknowledging the racist foundations of *terra nullius*, the Mabo judges' decision marked a major transformation in the underlying legal and moral premises of European colonisation.

This change was both a divisive and unifying force in Australian politics in the 1990s. The full legal ramifications of Mabo, and subsequent legislation like the Native Title Act of 1993 stemming from it, need not concern us here, and we will return to questions of nationhood and citizenship in the final two chapters. What we should note are the parallels between multicultural and indigenous discourses about cultural diversity, unity and social justice. In Keating's speech, and subsequent orations, he juxtaposed the legal dilemma of Mabo to the moral quandary of multiculturalism. As Povinelli argues, in post-Mabo Australia the abstract language of law, citizenship and rights became blended with a language of shame, reparation and reconciliation in 'a public purging of the past' (Povinelli 1998: 580). The acknowledgement of native title, whatever the legal niceties, became a symbolic benchmark to place alongside multiculturalism in the repudiation of 'White Australia'. Nonetheless, these discursive links were hardly matched by political practice.

The *National Agenda* had alluded to the situation of indigenous peoples in its sections on A&E and community relations programmes, and race relations legislation, but most of its policy initiatives were still directed at immigrants. By the time the *Next Steps* report had emerged (in 1995), the ALP government had established a Council for Aboriginal Reconciliation and it had liaised with the National Multicultural Advisory Council in the writing of the document. This contained more detail on aboriginal issues, such as social justice, than its predecessor, but there were few concrete proposals about how multiculturalism could address them. Many aboriginal persons remained, at best, sceptical about what they perceived as 'ethnic' policies. At worst, there was resentment about the perceived better treatment immigrants had received, particularly when they often seemed as accepting of racist stereotypes of aboriginal peoples as sections of the Anglo-Celtic population. There was little overlap between immigrant and aboriginal associations at the grassroots level, particularly when rural and urban politics are distinguished. The coalitions that did occur mainly operated within those bureaucracies and consultative bodies created to manage immigrant and aboriginal minorities, but these still tended to be compartmentalised according to organisation and issues. Neither immigrant nor aboriginal politics were sufficiently powerful or unified to form viable ethnic (in the broader sense) blocs.

Whether the forces opposing multiculturalism and aboriginal rights will eventually promote new alliances remains an intriguing prospect. Over the 1990s bipartisan parliamentary support for multiculturalism and reconciliation has weakened. John Howard, the current Liberal Premier, campaigned unsuccessfully in 1988 on a 'One Nation' platform. A decade later, with Howard in the Premier's office, this theme had more resilience. The retrenchment of multicultural and immigrant settlement services continues, and the repeated affirmation of a core of 'mainstream Australian' values within a more universalistic citizenship model, reveals the consistency of conservative views.

A somewhat different 'One Nation' named player, also emerged in the late 1990s. Pauline Hanson's party acquired 11 seats in the Queensland state legislature in the 1998 using this unitary symbol, and less weighty if still noteworthy backing in subsequent state and senatorial elections. Much of her popular support rested on populist economic policies appealing to small-business persons, farmers and other sectors of the population disillusioned with the main political parties. Undeniably, however, much of the One Nation Party appeal rested on Hanson's overt anti-Asian, anti-aboriginal and anti-multicultural stance. While this clearly suggests a more strident backlash against 'immigrant' and aboriginal reform, an unintended consequence has been an increased tendency for closer co-operation between immigrant and indigenous associations, for example, in recent demonstrations seeking a formal apology from the government for the forced dispersal of an earlier 'stolen generation' of Aborigines. At the time of writing no such apology was forthcoming. Yet neither conservative extremism nor ethnic minority rapprochement has been typical of Australian multiculturalism. If there is an overall theme in political processes still marked by ad hocery, it is the separate institutionalisation of aboriginal and immigrant minorities within a polity and society whose core characteristics remain unchanged.

New Zealand 'culturalisms': redundancy or renewal?

At the end of the 1980s biculturalism seemed entrenched as an official national icon and procedural framework for local governance. The 'ism' incorporated an historicist vision of the founding bedrock of the Treaty of Waitangi leading to a perception of a nation with a twin ethnic core and a state partnership between Maori and the New Zealand Crown. Grafted onto these dualities was a growing acceptance of more numerous and heterogeneous immigrant 'others'. In effect a bi-ethnic template was overlaid by a framework of greater cultural diversity. Biculturalism talked of partnership between autonomous groups whose jurisdictions nonetheless overlapped in a collaborative effort of state remaking and national rebuilding: on the face of it a remarkable experiment in post-colonial coalition between colonisers and colonised. Multiculturalism, a much weaker component, related to a recognition of changing immigration patterns heralding a more diverse demographic New Zealand future and the need for the institutional accommodation of cultural plurality.

The Royal Commission on Social Policy (in 1988) had given this model its blessing and various legislative acts had firmly established the precedents that the Treaty had become part of the principles of at least public sector procedures. A 'Maori dimension' had become commonplace in official business, and flowed through, to a more limited extent, in increased media and linguistic usage in everyday life. Meanwhile the Waitangi Tribunal, although still essentially an advisory body, had acquired extra membership, legal persuasion and research capacity to deal with the rapid accumulation of resource claims, material and symbolic, falling within its purview.

A decade later, state elites and a Pakeha intelligentsia had not discarded the design and application of bi/multiculturalism, but their Maori counterparts were increasingly pursuing resources and power sharing using different motifs. Four broadly linked trends, some of which we will return to in subsequent chapters, shaped 'culturalist' politics in the 1990s.

First, the introduction of proportional representation in the New Zealand parliament; second, the move towards direct state negotiation of Treaty policy without relinquishing indirect social and economic policy initiatives; third, the fission and fusion of Maori politics; and, finally, the changing climate of majority opinion about immigration and 'Maori issues'.

In 1993, reflecting their disillusionment with parliamentary politics and politicians rather more than support for a system promising greater representation for minorities, the New Zealand electorate opted by referendum for a system of mixed member proportional representation. Maori voted two to one for the change. The first election, in 1996, under this regime, saw the arrival of several new political parties and the realignment of old ones. The New Zealand First Party was the most prominent new feature. Led by Winston Peters, a charismatic Maori ex-National Party member, New Zealand First lived up to its name by tapping a large vein of discontent in the body politic about the relentless neo-liberal restructuring following the Labour victory in 1984. Peters cobbled together an unlikely alliance between discrete Pakeha and Maori interest groups who were fearful and angry about the pace and direction of economic and political change. These broad voting categories were hardly aligned on most issues, but the idea of putting New Zealand first in the face of increasing foreign ownership and rising levels of 'foreign' immigration, struck a similar chord in both camps.

New Zealand First's share of the vote gave it an interim balance of power since neither of the major parties gained enough seats to make them the government, and history dictated they would not sit on the front benches together. New Zealand First took all the Maori seats away from Labour, but still surprised many of their supporters by opting to form a government with National. The fragile coalition government, which lasted until 1998, had three Maori members in Cabinet, including Peters as Deputy Prime Minister and Treasurer. In total, 15 Maori were elected. Thus, Maori for the first time had acquired a level of representation proportional to their numbers in society. The increased numbers of women members, and to a lesser extent, representatives from other ethnic groups, had also injected a greater pluralism into parliament. Unfortunately, the range of 'minority' affiliations reflected in the new chamber mirrored their political fragmentation. For example, despite the influence of the New Zealand First Maori MPs, the dispersal of other Maori members across the broad spectrum of an outmoded 'right' and 'left' nullified their influence as a unified parliamentary force.

A similar trend was discernible in the wider political arena. Post-Second World War Maori political associations had always reflected a layering of affiliations based on descent, region, religious and ethnic ties. A tension between tribal and pan-Maori affiliations, which had some correspondence with rural and urban differences, became heightened in the climate of Treaty claims and the entrenchment of government commitment to the devolution of Maori service delivery. A focus on the Treaty inevitably placed an emphasis on relations between the Crown and iwi and hapu groups, since these had been the signatories in 1840. Claims to the tribunal about land, fishing and local resource management were therefore tribally or sub-tribally pursued, although broader questions about the Maori language or broadcasting, for example, could be considered in a more expansive bicultural manner. Moves to devolve (contract out) services like health, welfare and criminal justice to local groups also encouraged a resurgence of *iwi* (tribal) and *hapu* (sub-tribal) reorganisation and affiliation in the scramble for funding. Some multi-tribal initiatives, like the formation of a Maori Congress (in 1990), tried to provide a forum which would preserve *iwi* autonomy while simultaneously strengthening a broader Maori identity. But the conflicts between competing bases of political identification proved particularly intractable. Not least because a majority (approximately 70 per cent) of Maori were urban-based, and many had lost contact, some totally, with their tribal roots. The growth of urban pan-Maori authorities was the result.

A power struggle between 'tribal' and 'ethnic'-based interest groups, over access, control and recognition within Treaty and bicultural resource areas eventuated. Urban authorities, indeed, sought redefinition (ultimately by litigation) as '*iwi*' to be able to compete on more equal terms with rurally based tribes of common descent. The National, then Coalition governments', move towards direct settlement of Maori claims exacerbated this situation. The Waitangi Tribunal still served an important research and educative function (Sharp 1997: 389), but there was increasing impatience in the polity and electorate about the rapidly mounting number of claims and the slow rate of progress in dealing with them. In this climate the state chose, initially, to place a firm figure and time limit on claims procedures. It brandished a 'fiscal envelope' containing one billion dollars as a finite offer for paying off all reparations by the millennium. Not surprisingly, Maori unanimously rejected this overture and sparked a wave of political protest in the mid-1990s. But the stage was set for an escalation in direct negotiation. In some instances the Crown sought agreement with multi-tribal and pan-Maori intermediaries, self-proclaimed and/or Crown designated, like the Maori

Council and Maori Congress, who took a major role in putting together a nationwide fisheries' quota settlement. In other circumstances, land and resource settlements were negotiated with individual *iwi* Treaty claimants.[5]

Treaty claims procedures in general, and the fisheries deal in particular, highlighted how some *iwi* 'partners', rural and urban, were far better resourced and positioned than others for moving into an era of 'tribal capitalism' (Rata 1996). The problems of apportioning resources or profits within a complex matrix of 'traditional' and 'modern' indicators of 'tribe' and 'Maori', also brought into question the simple nominalism of a bicultural model. Even more significant was the noticeable shift among Maori and *iwi* interest groups away from biculturalism towards discourses of self-reliance and self-determination (Durie 1998: 219–20). In some circles this meant allusions to Maori 'first nation' constitutional recognition, in others it signalled 'real' power sharing for local *iwi*. Yet there was little sign of the state and polity developing a comprehensive Treaty policy moving beyond claims settlement and needs-based resourcing of social and economic policy initiatives. Bicultural partnership was still primarily concerned with the institutional accommodation of diversity rather than power sharing (Fleras 1998). These words are resonant of comparative multiculturalisms, but in New Zealand this 'ism' remained floating in the eddies of official slogans, periodically revitalised by sporadic waves of popular resentment about bicultural alternatives.

As we have seen, the rise in non-British immigration since the liberalisation of entry requirements in the late 1980s, prompted a sizeable increase in the number of, particularly Asian, new migrants. The fact that most of these newcomers paid their own way, or received miserly state assistance, did little to dispel popular anxieties and animosities. Much of New Zealand First's appeal was focused on resentment about 'overseas' intrusion, and little imagination was required to elide 'foreign' and 'Asian'. A combination of economic downturn and a less welcoming social climate provoked a dip in Asian immigration. New Zealand immigration figures reflected a return in ascendancy of the traditional British source, supplemented, for example, by rising numbers of white South Africans. Nevertheless, the continuance of a market-driven skills-based immigration programme, and the sizeable number of Pacific Island and Asian persons in New Zealand, still support projections of a future population whose heterogeneity considerably complicates a bicultural model: a prediction promoting familiar calls, within the state and academy, for a closer look at citizenship as a unifying practice. There are few signs, however, of any tangible move towards multiculturalism, beyond its mild resurgence as an official or popular slogan for endorsing or undercutting cultural pluralism, alongside or against fading Maori/iwi bicultural aims and more vigorous binational aspirations.

Multiple multiculturalisms

Even the briefest of glances at the array of 'culturalisms' described above confirms that, if we are all multiculturalists now, it is in rather different ways with widely differing degrees of voluntary and forced allegiance to the ideas and practices loosely clustered under a diffuse label. American and British brands of multiculturalism are unswappable, and the distinctions between our post-settler case studies are as prominent as their commonalities.

American multiculturalism is not an overarching official federal policy, and the degree to which it is embedded, institutionally speaking, at the state level, varies considerably in light of the ethnic profile of particular regions. Multiculturalism embraces wide-ranging and loosely linked debates about economic, political and social affirmative actions and forms of cultural expression arising largely from the interest groups who seek minority rights and recognition. Affirmative action policies stemmed from a further step in the unfinished quest for Black and Native American equality, compounded by the most recent waves of immigration. This process of 'remediating historical injustice' (Heller 1997: 5) spread to other racial and non-racial categories as the rights-based American political system provided fertile soil for the propagation of a competitive *modus vivendi* between minority groups (Favell 1998a: 123–4). Within the institutionalised framework of post-civil rights legislation, minorities are enabled to bargain for political power as racialised collective interest groups, with innumerable juries still out on whether this is subversive or submissive to WASP supremacy.

The pursuit of cultural recognition is frequently tied to the quest for equality when claims for a collective public status for minorities bolster their demands for resources on this basis, yet the tenor of debates in American tertiary education, for example, goes far beyond affirmative action and political representation. Here again, there is little agreement about whether this signals a profound critique of monocultural hegemonic orders or, that making a 'fetish of diversity' blunts critical discourses (Higham 1998: 218). Not surprisingly, these attacks on varying models and methods of universalism have met with equally vociferous responses from defenders of the English linguistic Canon and/or the American political Creed. The varied nature of these sources of ethno-racial political competition and cultural theorising and practice explains the emergence and persistence, of what Wievorka (1998: 887) calls a distinctive form of 'disintegrated multiculturalism'.

Affirmative action and cultural recognition for minorities are comparable themes in British politics. Here too, we can see the firm 'imprint of Imperial formulations' (Hesse 1997: 378). However, the source and institutional timbre of multiculturalism are decidedly different. British multiculturalism is a direct consequence of the arrival of 'the children of Empire' and the emergence of a paternalistic consensus among liberal elites that social harmony was best achieved by vigorously patrolling the borders of the state while endeavouring to maintain public order within them. Given the much smaller size and fragmented nature of immigrant politics in Britain, the formation of powerful racial and ethnic political blocs was never achievable, although recurrent local protests forced some concessions. The lack of a rights-based constitutional tradition also precluded the litigatory style of American reform. There has been little stress in Britain on positive discrimination and far less debate about the politics of recognition in education and other institutions. Accordingly, although there are important elements of minority-based forms of empowerment, British multiculturalism was more an incremental, pragmatic state strategy of containment – of immigrant flows and the actions of racist and anti-racist 'extremists'. A combination of draconian immigration and more enlightened 'race relations' legislation, mollified white electors perturbed by 'diversity', accommodated 'moderate' ethnic lobbies, and effectively confined multiculturalism to the shallows of mainstream politics. In sum, British multiculturalism represents 'a kind of benevolent isolation of minorities' (Vertovec 1996: 52).

Set against this US/UK counterpoint, Canadian and Australian multiculturalisms are far more integrative, in overlapping and contrasting ways. Both states originally employed multicultural imagery and policies to manage the greater diversity produced by mass post-Second World War immigration, and went through similar stages in moving from token recognition of ethnic difference to a more affirmative national model of multiple origins. Despite recent cutbacks and varying levels of commitment within federal structures, both states officially subscribe to the view that post-settlement migrant services are a normative requirement of public provision. They also accept in principle, and varying degrees of practice, social justice prescriptions for pluralistic special needs, and acknowledge the economic payoffs of such policies, although Canada, with greater numbers of 'visible minorities', and more sensitive to American experience, has drawn stronger links between employment equity and anti-racist policies. Notwithstanding this trend, the recent move in Canada to shift multiculturalism away from a special concern for 'immigrants', 'ethnics' and racial minorities, towards a general citizenship model for 'all Canadians' illustrates a further parallel with Australia.

But Australian multiculturalism has so far eschewed legal enshrinement and has moved much more tentatively towards constitutional attempts to reconcile collective and individual rights claims. There is no equivalent to the Canadian Charter of Rights and the Australian state has refrained so far from embarking on the constitutional experiments featuring so prominently in the Canadian political landscape. Marked similarities between aboriginal demands for self-government and more general appeals for reconciliation have figured in both countries, but the answers have been framed in different historical contexts. Perceiving aboriginal peoples as 'First Nations' has yet fully to enter official and popular Australian national imaginings. And, of course, there is no analogue to the perennial question of Quebec. If America and Britain still confront the legacies of slavery and Empire, Canada continues to feel the tremors of its non-aboriginal, bicultural fault-line. Thus far, the Australian state has been more inclined to keep apart what its Canadian counterpart has sought to glue together. Australian multiculturalism still resembles a model of ethnic parallelism within which the state separately manages aboriginal and immigrant minorities within a growing sense of national civic unity. By comparison, we might best describe the Canadian tradition of more ambitious aims to construct a model of multicultural coexistence as a form of frustrated consociation.

With New Zealand we re-enter a society with a historical duality, where talk of 'two races' persists, and models of partnership prevail in official state discourse. A bicultural Maori/Pakeha model still overshadows multicultural possibilities. Bicultural principles and policies have been institutionalised within the matrix of legislative and political readings of Waitangi Treaty texts. In effect this has meant the incorporation of a 'Maori dimension' into state practices and national symbols, and a series of collaborative attempts by Maori and the Crown to devise laws and institutions protecting Maori interests. Both processes have been enhanced by the increased proportional representation of Maori in the mainstream of New Zealand politics and the, much contested, momentum of Pakeha intelligentsia support for a reworking of old myths to reflect new destinies. In tandem with or counter to these trends, Maori and iwi politics increasingly reflect a shift from bicultural to binational imaginings, alongside tribally based intracultural imagery and action. In this scenario a major reformulation of power sharing and recognition is envisaged involving the renegotiation or dissolution of a model of binary accommodation that currently leaves the 'core business' of governance and resource ownership firmly in post-settler elite hands.

New Zealand bicultural and post-bicultural developments remain awkwardly situated alongside still residual multiculturalisms. The more diverse character of New Zealand's recent immigrant flows, although pale imitations of Australian and Canadian trends, have nonetheless revitalised multicultural agendas. In official parlance this adds up to little more than a bland, consensus-style broadening of bicultural accommodation, or tacit support for mild citizenship reforms. The critical polarities of New Zealand multiculturalisms are still most sharply defined by strange bedfellows, whose politics echo those in other post-settler societies. On the one hand, are those persons, including members of immigrant minorities, who question the replacement of mono supremacy by binary exclusivity. On the other hand we find some 'European/white' New Zealanders (they will reject the Pakeha tag), resenting or fearing what they see as Maori bicultural (or post-bicultural) empowerment, turning to multiculturalism as a useful dissembling device to retain the very resources and status other 'multiculturalists' pursue.

Conclusions

This chapter has considered whether various multi-culturalisms are similar phenomena in different places, or rather different things which merely happen to share the same label. These alternatives are not mutually exclusive. There are some broad similarities across all the societies examined above. Most consistent is the clichéd, and often reified, concern with 'culture' and plurality: as the basis for socio-demographic description and lived experience, as a recipe for political change or containment within a set of distinctive public policies and institutional arrangements, and as a vehicle for academic and popular scrutiny. In all of the societies we have scrutinised, 'cultural' discourses invoke representations of ethnic and 'racial' categories within the state and 'nation'. Such images provide a focus for the political actions of those in power and those who seek empowerment. In all their various guises multi-culturalisms can critically challenge, relativise and revise ethnocentric ideas and institutions, but they can also license political and intellectual separatism. Yet what is sometimes portrayed as a general feature of Western liberal democracies, is, as our analysis shows, customised by pre-existing structural conditions in specific locations. This applies as much to comparisons across our particular post-settler case studies as it does to the contrasts with America and Britain.

Comparatively speaking, 'culturalist' models retain a hierarchy of resourcing and recognition resting on pre-existing power imbalances, often as much to do with regional and class distinctions as ethnic differences. And the boundaries new 'culturalisms' follow, ironically, often trace the shapes of old 'races' they were meant to replace. If immigration remains a key trigger of multicultural musings and reforms, the place of aboriginality (plus for Canada, Quebec) persists as a central unanswered question. This issue is no longer of British concern, and, given the scale of competing ethnic categories, has a far more muted presence in America. In contrast, the immigrant/aboriginal axis is pivotal to our case studies. The recent character of this relationship confirms the endurance of modernity in post- or late-modern times, and reminds us of the incomplete processes of decolonisation and deracialisation of minority worlds. Multi-culturalisms, moreover, are as much to do with the imaginings and practices of 'majorities' as those of the minorities in their midst. The persistent reconfiguration of an analytic triangle – aboriginal/settler/immigrant – is, therefore, *the* quintessential feature of ethnic politics in post-settler societies.

7
Nationalisms

'Who are we as a people now?' (Cairns 1992: 35). The poser of this question is a Canadian, and bookstores in his country are replete with titles on national belonging, dissolving and reimagining. The complexities of Canadian national identity give the 'who are we' question particular piquance, but it has much wider comparative appeal, although whether 'appeal' is quite the right word is debatable, given the angst often evoked by the query. Americans might approach the topic in terms of racialised, multicultural machinations, the permeability of their state borders and some loss of post-Cold War imperial pre-eminence. The British may still ponder on the fading of their imperious reign, and reflect on its recurrent consequences for domestic 'race' relations. But now there is more conjecture about persistent and resurgent national autonomies within British boundaries, and, once inconceivable, European imaginings beyond them.

For post-settler populations, the past two decades have seen a flourishing of regional and aboriginal nationalisms, provoking a mix of long-settled 'majority' reactions, with more recent migrants also wondering where they fit in. Do these trends herald new freedoms for those on the margins, or will the 'old' centre hold? Is the current status of national projects and state recrafting the portent of further expansive late or post-modern realignments? Or are they a sign of the imploding of deep-seated flaws in the modernist make-up of post-settler regimes? Such questions will remain prominent in the final chapter, but, for the moment, let us take stock of the trend and current character of these 'new' nationalisms and see how they relate to the 'old'. For a Canadian, Quebec is a likely starting point to consider these questions.

Quebec: quasi-state nationalism

If we can see the roots of Quebec nationalism in Canadian history clearly enough (see Chapter 3) the most recent outgrowths of national sentiment are more densely tangled. Quebec, alongside cases like Scotland and Catalonia, is often described as a neo-nationalist, or ethnoregional movement. Such movements are portrayed as basically autonomist rather than separatist, reflecting an inadequate political incorporation of regions, whose economic status makes them far from impoverished and powerless peripheries (McCrone 1998: 126–7).

In McCrone's view, drawing on Keating's (1996) analysis of the above three cases, neo-nations are characterised by having a coherent civil society not an independent state. This coherence provides the cultural underpinnings for a potentially greater identification with 'their nation' than the state in which they belong. Nevertheless, they have multiple nationalities. Quebeckers are Canadian and Scots are British. These dual associations promote free-floating links between recent nationalist movements and political parties. Neo-nationalists have an eye for the main chance, with economic gains often complementing or overriding ambivalent political and cultural considerations. Such ambitions neatly coalesce with the increasing possibilities for establishing economic and political corporatist links with suprastate bodies like NAFTA and the EU. In sum, Quebec typifies a civic, 'niche nationalism' of relative privilege.

In the Scottish case, as McCrone sees it, the Treaty of Union in 1707 was not negotiated in a climate of defeat, it was more a settlement between Scottish and English elites for mutual economic and political gain. The peculiarity of Britain's ancien régime, with its loose fit between state, nation and society, allowed Scotland to retain its own legal, religious and educational institutions, while Scottish entrepreneurs and administrators could take full part in British imperial expansion. A process of further devolution of administrative powers forestalled greater demands for direct democracy, although, as he points out, the more a semi-state was created the more obvious a democratic deficit became apparent (ibid.: 132). A twentieth-century cultural renaissance combined with economic reinvigoration (the discovery of North Sea oil, fading manufacturing industries superceded by hi-tech replacements, and the emergence of the Common Market), coincided with the decline in the Imperial project. Political union with Europe offered a replacement market and the possibilities of enhanced status as part of a multinational Britain in a multi-state region. In this environment being culturally Scottish and politically British became more inconsistent, and, more to the point, the profits of greater parliamentary autonomy outweighed the losses of privileged dependence.

How far does the Quebec situation match the Scottish case? From an outsider perspective, French Canadians in, and to a lesser extent beyond, Quebec, have 'enjoyed' a degree of civic equality, parliamentary proportionality and representation, and economic and territorial security, the envy of many other Canadian provinces and most First Nations. Like Scotland, Quebec has retained its own core cultural and civic institutions, and this has been further strengthened by a history of strong linguistic continuity. But Francophone/Anglophone relations are marked by a deep ambiguity of relative political advantage and deprivation, and fluctuating economic fortunes. A switching of allegiance between Liberal, Parti Québécois and other minor parties, and an uncertainty about the merits of increased autonomy or outright secession, reflects the niche-like parallels that McCrone develops. Nonetheless, there are fundamental differences between the Quebec and Scottish case. Quebec is still enmeshed within a heritage of memories and symbols of 'conquest', and a myth of co-founding nations in a settler state. These narratives are set within a confederal provincial arrangement that is complicated by the recent political assertiveness of aboriginal peoples and the arrival of increasing numbers of allophones. Quebec is the pivotal feature of Canadian multinational politics within this scenario. Québécois nationalism and quasi-statehood are the fulcrums upon which English Canadian, aboriginal and immigrant national imaginings are so frequently balanced.

Where other national ties are unwinding or still emergent, Quebec nationalism retains a consistent cultural and political core of elements linking origins to destiny. In the space of a few decades the locus of Quebecker identity and politicisation has shifted from '*la survivance*', through '*la revolution tranquille*', to 'Quebec Inc.'. Both old and new elites used primordial sentiments to sustain their power and wider ambitions, but whereas the founding Catholic hierarchy viewed 'culture' as 'an antidote for political nationalism' (ibid.: 135), their commercial successors used it as a still potent force *within* their political project. The appearance of *Je Me Souviens* (I will remember) on every Quebec province vehicle licence plate provides a neat juxtaposition between ethnic memories and civic reminders. The cleric vision did not extend beyond a stateless nation within Canada, but the more worldly prophecies that replaced it embraced a vision of sovereign status within a global order of states. This ambition was made more realisable by the increasing contiguity between identity, territory and political-economic viability.

A pan-Canadian Francophone identity was steadily replaced, if not completely eradicated, by a more powerful Quebec-based consciousness. Language politics, at the forefront of nationalist sentiments in the 1970s, remained a key boundary enforcer. Despite Trudeau's attempts to bolster a Canadian-wide bilingual national identity, an overwhelming majority of Francophones clustered in the one province. Although the percentage of Canadians with sole French origins declined as a percentage of the total population, their numbers residing in Quebec remained unchanged.[1] Consequently, an ethnic core remained in place to construct and reconstruct the mythic sites of invention that provided a primordial continuity for a contemporary social movement that was overturning the very order it romanticised.

The pursuit of collective rights for French language users, not only symbolised a claim for the redress of old injustices and the enhancement of contemporary recognition, it also signalled material upward mobility by removing forms of linguistic closure to the higher echelons of paid work and capitalist ownership. In essence, the language wars typified a reconquest by the French-speaking majority in Quebec. Although only a hardline minority (in numerical terms) unequivocally supported French unilingualisim and full-blown Quebec separatism, events in the 1980s and 1990s cemented a trend towards a particularistic territorialism. A cultural nationalist project was firmly embedded within a quasi state whose political and economic clout pushed claims of independence far beyond rhetorical limits.

The persistence of ethnic attachment, combined with what Breton has called entrepreneurial nationalism, provided a two-pronged strategy for the Parti Québécois, and the elites and intelligentsia that supported it, to move the focus of national attachment from federal state to province (Breton 1998: 78). Surveys show that in 1970 a third (34 per cent) of Quebeckers saw themselves as *Canadiens*, by 1990 only 9 per cent did so. Over the same period the numbers calling themselves Québécois rose from 21 to 59 per cent (Keating 1996: 83).

This change in self-naming is important as both a definer and illustration of the tenor of regional and national politics. Such labels generate strategic resources and levels of solidarity by invoking the limits between 'them' and 'us'. As Jenson (1993: 337) argues, 'choices of names configure the political opportunity structure'. They also mark discursive boundaries of meaning that prioritise claims for recognition and resources. How one chooses to name oneself has vital consequences for state relations, since avenues of representation may be opened or closed according to title. When Trudeau was printing the invitation cards,

French Canadian or Quebecker gained entry to the federal club, since these names legitimated Canadian nation-state models of linguistic alliance or a compact between provinces. The indépendantiste Québécois label met with sharp rebuffs. In turn, Anglophone Canadians grew weary of hearing *non* to what they saw as ever-widening concessions. Recent constitutional experiments, designed to ameliorate the situation, compounded matters.

Quebec's distinctiveness was acknowledged at Meech Lake, but agreement foundered on the rocks of provincial rivalry and other claimants for uniqueness. At Charlottetown the edges of distinction became decidedly blurry, particularly as aboriginal peoples were pressing further with their own name claiming (Webber 1994: 161–5). Canada was now perceived in terms of three levels of governance and innumerable founding nations. In this climate, there was a stronger push in Quebec for the fulfilment of: 'A wish to replace loss of recognition and status as a "founding people" to international recognition and status as a nation-state' (Breton 1998: 83). Since the 1980s, with the advent of the Free Trade Agreement (FTA) and NAFTA, Quebec's business links with the United States grew steadily tighter. By the mid-1990s three-quarters of Quebec's exports were heading south, and almost half of its imports were passing them en route (Keating 1996: 104). If many Canadians were queasy about neo-liberal restructuring, deregulation and free trade, Quebec's commercial elites welcomed a rapprochement between multinational corporations and a, still state-driven, Quebec Inc.

Politically speaking, these moves drove another wedge between English Canadian and Québécois nationalists. Whereas the former vigorously opposed any further McDonaldisation of Canadian culture and increased privatisation of Canadian institutions, the latter were prepared to risk greater cultural intrusiveness and potential erosion of the welfare state, for the payoff of political independence. In 1995 another referendum on separation produced a wafer thin majority vote for the status quo. Jacques Parizeau, the Premier of Quebec, was quick to blame *les autres* (the others) in his bitter postmortem. But there was more than a grain of truth in his prognosis. Like Canada, Quebec had experienced significant 'foreign' immigration and a resurgence of aboriginal politics. Both trends had altered the classic colonial duality.

As expected, support for separation was clearly strongest among Francophones, but ambivalence was still prominent.[2] Opinion polls consistently showed most Québécois preferred to remain in Canada, within an asymmetrical federalism that reflected a strengthened bilateralism between Quebec and the rest of Canada (ibid.: 184). They wanted to preserve their culture and identity, retain their collectivist state apparatus, and improve their economic standing. Few had any interest in foreign diplomacy or defence – the classic affairs of states. Federal asymmetry assumed a divisible sovereignty and multicultural/regional identities. Some Canadians would say this state of affairs had always been so, but non-Québécois within, and certainly beyond Quebec, would not concede any further enhancement of a 'super province' within Canada. Quebec, seemingly, had reached the ceiling of tolerance towards a neo-nation and quasi-state. This left a choice between the status quo and secession. Québécois would not contemplate the former, the multiple 'Others' stopped well short of encouraging the latter. Thus, both combatants, as Keating wryly notes, were left with their second choice, an ironic unplanned outcome that may still eventuate (ibid.: 185).[3]

Neo-nationalisms like the Scottish and Quebec cases, are not just historical memory traces or regional, civic sideshows detracting from the greater sway of social class actions and global realignments (McCrone 1998: 148). For McCrone, the sentiments and power struggles of neo-nations are important facets of broader issues of contemporary national identity and state reconfigurations. I agree; but Quebec nationalism is not as new, more ethnic, and even more crucial than McCrone suggests, because of the peculiarities of settler and post-settler states – a point underlined by consideration of other forms of nationalism.

Aboriginal 'first nations'

North America

At first glance, recent aboriginal politics could be seen as embracing another form of neo-nationalism. Given their post-1960s resurgence and the prominence they have attained in recent Canadian constitutional discussions, fruitful parallels between First Nations and Quebec can be drawn (Gibbins and Ponting 1989: 34). Nationalist rhetorical flourishes of Quebec origin have been readily adopted by First Nation spokespersons. Québécois and aboriginal peoples have an analogous wish to preserve a cultural and territorial contiguity of 'distinct societies' in a remodelled confederation. The Inuit people of the Eastern Arctic are now experiencing living in Nunavut ('our land') as a self-governing territory with the prospect of becoming a fully-fledged province. The Nisga'a people in the north-west of British Columbia have lesser powers,[4] but they too exert considerable control over reserve and resource management, including the provision of education and health services. These are but two examples in a worldwide move towards greater aboriginal control of their own political, economic and social destinies.

Despite similarities between Quebec and some Canadian aboriginal peoples, their 'ways of *being* nations differ radically' (Sigurdson 1996: 60, original emphasis), as does their potentiality for statehood. Hence many of the parallels between them remain at the level of rhetoric. Despite an increasing intercultural and aboriginal presence, Québécois have a unified language and culture within a contained territory. Quebec is also a provincial state, with all the institutions for political sovereignty in the full modernist sense. Arguably, Nunavut may approximate Quebec. Most other aboriginal 'nations' do not. Hundreds of culturally and linguistically varied aboriginal groups are spread across the continent in non-contiguous reserve lands. A majority of aboriginal persons reside off-reserve. Many have no land base at all. How can such peoples, as distinct entities or *in toto*, sustain national imaginings, let alone contemplate statehood? A great deal depends on the meanings and aims of 'first nationhood' and 'self-government'. This is rarely clear-cut and the ambiguity is compounded by the embeddedness of aboriginal politics within Western conceptions of nations and states.

Much of the impetus for Canadian 'first nation' naming, derives not only from Québécois influences, but also from American and Third World origins. Once colonised, Native Americans were forced into an ambiguous zone between settler state citizenship and domestic dependency. Marshall's 1830s' judgements in the USA established a deep-seated administrative convention of perceiving tribes as 'territorial polities holding residual sovereign status' (McHugh 1998: 172), a tradition revitalised in recent decades by post-civil rights movements, Third World decolonisation, and state management responses to calls for self-determination. Self-government, Deloria observes 'is not an Indian idea' (Deloria 1998: 15). 'Traditional' American Indian conceptions of nationhood, and Western ideas of self-government are entirely different, although the distance between them widens and narrows according to the forms of group organisation and identity encountered within 'Indian' political circles. Deloria draws an analytic distinction between what he calls 'tribal' and 'ethnic' Indians. For tribal Indians, a perception of the continuities of land, descent, language and religion have preserved indigenous 'nations within'. Tribally naming oneself implies a process of communal decision-making relating back to pre-contact times.

In contrast, for 'ethnic Indians', often urban-based and more sympathetic to supra-tribal coalitions, Native American self-government is a recent post-contact phenomenon. The politics of pan-ethnic Indian nationalism embraces similar strategies and fights for comparable resources as other 'cultures' in multicultural America (ibid.: 255). Much like 'Black' and 'Asian', as we saw in Chapter 6, an ethnicised and racialised name of 'otherness' is revalorised to become a new national and self-identification. But the links between 'tribal' and 'ethnic' Indians are retained in the naming and legitimation processes so vital to the preservation or reinvention of 'tribal nations' and the promotion of 'transnational' ethnic identities across the United States.

Most Native Americans carry, value and defend a range of individual, local/regional and national identities (Cornell and Hartmann 1998: 112). Thus distinctions between 'tribal' and 'ethnic' Indians are not sharply defined. Whether indigenous 'nations' are conceived of as primordial communities or recently formed political instruments, both rely on a land-based connection between pre- and post-contact imaginings, and are thoroughly entangled in a history of relations with states. In the early contact period Indians played a leading role in tribe/state relations, then the pendulum of Bureau control swung in an assimilative arc, almost undisturbed until the 1960s. It stopped momentarily in the New Deal era, when Bureau policy shifted from outright assimilation to recognising a form of aboriginal control. The reserve was the standard, and state-imposed recognised unit of governance, and newly elected tribal councils bore little relation to 'traditional' political organisation. Tribal membership, once largely a cultural construct, became a distinct legal category (Cornell 1988b: 41). Assimilation policies returned with new vigour in the 1950s, until the twin forces of self-determination and rights claims pushed the pendulum back towards political autonomy. From the Nixon to the present Clinton administration, 'sovereignty-talk' has been fashionable, and, at least at the federal political level, state–tribal dealings have reacquired a relational self-governing flavour.

What is being traced through this period of oscillation are fluctuations in the form and degree of external constraint, and shifts in the relationship between conceptual and political communities. In the recent moves to consolidate tribal councils, encourage Indian administration of economic and social programmes and services, and widen the powers of still circumscribed jurisdictions in tribal courts, self-determination in the eyes of the state basically means 'tribal' determination. This does not reflect a state/nation relation return to early-contact times. Recent trends illustrate the restoration of a modest degree of power within the highly varied and complex set of conditions that governs the universal insertion of 'Indians' qua 'Native Americans' into the federal and state polity, judiciary and economy. Culturally speaking, the situation is far more varied. Aboriginal identities and *mores* may reflect centuries of continuity, or decades of reimagining. In both cases, the process of weaving myths of origin and destiny into national tapestries, ensures an intricate entanglement of 'old' and 'new'. Within these settings, continuity, resurgence, dependency and decline, are occurring simultaneously. Ethnification operates in tandem with tribal nationalism, while supra-tribal national sentiments coexist with still pervasive interpersonal assimilation. Thus, the 'tribe' is both a cultural survivor and political creation of relations between peoples and states.

Canada

This matrix of identity, nationality and political positioning in the United States has many parallels in Canada, Australia and New Zealand (Perry 1996; Fleras and Elliott 1992). Yet none of these societies has the American philosophic and legal traditions of recognition of limited indigenous sovereignty shaping United States 'government-to-tribe' relations today. Unlike their American counterparts, Canadian Indians were not inserted into state relations in a comprehensive manner as residual sovereignties. Far from all Indians in Canada, you will recall, signed treaties, and the highly varied agreements they entered into were not seen by the state as politically bilateral. Band/tribal administrations were created on reserves, but these were primarily state-designed to facilitate state wardship, not sovereignty. Only status Indians were administratively perceived as an aboriginal people, with Métis and Inuit having their own distinct histories and relations with the state outside of this designation. 'National' discourses resurfaced sporadically during the twentieth century, but achieved most momentum in the concerted reaction to the 1969 White Paper's renewed assault on separate 'Indian' status. Further impetus was achieved during the constitutional ferment of the past two decades. The phrase 'aboriginal peoples of Canada', as an all-embracing constitutional category, was not coined until the 1982 Constitution Act.

This description lies at the heart of the recent voluminous report (1996) of the Royal Commission on Aboriginal Peoples, most of whose commissioners were indigenes. The report sees aboriginal peoples as 'collectivities of unique character', having the 'inherent right of governmental autonomy'. A primary recommendation (of the report), is the reconstitution or creation of multi-band units to construct 'modern nations'.[5] What seems to be envisaged, building on recent constitutional debate, is a clustering of peoples comprising a new order of government within the federation. This vision encompasses an intriguing possibility of 'a virtual province or an indigenous archipelago', linking hundreds of aboriginal groups into a single political structure (Coates 1998: 65). That structure would be represented in a House of First Peoples, an Aboriginal Assembly advising the House of Commons and Senate.

Although this prospect, indeed much of the report, is still on the table, what is most likely are varying levels of 'internal sovereignty', ranging from quasi-provincial autonomy, through municipal-like jurisdictions, to nominal control over specialised service provision (Fleras 1998: 199). Sovereignty-talk runs through all these levels as a potent rhetorical device for underpinning claims of cultural and political autonomy. Yet the most consistent recent trend has been for the federal state and provinces to offer selective and limited local self-administration to be negotiated on a case-by-case basis.

Some treaty-based First Nations, like the Mohawk, have maintained strong sovereignty claims, to the point of military confrontation,[6] but few aboriginal communities contemplate secession. Nationalist rhetoric, however, is pregnant with separatist imagery and the profundity of difference. On the one hand, much influenced by Third and Fourth World anti-colonial movements, adherents of strong 'national' claims espouse a political status of prior claim and original occupancy, by adopting Euro-Western concepts of sovereignty as analogue for a traditional status of 'nationhood' (Boldt 1993: 133). On the other hand, the goal of cultural resilience or revival is constructed by perceiving 'Whites' as the 'Other'. In both cases, a discourse of displacement – of the state and an alien culture – tends to overshadow equally or more pervasive dialogues of coexistence. This situation part-mirrors the Quebec paradox noted above, since hardline 'first nation' imagining 'presupposes a goal that for the overwhelming majority of Aboriginal Canadians is neither sought nor practicably attainable' (Cairns 1995: 254).

Australia

In Australia, there is also an increasing tendency for aboriginal spokespersons to use national imagery, although local and regional affiliations still predominate. Similar historical narratives of the confluence of race, culture and ethnic descent are fashioned, signifying a celebration of continuous survival and a political project of cultural retrieval and economic recovery (Pettman 1995: 75–6). Here too, we find a familiar continuum of views on the possibilities of 'self-determination' and political autonomy. The formations of federal aboriginal representative bodies, regional land councils, outstation movements, and local health and legal aid centres, have fostered a rich profusion of political identities and strategies within the gamut of local communities and broader ethnic categories. Nationally speaking, these range from the ATSIC framework of regional constituencies under a federal umbrella; through land-based models of local autonomy along Canadian lines of inherent jurisdiction; to rarer sentiments of separate statehood and secession. ATSIC is likened by some commentators (see Havemann 1999: 474), to being the nearest Australian equivalent to the Canadian Royal Commission's notion of a First Nations assembly. Formed in 1991, it consists of a national Commission and elected or nominated regional councils, some of whom, particularly in north, west and central Australia, bear some relation to pre-colonial groupings. Most councils, however, are artefacts of the evolution of state administration. Their 'regions' are not coincident with socially and politically integrated communities (Rowse 1994: 163). ATSIC is an accountable statutory government authority that contains important elements of participatory local democracy and economic development,[7] but this mix reflects inbuilt contradictions. Aboriginal talk of 'self-determination' rubs up against state-speak of 'outputs and outcomes'. The resulting friction has prompted widespread debate about whether ATSIC should be seen as cementing welfare dependency or enhancing cultural and political autonomy, although, as we have seen, these processes are not mutually exclusive.

The *Mabo* decision revitalised sovereignty claims, but also triggered a backlash. Some aboriginal lawyers and political spokespersons hailed the affirmation of legal inherency, while assorted pastoralists, mining companies and politicians predicted disastrous consequences for their 'national' interests. The current Coalition government seems more wedded to the latter view. Although some post-*Mabo* decisions consolidated native title, the government moved to amend legislation to favour pastoralist and mining aspirations over aboriginal rights. Echoing Canadian experience, the prospects of meaningful internal sovereignty rest on degrees of congruence between land bases, human and economic resources, and the level of non-aboriginal support. Self-government is most likely for territorially distinct Torres Strait Island communities, and the major land councils in 'remote Australia' (Reynolds 1996: 145–6). Topographically and climatically, the Arnhem Land reserve in Central Australia, for example, hardly compares with Northern Canada. Yet the administration of a vast territorial area, whose sparse aboriginal population is nonetheless a numerical regional majority, begs some comparison with Nunavut. In both settings, isolated aboriginal peoples can draw on public support as, often romanticised, exemplars of 'real' Aborigines or Indians, whose struggles against the government, multinational developers, and a harsh environment, strike sympathetic chords in an urban populace viewing events from a safe distance. The prospects for 'mini-nations' in the midst of majorities are much less propitious.

New Zealand

In some ways the New Zealand situation offers a test case for urbanised aboriginal minorities. The vast majority of Maori now live in towns and cities, and a substantial minority (numerically speaking) claim no tribal affiliation.[8] For them, despite periodic visits to their ancestral areas, 'tribalism remains an ideology only' (Walker 1999: 115). Ideologies, however, are powerful forces, particularly when resources and identity are at issue. Maori is an ethnic category, providing a national group identity with the potential for political community. Recent binational imaginings, reworking earlier regional positions, envisage a bicultural model of dual assemblies. This encapsulates Western and Maori political concepts within a constitution reshaped by Treaty principles (see, for example, Durie 1998). In some manner, the equally historicist meanings of Crown and chiefly authority can be reconciled by a new divisibility of sovereignty within and across ethnic divisions. So far, there is little sign of political will on the part of state elites to bifurcate 'their' polity, and Maori unity is constantly threatened by tribal, corporate and class divisions. Unlike North American and Australian federal arrangements, the unicameral history of the New Zealand settler state is even more aligned with a notion of 'a unified and centralised paramount power' (McHugh 1998: 143), that pays scant attention to 'other' sovereignties.

After years of seeking to encourage pan-Maori entities as a means to co-opt aboriginal minorities into the state- and nation-making process, the re-emergence of the Treaty as an icon of national origin and instrument of state administration, provoked a 'tribal' resurgence and reinvention of political and cultural communities. As we saw in Chapter 6, the Waitangi process made *iwi* corporate and political entities, and created careers for a 'new Maori middle class' of capitalist and cultural entrepreneurs (Rata 1996). Linguistically, *iwi* can mean 'people' or 'tribe'. This flexible naming, compounded by Treaty textual ambiguity, provided ample scope for revitalisation and radical redefinition. The Crown continued to negotiate with pan-Maori groups, as the national fishing agreement revealed, but access to resources still relied on 'sub-national' membership. Another 'battle of the name' resulted, between mainly rural and urban Maori, over 'tribal' legitimacy. The forces of 'tradition' played the forces of genealogical and territorial displacement, with a Western judicial referee.

Unlike their counterparts in our other societies, Maori have sufficient numbers, at least if the current proportional representation parliamentary system is retained, to exert more influence through the ballot box and the political party process. Some iwi, as reimagined primordial communities and/or contemporary, instrumental corporate entities, have the resources to acquire or consolidate increased devolutionary powers and enhanced levels of economic sustainability. But reserve-based North American models of aboriginal self-government, one suspects, have little purchase in New Zealand, beyond the aspirations of 'a politically active and educated elite' (Maaka 1994: 329). And the ethnic and spatial proximity of 'the two cultures' preclude 'remote' Australian possibilities. This degree of intermixing and intimacy reinforces the importance of 'majority' nationalisms in promoting or preventing regional and aboriginal national projects.

The indigenising of dominion diaspora

If the image of conquest still serves as a founding moment for Québécois, and dispossession performs the same function for aboriginal peoples, 'majority group' myths of national origin are far less continuous and increasingly contested. Cohen, affirming the ephemeral nature of dominion diaspora, notes that 'the automatic and unthinking affinity between the British diasporic communities and "home" is now largely gone' (Cohen 1997: 78). Social and political elites are now firmly anchored in ex-dominion societies. His thoughts on disaffinity are perhaps more secure than the moorings of the post-diaspora. The unhitching of the fraying tie cast some of the majority population in these societies adrift in uncertainty.

The very nature of diasporic relations requires us to explain their demise in transnational terms. Changes in post-settler states need to be set against transformations in Britain. The collapse of Empire and upsurge of the 'new Commonwealth', the subsequent moves to bolster British border control, and, most painfully, the 'mother country's recent alignment with Europe, further damaged an already weakening relationship, particularly between Britain and Australasia. The 'fires of imperial enthusiasm' were finally, formally extinguished in Canada in 1982, although the flames had dimmed decades before this (Francis 1997: 85–6). The Antipodean diaspora's self-conception as 'better' or 'best' British within the imperial *commonweal* was more resilient. But, despite the vote in 1999 to keep the status quo,[9] Australian republican status cannot be too far away, and New Zealand will doubtless follow eventually in these footsteps.

Recently, 'the British' in Britain, have been more concerned with internal family matters, than receding memories of kin beyond their shores. But shifts in 'Anglo' identity in post-settler societies are not simply attributable to parental neglect, nor a narrative of maturing offspring, although metaphors of growth and family obligation are still liberally sprinkled in national discourses. And one must be continually mindful of the slippage between the musing of elites and intelligentsia and the national self-images of the masses. The upper classes were always the most attached to British diasporic connections, while their 'chattering' counterparts remain at the forefront of those who now reject 'older' European, and newer American benchmarks of attainment and respectability, often with a stridency that still reveals a tinge of insecurity. Intelligentsia commentary, particularly in Canada, often suggests the populace are neurotically wandering the streets, wringing their hands over the state of the nation. Neither opinion surveys nor my direct observations bear this out, but an air of unease about rapid social change and national identity is undeniable.

Demography is once again important in mapping the sources of change, with certain trends confirming a movement beyond the ambit of Britishness within and outside the Empire. Census shifts over the twentieth century in Canada clearly portray the transition from a society dominated by British and French influences to one in which no one category clearly predominates (Pryor et al. 1992: 217). From 1901 to 1986, 'the British' shrank from being almost 60 per cent of the total Canadian population to approaching a third. French decline was far less noticeable, although they started with a much lower base, moving from close to a third (30 per cent) to roughly a quarter of the populace over the period. The fall in the numerical dominance of the British and French was matched by the rise in numbers of multicultural and aboriginal 'others'. In 1901, these diverse categories made up approximately 11 per cent of the total surveyed. By 1986 their numbers almost equalled the French figure, and in the last decade they have surpassed it. Just as striking are recent shifts within and across British/French/Other census categories. Since the mid-1980s, the numbers of people naming themselves as 'Canadians', in sole or hyphenated form, or stating a single or multiple aboriginal status, has risen sharply.

These trends in self-naming, with obvious omissions (the French), are repeated to varying degrees in our other post-settler societies. In 1986 nearly half (48 per cent) of the Australian population still described themselves as 'British', but the numbers of persons stating 'Australian' (approximately 20 per cent of the total in 1986) continues to rise in census returns (Inglis et al. 1994: 7). Hyphenation grows apace in tandem with ethnic intermixing. Almost a third of Australians (30 per cent in 1986) claim multiple ancestries revealing they have crossed the Anglo-Celtic/Other line), while less than half (42 per cent in 1986) of the Aboriginal and Torres Strait Island (TSI) population had 'unmixed ancestries' (Price 1991). Recent, striking increases in Australian aboriginal census enumeration follow the Canadian pattern, with Aboriginal/TSI self-naming increasing by a third between 1991 and 1996 alone.

In New Zealand, the numbers of 'still British' (or 'European') remain prominent, the tendency towards hyphenation is less apparent, and the growth of the 'official' Maori population, although steady, is less dramatic than in Australia or Canada. But the trend of self-identifying in multiple ways, within and beyond the central Maori/European axis, continues to strengthen. And the propensity for naming oneself 'Pakeha' and/or 'New Zealander' is becoming increasingly common.

These comparative census numbers are as attributable to changes in the method of the state administration of naming, as they are to shifts in ethnic or national identification. One can only speculate on what responses might have been in earlier decades if populations had been given the opportunity to name themselves as an open-ended option (or, indeed, if some aboriginal people had been offered any option at all). But given the attenuation of British ties, the inrush of heterogeneous newcomers, and the vigour of aboriginal and regional subnationalisms, one can surmise that many naming changes are of relatively recent origin. What the above comparative census figures suggest is that we are witnessing a shrinking, but more consolidated sociodemographic indigenisation, of post-settler majorities, that parallels the reconstruction of the national identities of aboriginal peoples (and in Canada, Québécois), with both processes affected by more diverse immigration flows. Politically, these trends indicate a strengthening ethnicification of elements of the majority group is coincident with a resurgent pan-ethnic, nationalism of aboriginal minorities. Interestingly, this dual tendency reflects both conflict and compromise between old and new nationalisms as nativism is juxtaposed to pluralism.

Only a couple of decades ago English-Canadians appeared to have made the transition from grounding their national/self-definition in British memories to 'a more open society sensitive to its own heterogeneity and united by English language' (Cairns 1992: 7). As late as the 1980s, at least within left-nationalist circles, there was some sympathy for Quebec's pursuit of greater recognition. Opinion polls showed that multiculturalism had mixed but moderate approval, while the plight of aboriginal people had much firmer public support. A decade later, however, the same Canadians were far less sanguine about multinational diversity. The assertiveness of Quebec's business elite, and their close links with United States capital, irritated or saddened English Canadian sympathisers concerned about economic sovereignty and the inroads of 'the American way of life' (Ayres 1995: 188). The forceful demands of some aboriginal spokespersons and 'multiculturalists' met a similar fate. Survey results on aboriginal issues are hardly clear-cut, and display important regional variation, but recent overviews demonstrate a hardening in public opinion against what are perceived to be 'radical' demands (Ponting and Kiely 1997: 176). Substantial minority support remains for individual land claims, and aboriginal management of education and welfare programmes, but polls of opinion in the 1990s revealed a growing disenchantment with general attempts to establish forms of self-government with unrestricted provincial powers. Strong reservations about the limits of multiculturalism are in tune with these sentiments. Multiculturalism as a national motif retains substantial support, but, notwithstanding the recent cutbacks in already modest multicultural programmes, most Canadians still cavil at the prospect of funding ethnic minorities to preserve their customs and traditions (Hjerm 1998). A move away from overt assimilation has been accommodated, even applauded, but the Canadian 'majority' stops well short of supporting full-blown pluralism.

This shift in sentiments is broadly echoed in Australasia. The cross-national survey results Hjerm draws upon, show even fewer Australians and New Zealanders are enamoured with the idea of bankrolling minority 'cultures'. Majority opinion on aboriginal and Maori issues, much like its Canadian counterpart, is similarly fluid and inchoate, as viewpoints shift in the winds of political contingencies. Generalisation is hazardous. Yet the maxim that special rights should stop short of separatism is consistently repeated in the 1990s. Forms of limited self-management are one thing, sharing sovereignty is quite another. Encouraging 'ethnics' to maintain their 'culture' is fine, as long as we don't have to pay for it, and 'they' still make an effort to 'fit in'.

These comparative ethnic trends need to be set against broader socio-economic influences, some of which, like globalisation, we will return to in the final chapter. Changes in gender and class alignments are a case in point. The 1960s was the highpoint of the providential state and new cultures of entitlement in post-settler states. But by the 1980s, providence was being rapidly privatised and, in some eyes, 'minorities' were getting all the privileges. Sections of the middle classes (particularly males), for example, felt particularly aggrieved as they saw themselves sandwiched between 'the rich' visibly capable of taking care of themselves, and 'the poor' apparently still receiving generous state assistance. Meanwhile women were making increasing inroads into public arenas where masculine domination had once seemed assured. Deteriorating job opportunities and declining education, health and pension rights, promoted a sense of economic insecurity, compounded by perceptions of social, cultural and political displacement. These envies and anxieties were heightened by the awareness of once-marginal constituents moving to the centre of political debate. Even more immediate was a transformation in the daily experience of public discourse and private lives where 'other cultures' were encountered to an unprecedented degree. In some neighbourhoods, tangible increases in the numbers of 'foreigners' fuelled more expansive images of society as a stranger place.

Such feelings were not confined to 'Anglo' groups. Other, older generations of migrants, from Southern or Central Europe for example, saw the traditional image of working one's way up the ladder of opportunity upended by equity and affirmative action programmes they never experienced. Difference, once an obstacle to be borne stoically and overcome, had seemingly become an advantage. Victimhood was a viable weapon for advancement. Particularly upsetting was the sight of new, wealthy arrivals displaying outward signs of instant rewards. Groups once ignored or despised had taken on an unaccustomed prominence. The new status of 'Aboriginal' or 'Asian' was set against very different histories and current conventions, but both evoked a sense of dissonance between past and present. Thus, new patterns of status inconsistency blurred the old lines of ethnic stratification, already rendered more complex by changes in gender and class differentiation.

Perceptions of relative deprivation fostered nativistic tendencies. A rise in right-wing populism was one demonstrable outcome, reflected in the emergence of ultra-nationalistic political groups, or the strengthening of such sentiments among more centrist parties. The National Party in Canada, One Nation in Australia, and New Zealand First, all garnered votes using fear and envy as effective, if somewhat blunt, political weapons. Yet one should not overdraw the links between perceived threats to cultural identity and 'the nation', and direct political action. Nativism is best seen as a set of beliefs and attitudes that extends across a wide spectrum of social groups, most of whose members abstain from supporting the more extreme manifestations of enforcing conformity to an exclusive sense of order and tradition. More common is a more muted sense of uncertainty and contestation over symbolic-cultural representation and material resources.

Naming is a key process of ethnic and national positioning, as our discussion of regional and aboriginal politics reveals. The self-identifying of 'majorities' has always been enigmatic, and, as their numerical supremacy declines, the definition of relative powerfulness becomes even more problematic. The name 'English Canada' remains ambiguous, conflating common language usage with a diversity of ethnic affinities. Since the resurgence in separatist sentiment of Quebec and First Nations, a 'Rest of Canada' (ROC) national neologism has introduced further equivocalness. ROC is neither a nation nor a state, but a nascent, national sentiment of 'necessity responding to a reluctant recognition of potential loss' (Cairns 1992: 5). An acknowledgement of waning British influences is linked to a heightened awareness of the potential dismemberment of pan-Canadian unity by sub-state nationalisms and multicultural plurality. The displacement of a British/English prefix by a 'Rest of' qualifier neatly illustrates the repositioning of 'the majority' who, once automatically saw themselves as 'Canada'.

The break-up of Australia or New Zealand is hardly imminent. Despite talk of aboriginal sovereignty, there are no manifest signs of secession, and the demographics of ethnic identity still paint a rather different picture to Canada. The British heritage of national institutions is still easily discernible. But the naming of the 'majority' remains elusive. Language might be a comparable basis for majority group definition in Australia given the official marking out of those with Non-English Speaking Backgrounds (NESBs). Curiously, however, there is no equivalent category of ESBs. In popular parlance we have 'ethnics' (or 'migrants'), 'Aborigines' and the remainder, variously described by commentators as Anglos, Anglo-Celts or Whites. Yet none of these terms is widely used as a term of self-categorisation by those who are so labelled. Whites, Anglos (maybe Celts) more commonly, simply call themselves Australians.

Their equivalents in New Zealand also use a national identifier to describe their origins, although a small, but growing number, now uses the term Pakeha, to signify their status as descendants from British settlers, or, more simply, non-Maori. Most prominently used among a white, ethnic intelligentsia, seeking to achieve a new, bicultural national project, 'Pakeha' has the potential to do the work of creating a sense of ethnic groupness that English-speaking Canadians or Australians so far show little sign of achieving, particularly since the category is now widely used in educational texts, the media and in official parlance. Current Pakeha national narrators have brought together a set of nineteenth-century representations, added in the process of indigenisation and rupture from Britain, and mixed these ingredients into an innovative nationalist recipe.

Themes of continuity and supersession are both discernible in recent Pakeha discourses. One strand stresses the coherence of Maori and Pakeha mutuality in occupying the same territory, in forming unique identities and relationships within that space, and the continued relevance of past contractual agreements, never irretrievably broken by colonial neglect or perfidy. In this story European origins are not dismissed or forgotten, they are reworked through the indigenisation process that 'Europeans' have undergone in the Antipodes. An alternative narrative places far more stress on superseding those origins, although the Treaty foundation myth is retained, within a spirit of atonement for colonial misdeeds. In this light, Levine (1997: 158) suggests, 'becoming Pakeha' as a nationalist project is more to do with the creation of a 'community of assent' (cf. Morris 1996) than the reconstruction of a community of descent. Stressing the religious analogy, Levine argues 'white biculturalists' have adopted a progressive 'Pakeha' narrative that truncates British origins and replaces them with new myths of destiny pursued with mission-like zeal. Allegiance to a bi-cultural community of assent: 'provides the body of shared truths, complete with a version of original sin. The children of rapacious, capitalistic settlers renounce their origins (Britain as home) and adopt a set of progressive values to define a new community' (ibid.). Leaving aside the hint of cynicism here, Levine is touching on an important nerve centre that is present in Canada and Australia, namely, the desire, at least among some members of the majority, to overcome the competing national claims of dominant and minority peoples through a process of redemption and, what they see as, positive appropriation.

Questions pertaining to 'reconciliation' in Australia, and 'healing' in Canada, both capture the mood of recent moves to redeem histories, in states whose foundational myths, once constructed on national and international pride, now evoke sentiments of guilt and shame. The quest 'for legitimacy and self-respect is the great underlying theme of settler nationalism' (Moran 1998: 107) that takes on new twists in post-settler times. Moran, writing of Australia, notes the historical debates about the 'convict stain', aboriginal dispossession, the dependency relationship with Britain and the 'cultural cringe' reflected in constant evaluation of self and national worth through international comparison. Canadians and New Zealanders do not have the convict element, and their local narratives about dispossession contain their own tales of comparative advantage in which Australia (and the United States and South Africa) will likely figure, but most of the themes Moran alludes to are immediately recognisable within their own distinctive contexts. Revisionist histories that proclaim settler societies were always multicultural are now thoroughly in vogue. As are the varied attempts by post-settler intelligentsia to reconcile their myths of origin with those of aboriginal peoples, whom they now perceive as having achieved the moral high ground as 'first peoples':

> By grafting Aboriginality onto a settler identity that seems too 'light', too lacking in historical depth and continuity with the territory it wants to fuse itself with, such an identity would be indigenised. But there are other settler responses. One is to repress envious feelings by establishing an equivalence between settler and indigenous connections with land. Another is to deny the continuing Aboriginal connection with land, or even to deny that such a connection ever really existed. (ibid.: 111)

How far these sentiments are reflected in the minds of most members of 'white' majorities, as Moran acknowledges, is a moot point. If national surveys are a guide, Australians, Canadians and New Zealanders in general still exhibit high levels of pride in their countries and ancestry, although qualified support for particular state actions and unqualified disrespect for politicians firmly belie a blind patriotism. Public record offices are clogged with enquiries from amateur genealogists seeking out their roots. Hence there are demonstrable indicators of widespread national belonging and more particularistic ethnic reconstruction. And these signs, plus majority group support for local variations on the same refrain, 'We're all Australians, Canadians or New Zealanders', have a positive ring of inclusivity, embracing multicultural and bicultural destinies. But this chime has a flawed note. By adopting an all-encompassing sense of the nation, majorities, in some cases admittedly unwittingly, are still reaffirming their dominance.

Reframing nations

Post-settler societies are characterised by a mix of nationalisms that reflect the positions of dominant, minority, and in Canada's case, ethno-regional, groups. These nationalisms are thoroughly interlaced but separate elements are still distinguishable. Closer examination of the relationship between nation, state and civil society brings them into a clearer focus. Rogers Brubaker's insightful distinction between state-framed and counter-state conceptions of nationalism and nationhood is useful here. In the former, Brubaker, suggests: '"nation" is conceived as congruent with the state, as institutionally and territorially "framed" by the state; in the latter, it is conceived in opposition to the territorial and institutional frame of some existing state or states' (Brubaker 1998: 300). Using this contrast, majority group understandings of nationhood and forms of nationalism still tend to be 'framed' by the state. Such groups view themselves as representing 'the nation', and the state is the major point of reference for this abstraction, since it is the chief vehicle through which their everyday dominance is portrayed. Both nation and state are, frequently reified constructs, reproduced and refurbished through the mundane trivialities of everyday life and occasional, more extraordinary defining moments. Both so-called 'high' and 'popular' culture are reference points for continuance and change of the categories and institutions through which people define who 'they' are. For 'majority groups', there is a likely linkage between their perception and experience of state, nation *and* their ethnic identity. It is no surprise to find persons of English ancestry, for example, in post-settler societies defining themselves as Australians, Canadians or New Zealanders, or providing a hyphenated (English or Anglo) expression of affiliation when asked for their 'ethnic' background. One can surmise that this is because any sense of 'English' ancestry is constructed within systems of dominance where their personal origins were, and largely remain, defined through national public attachments (Pearson 1990: 218). As we saw in Chapter 3, Englishness may have persisted, but more likely it was conflated with 'Britishness, before, or through the process of, migration and settlement. Over time, as suffix or prefix depending on the weight of national allegiances, a largely figurative, hyphenated 'Britishness' emerged. Ultimately, for many local-born, the 'British' qualifier was dropped, although new waves of British migrants would reinvigorate the process of remembering and forgetting. Ethnic and national symbols were, therefore, elided or interconnected. More recently, however, a repositioning in multicultural contexts, prompted by greater ethnic heterogeneity and the reformulation of official ideologies and labels, has revived the qualifier in a more tangible hyphenated form, or a single national signifier has been more strongly adopted.

For majorities, the rituals of civil society and economic existence, the functioning of state institutions and the public celebrations of myths of origin and destiny are thoroughly interwoven. The organisation of mass education, the conduct of governance and law, and the codes and currency of monetary exchange, are expressed through the medium of a national language (or languages) and institutions within a common territory. For much of their histories, dominant settler populations supported a modernist nation-state project based on unity and sameness. This was never fully realised. English Canadians, for example, were forced to don cultural bifocals by virtue of the 'French fact', and British New Zealanders conceded Maori a far more marginal membership. Still, racial and cultural homogeneity was the national norm and any border crossing was subject to assimilative sanction. The 'real' British had an immemorial, organic, continuous narrative of nationhood to draw upon that glossed alternative identities in outlying regions. The Americans' revolutionary moment provided a historical benchmark and an ideological political foundation displacing ethnic diversity in the pursuit of a common destiny. Our other 'nations by design' (Smith 1991), however, had recourse to neither of these narratives. This only became problematic, at least for 'Anglo' political elites, when the weakening of the British connection and the strengthening of ethnic and regional heterogeneity made 'sameness' nationally and internationally unsustainable. Unity, however, was still firmly on the agenda, set within a new climate of diversity.

Canada and Australia were nationally reconstituted by the state as multiculturally unified through difference, with New Zealand seeking to take a similar route to a bicultural destination. Homogeneity and assimilation seemed to have been superseded, and for those members of the dominant majority supporting an unfettered cultural pluralism, a radical uncoupling of settler nationalism is envisaged in post-settler times. But this position, currently, has neither unqualified elite nor mass support. There is still an emphasis on 'core' national values, and strict limits to sovereign authority and the boundaries of cultural acceptance. Despite recent acknowledgement and acceptance of greater regional and ethnolinguistic autonomy, a persistent *normative* belief in an overlaying territorial, political and cultural symmetry remains. The national identities of most members of post-settler majorities are still framed by the state.

English-speaking Canadians, Kymlicka observes (and his remarks seem pertinent to similar groups in our other societies), do not see themselves as some national subset, they view themselves as 'members of a (Canadian) nation that includes all citizens, whatever their language or culture, from sea to sea' (Kymlicka 1998: 141). In seeing the nation in this way, dominant groups are seeing themselves in an abstract, territorial, statist manner. In Sally Weaver's (1985) terms, a link is still sought between what she calls public and private ethnicities. National motifs are ubiquitous public ethnic signifiers. The Maple Leaf *is* Canada, as the kangaroo or fern leaf is in our other two societies. Such symbols become banal through their ubiquity (Billig 1995). They appear on flags, government letterheads, commercial products, and the coins in one's pocket. When emblazoned on the clothes of 'our' sports teams, 'they' become 'us' in national terms. By becoming familiar and taken for granted, a conjunction between public and private symbols of common descent is unreflectively realised, and not readily articulated in 'thick' ethnic terms because of the elision of national and ethnic attachment. Thus, 'thin' ethnicities, far from indicating a lack of 'cultural assurance', are often signs of quite the reverse.

Majorities in post-settler states have experienced considerable change in public representation and private experience of national identity in recent decades. New national flags are contemplated, to replace or put beside the old, and sub-national flags acquire legitimacy in certain contexts. National museums now prominently position 'first peoples' as co-founders or precursors of 'the nation'. International sports meetings, Olympic and the Commonwealth Games, for example, provide public occasions for multicultural display. There are new 'cultural' dates on national and regional calendars, reflecting shifts in linguistic, religious and political representation, evoked through carnivalesque events. Transformations in cuisine, dress, and musical, linguistic and artistic expression, underpin a move towards cosmopolitanism and plurality finding support among intelligentsia in education, the arts, and those sectors of state bureaucracy designed to promote or represent 'multiculturalism', with more mixed allegiance from the polity and the masses. Are these changes indicative of a new era of tolerance supplanting a previous period of officially sanctioned intolerance? Or are we viewing a strategic set of reformist policies designed to forestall more radical possibilities arising from the challenges to domination by minorities? Much hinges on the meaning of 'tolerance' and its linkage to the word 'tolerate'. As Hage notes, the key factor in this link is: 'those who were and are asked to be tolerant remain *capable* of being intolerant or, to put it differently, that the advocacy of tolerance left people *empowered* to be intolerant' (Hage 1998: 86, original emphasis). In sum, there are clear limits to tolerance. Multicultural forms of inclusion always have an exclusive edge, by virtue of their interconnection to a common theme of 'different thresholds of tolerance' (ibid.: 92). Cultural diversity, at the end of the day, must not undermine unity viewed in nation-state terms. Tolerance, therefore, is fully ensconced within a normative acceptance of 'the nation' still being framed, territorially and politically, by the state.

In contrast, national minorities have to choose between potentially divided state, nation and ethnic loyalties. Aboriginal people, and Québécois, are far more likely to have counter-state understandings of nationhood. Their nations and nationalisms are partly conceived in pre-state and/or extra-state terms. The territories they owe first or shared allegiance to are imagined or directly experienced places existing prior to, formed within, or extend beyond the borders of the nation-state the dominant use to frame their attachments. Dissonance from multiple identities and affiliations is not a reflex expectation of national majority or minority membership in post-settler societies. Most persons, including members of aboriginal and immigrant minorities (and Quebeckers) move freely between multilayered attachments. Yet dominant nation-state institutions are far more likely to be perceived as secondary or alien sites of affiliation for aboriginal and regional 'nations within'.

Alternative national and transnational imaginings are also a feature of some immigrant minorities, particularly diaspora, but national sentiments for 'old' homelands rarely hinder their affiliation to 'new' abodes. Immigrant minorities are more likely than settler majorities to hyphenate their national naming, but evidence suggests some semblance of national belonging is soon acquired by subsequent generations. If not, the problem is seen as one of non-acceptance, or non-recognition of cultural diversity within the state, not the establishment or reproduction of separate nations. Greeks and Macedonians, or Serbs and Croats, to use deceptively solid signifiers, may replicate the conflicts of geographically distant national projects within their diasporas. But these extra-local cultural and social attachments, although possibly weakening allegiance to their societies of settlement or sojournment, have not involved counter-state nationalisms within them. These are the preserve of aboriginal, not immigrant, minorities.

Such thoughts on public and private ethnicities, and state and counter-state nationalisms, add to my argument (touched on in Chapters 1 and 3) that we need to be very wary about drawing firm distinctions between civic and ethnic conceptions of nationhood, especially if we wander into the minefield of normative assessment of 'good' and 'bad' nationalisms. Analytically distinguishing between national sentiment on the basis of ethnic descent or rational legal citizenship, for example, has ideal typical merit, and aids the task of sketching the nuances of comparative shifts within or across histories of nation and nation-state making. But each of the nationalisms discussed in this chapter have both ethnic and civic components. Brubaker, rightfully, rejects any attempt to draw an over-simplistic contrast between civic state-framed and ethnic counter-state nationalisms (Brubaker 1998: 301). State-framed nationalisms may be ethnicised, while counter-state national definitions often contain civic elements, as discussion of the above nationalisms demonstrates.

Conclusions

Core support for Québécois independence still rests on ethnic memories, myths and blood-ties. Yet the task of reconciling a diversity of aims between French and English interest groups within Quebec, most demonstrably in Montreal, and incorporating immigrants and aboriginal persons within quasi-state borders, is set firmly within the civic institutions of liberal democracy. A departure from Canada depends on corralling enough citizen votes, and establishing one's own bounded nation-state that may very well mirror in most respects the institutional framework of the state seceded from.

At first glance, aboriginal minorities seem most ethnic in their orientation. Their nationalisms commonly embrace primordialist, cultural invocations of shared ancestry and history shaping their aspirations for self-determination. These national imaginings, however, are thoroughly embedded within the civic political and legal institutional frameworks they have become enmeshed within since colonisation. They also frequently assume a modernist conception of territorial boundedness overlaying pre-modern conceptions of relations with the land underpinning claims to distinctiveness. Recently instituted forms of self-governance therefore reflect a mix of, putatively retained, revitalised and introduced beliefs and practices defying neat ethnic/civic distinctions. Nevertheless, while few nationalist aspirations are anti-state to the point of secession, the countering of a dominant group conflation of nation and state is axiomatic of aboriginal self-determinative projects.

Majority group nationalisms are civically centred in so far as they retain a sense of symmetry between state, territory and citizenship, but multicultural and bicultural models clearly have ethnic constituents. Attempts to position oneself, and one's category, within these models has also initiated a 'thicker' form of ethnic identification among some majority group members. Yet most dominant group national sentiments are still framed within rather than run counter to the state.

But are all these nationalisms ephemeral in a world where states are rapidly becoming redundant in the face of globalisation, where post-settler nations are supposedly becoming post-colonial, and where new global citizens will reduce outdated conceptions of sovereignty and societal membership to anachronisms? Such questions return us to those posed at the beginning of this chapter and take us beyond them into the final chapter of this book.

8
Beyond Nations and States?

Who now reads Louis Hartz? The Hartzian contribution to the argument about the weight of internal and external forces shaping New World societies is now largely ignored, but within his (1964) analyses of settler societies there are still familiar themes indicating some prescience of current preoccupations. Hartz portrayed British settler colonies as chips off the old block of an imperial Britannia. Each fragment had its own character, reflecting different combinations of feudal traces, and how these shaped local patterns of preservation and departure from European institutional and ideological forms. Musing about 'The New Era', he observes how far the fragments have drifted from their source, as the descendants of settlers became, in my terms, indigenised within post-settler societies. Of particular note is the way Hartz recognizes, at a time (the 1960s) of increasing diversity and cosmopolitanism, how settler generations had broadened their field of experience and imagining, from a local/Europe to local/World configuration, while retaining, in his words, 'the intolerable ambiguity of being part of a whole and isolated from it' (Hartz 1964: 64). Part of this intolerability, Hartz suggests, stems from current generations remembering what their predecessors forgot, as they seek, simultaneously, to disentangle and reposition themselves in local and global identity terms.

Indeterminacy and ambivalence still characterise ethnic relations within our case studies and their position in the world, and the process of forgetting persists alongside remembrance in national imaginings. How much of this uncertainty is due to general features of globalisation or the particularities of continuous semi-peripherality remains an intriguing question. If we define globalisation as a multifarious stretching and deepening of relations and institutions across space and time (Held 1999: 92), fragmentation is often seen as a corollary. Replacing a pattern of territorial empires subjecting a single political and economic system over much of the world, we now have: 'a proliferation of international organisations, transnational practices, and networks of exchange (in industry and banking, in information and communication, in travel and cultural interchange)' (ibid.: 95). The interweaving of these global and fragmentary dynamics can have explosive or benign ethnic outcomes depending on whether one sees worldwide, regional and local effects as competitive or complementary. On the one hand, there are doom-laden images of 'a world becoming one and uncontrollable at the same time' (Joppke 1998: 12), as ethnic 'tribes' compete in a global tournament of warring 'civilizations' (Huntingdon 1996). On the other hand, there are those who suggest many new or renewed forms of ethnic and national political discourses and projects augment rather than conflict with global forces (Holton 1998). I am inclined to the latter view, but the jury is still out on these major questions, and I suspect in the unlikely event of a decision it will only be interim as rapid change promises swift relitigation. Answers, as always, tend to be contextual. Some states are rather better placed than others to promote as well as withstand global forces, and have adopted rather differing strategies in the process. This becomes abundantly clear if we re-examine our case studies and compare them with the two states they have been so intimately related to since their conception.

Contrasting exceptions

America

The United States is an exceptional post-settler society, while Britain's peculiarity stems from its role as an ex-imperial progenitor of global settlement. The historical link between them was their participation in a common Enlightenment project of the spread of Western civilisation and the creation of a world of states qua nations. More recently, the bonds were most apparent in the strategic solidarity between them during the Second World War and its aftermath. Post-Cold War, with the rise of Asian and European economic and political blocs, America has lost some of its pre-eminence, yet it remains, at least for now, as the one state with the size, wealth and technological resources to be as much in control as at the whim of globalisation. America, Hall and Lindholm (1999: 74) recently aver: 'has the capacity – uniquely so in an increasingly interdependent world – of deciding its own fate, relatively free of intervention from abroad'. Their statement is primarily addressed to geo-military and economic matters, but how does it square with the cries of concern about the porosity of migrant borders and its impact on domestic ethnic politics? What of the claims of multicultural Balkanisation, concern about enduring and more recent inequalities between racial categories, and the links drawn to immigration, particularly in those conurbations where the class and spatial divides between poor and not-so-poor ethnic enclaves are most sharply drawn?

This potent cocktail appears to lay bare the fragility of time-honoured civic sentiments of a non-ethnic constitutionalism binding the nation. Even America, or so the story goes, has become the victim of over-liberal immigration policies, and the racialised faults in what was always a flawed idea of 'the land of the free', have widened and spread into new ethnic fissures. The US Census Office predicts, over the next half-century Hispanic Americans will outnumber the combined total of American Indians, and African and Asian Americans, while Non-Hispanic Whites will decline in numbers from almost three-quarters to just over half of the American population – a forecast prompting thoughts about a United States post-Western nation whose public ideology will need to realign with future ethnic realities (Gray 1998: 130).

Current ethnic and national ingredients indicate a clash of flavours requiring new political recipes, but we need to be mindful of the origin of some constituents and countervailing blending agents in the reformulation process. Ethnic tensions in the United States are still as much to do with domestic politics as transnational pressures. Current immigration debate, consistent with earlier periods of American history, reflects a complex mix of localised moral panics about invasion offset by demands from business, ethnic kin, and anti-racist and rights groups, for continued, or increased migrant access. These interests, Freeman (1998) suggests, tend to be the most effective political agents. Consequently, immigration outcomes incline to remain expansionary. During the 1990s, at a time when many other Western societies were cutting back on migrant numbers, the United States increased its legal admissions. In spite of a much harsher national and regional statutory regime restricting the rights of entry of asylum seekers, and initiating clampdowns on illegal aliens, their numbers also continued to grow. This expansion *is* partly accountable to global trends, but it is also attributable to governments seeking to balance local electoral fears and lobbyist demands by reinvigorating civic inclusionary foundation myths while appeasing powerful domestic interest groups. Such myths paper over the racial cracks as much as they might seek genuine cultural renovation. Nonetheless, a lack of unity among and within racial categories about assimilation and separation, and the shared anxiety of the majority, often combine to reinforce the status quo. A recurrent anxious preoccupation with migrant others actually strengthens the nation-state. As Behdad recognises: 'On the one hand, we are a nation of immigrants; on the other hand we identify ourselves against our immigrants, as we try to control them' (Behdad 1997: 175).

A theme of civic stability amidst the outcries of ethnic doomsters is contentiously, but persuasively, taken up by Hall and Lindholm (1999) The authors suggest an underlying socio-political equilibrium is still discernible in the United States. It rests on a still unified establishment, widening political citizenship, a lack of state intervention in civil society, continued economic growth, and the absence of a genuine geopolitical global rival. Beside these relatively tangible signs of greater assurance, they argue, there is the more ethereal, but critically important persistence of ideological symbols that still win hearts, if not always minds. A shared, malleable creed of 'freedom', 'individualism' and 'equality' – an egalitarian belief in 'all you can be' – overlays all too apparent inequalities highlighted by a politics of difference. Thus, the States remain united because, not in spite of, foundation beliefs in diversity.

Britain

Arguments for United States post-settler exceptionalism rest on it being as much the source as a recipient of globalisation, and its special blend of civic national durability and ethnic elasticity. British exceptionalism is of an entirely different order. Despite recurrent local episodes of racial heat bringing Cool Britannia into sharp relief, the US clamour over immigration and multiculturalism is only palely reflected in the UK. In global and regional terms, British multiculturalism is peculiar for its lack of internationalism. A 'curious idea of multiculturalism in one nation' (Favell 1998a: 342) is preserved through tight border controls, restrictive immigration and bipartisan, self-styled progressive race relations legislation, for the small, ethnic minorities allowed to reside within. The result is a 'would-be zero immigration country' (Layton-Henry 1994).

In contrast to the United States, the main threat to UK national unity does not stem from assertive racial categories or the inrush of foreign migrants, but from internal neo-nationalisms and the promise of continental realignment. The formation and process of European union looms large on both horizons. The 'Euro' will soon become common currency. On one side of the banknotes is a new European motif, on the other the more familiar national emblem of particular states. This neatly symbolises the juxtaposition of national and supranational sources of authority of participating states. Britain, as yet, is not fully among them, but is hardly unaffected by the actions of her neighbours. Adrian Favell's summary of the trends of European integration over the past two decades, captures the new climate of change affecting British immigration and regional devolution policies:

> Within the context of the European Union (EU), European nation states are no longer self-contained bordered units within which immigrants must integrate. Common laws and new political institutions challenge the sovereignty of each state to make policies or to assert political control over immigration issues. Economic interdependence and the prospect of monetary union have rendered many government powers obsolete. Open borders make free movement and labour mobility much easier. Culturally, Europe as a whole appears to be fragmenting into a collection of smaller regional units and transnational cultural tiers, as well as moving towards a more Europeanised common culture founded (potentially at least) on a political unity of multinational and multicultural citizenship rights (Favell 1998b: 605).

This synopsis, as Favell acknowledges, requires cautious caveats. The EU was created to *preserve*, not undermine, state security and prosperity in the face of global economic and geopolitical change. Of the 'four freedoms' of movement, the flow of goods, services and capital has been far less restrictive than the travel of persons. In keeping with states having legacies of guestworker and/or post-colonial migrations, the EU migrant formula imposes stringent external immigration control, particularly over illegal migrants and asylum seekers, while opening internal borders to fellow members whose conditions of settlement are closely monitored. Hence the two-tier status of EU and non-EU nationals' rights and freedoms. Quasi-confederal co-operation seems to offer unprecedented possibilities for the enhancement of recognition and treatment of migrant workers within the system, but major question marks are raised about the rights and conditions of those outside of it. There is also considerable slippage between *de jure* and *de facto* conditions given the expanse of grey areas in a mass of bureaucratic regulation, and the ability of individual members to opt out, sidestep or quietly ignore rulings. The UK is a classic illustration.

As a domestic state confronted with a new set of international migrant human rights norms, it has used its parliamentary power, largely unchecked by formal constitutional restraints, to protect itself from 'undemocratic' intrusion of a Europe still viewed by much of its populace as an Other 'over there'. The resultant, distinctive 'race relations' politics, crosscut by class and gender lines, reflects the enduring problem (as perceived by political elites and much of their electorate) of racialised post-colonial migrants and more recent conflicts over religious cultural pluralism (Statham 1999). Neither of these smouldering issues, despite recurrent flashpoints, resembles the more expansive and deep-seated conflicts reminiscent of America and other parts of Europe – a fact British politicians never tire of reminding their transcontinental counterparts.

Notwithstanding resistance from a broad spectrum of local political interests to look beyond 'one-nation cultural pluralism' (ibid.: 620), the UK state is not immune from the administrative and *de jure* EU support for open borders and enhanced migrant rights. European Court rulings and European Commission conventions have had an impact on domestic immigration policy and the position of aliens and asylum seekers, if only, to be cynical, in initiating innovative ways of circumventing them. And whilst British ethnic minorities often seem as insular as the majority, some, notably local Muslim politics, are clearly framed within transnational settings.

The EU has also been an important impetus for regional devolution within the UK. Scotland, Wales and Northern Ireland have been granted varying degrees of autonomy within the British state. Their Home Rule projects were, and are, much influenced by perceptions that the EU political framework, bolstered by a common economic, and, less common, social welfare policies, enable smaller regional units to bypass English-cum-British state control and provide some protection against the incursions of global forces. For Scotland, and more so Wales, there seem only limited prospects of separate nation-statehood, although Northern Ireland may still look south to the Republic for independent unity. Nor is there much likelihood in the foreseeable future of the EU becoming the site for realistic federal state or cross-national imaginings (McCrone 1998: 184). Yet the united Kingdom is tangibly less so than it has ever been. 'Britain' has become explicitly free-floating, with its national margins more anchored than its core in new, devolved places.

Where does this leave England now? For the English, the UK state tended to be perceived, institutionally, as synonymous with England, with Britain being an even Greater image of themselves. Now, the fuzzy boundaries between the 'four nations and one' (Kearney 1991: 4), have become more sharply observed. Some pessimists might immediately espy another crisis of identity (there is an awful lot of it about!), but, one could equally argue regional and global fragmentary trends actually *reterritorialise* England. Your own boundaries become clearer when all around you others are loudly proclaiming their differences. Neo-national centrifugal forces, as Haseler (1996: 159) recognises, might ignite regional English identities as much as they could inject new life into English nationalism. But he does not discount a deeply ironic possibility that 'the British' (or does he mean English?), having experienced all manner of economic, political and cultural losses, might reverse their fortunes, and re-find themselves, by eventually embracing a European continent they have mistrusted for centuries. For Haseler: 'There never was a "British dream" to match "the American dream". British absorption in Europe – with its bounty of wider horizons and new frontiers – provides just such a possibility' (ibid.: 186).

Post-settler realignments

Are post-settler societies still 'semi-peripheral' states? Yes, but their location within a single Empire has been supplanted by a place of continued intermediateness within regional and global arenas in which the United States and Britain have also had to confront the ramifications of international realignments. Paradoxically, Haseler's imagery invests the dénouement of an Older Order with New World possibilities. In a spirit of new beginnings Britain's future lies in forging links with old continental neighbours as a defence against forces more cast in the role of economic than geopolitical enemies. Cautiously, but voluntarily, EU states are dismantling their economic frontiers while preserving much of their political and cultural differences in the construction of another complementary level of regional identity – a scenario rather at odds with memories of New World frontiers as the site of the conquering of continents in which rival cultures were required to be eliminated or swept aside in the name of economic and political progress. The Old Dynasties always saw Europe as a site of alliance as well as plunder. Now the masses, or at least some of them, are taking on a wider, regional mind-set. Britishness has become complemented by a sense, still, I suspect, far more strategic than emotional, of Euro-Scottish or Welshness. In the New World, elites saw 'Europe' as an emotional marker beyond Britishness, a distant source of civilised legitimacy for the displaced. Now those ties have unwound new bonds of, largely economic, attachments are contemplated, although their emotional proximity and strength of political legitimacy are more problematic.

Deregulation and the internationalisation of economic activities and markets have become hallmarks of all highly developed countries since the 1980s (Sassen 1999: 150). The post-Second World War Bretton Woods regulatory framework underpinning global expansion collapsed in the face of the economic 'shocks' of the 1970s, the growth of international capital markets, and the reshuffling of world political players. The relative decline of the US, the ascendancy of Japan and other 'Asian' states, and Britain's overtaking by European economic integration, reshaped political and economic alignments. In response to global economic trends and the neo-liberal philosophies fashioning the actions of governments, we have seen the recent formation or enhancement of burgeoning regional trading blocs. Since 1994, building on earlier free trade agreements, Canada, Mexico and the United States formed NAFTA. Other Latin American states, particularly Chile, are likely to join them. Australia and New Zealand remain in their longer-standing CER framework. All of these states are loosely linked to the Asia-Pacific Economic Community (APEC), as so-called Pacific Rim societies. None of these, ostensibly trading agreements, approaches the transnational level of political and juridical organisation of the EU. NAFTA does not affirm the free movement of workers, aside from professional and managerial staff connected to interstate investment. Indeed, much of its rationale is designed to manage illegal cross-border policies on the flow of persons and the (mainly) legal movement of products in the south-west and north of the USA. CER goes much further than NAFTA in eliminating barriers to trade, services, and migrants, and the occasional murmuring about a common currency and closer political relations might appear to have EU possibilities. But, as we saw in Chapter 7, there are far more signs of support for continued national independence than an Australasian merger. Similarly, NAFTA has not strengthened any national affinity between Canadians, Americans and Mexicans. Quite the reverse. Cross-border free trade heightens all the old fears in Canada of retaining national cultural integrity, with talk of US/Quebec interdependence adding to these anxieties.

The notion of a broader, imagined Asia/Pacific community is even more tenuous. The idea of 'the Pacific', Dirlik argues, was a Euro-American invention. More recently, the 'Pacific Community' concept is 'a baby whose putative parents are Japanese and American and whose midwife is Australia' (Dirlik 1999: 25). The APEC infant was born in virtual space with no natural geographical boundaries, no common historical or cultural ties, and no coherent identity. Unlike NAFTA it has no set of binding agreements; unlike the EU, there is no formal, institutional structure (Kelsey 1999: 283). APEC is basically an attempt to form a late-modern mercantile supra-region, bound together more by the pursuit of profit than cultural ties. It is hard to imagine any EU-type model of border-free migrant nationals emerging, given the mix of political regimes with very different levels of social democracy and human rights traditions across the region.

Post-settler societies have largely disentangled the threads of Empire dependence, but remain enmeshed in new networks of control and reliance as middle-range powers. The historical continuity of their global semi-peripheral position is now underlined by their relative 'core' positions in more localised regional zones in which Britain's sway has been largely replaced by American and 'Asian' (mainly Japan and China) supremacy – arrangements which have implications for aboriginal peoples and immigrants alike.

Globalising aboriginality

The politics of aboriginality has always extended beyond immediate territory, particularly when the intrusion of nation-states entrapped indigenous peoples within artificial confines. In earlier centuries, small delegations of indigenous leaders, particularly from North America and New Zealand, travelled across oceans to seek audience with the British monarch about the non-recognition of the treaties Crown representatives had signed with them or their ancestors. Occasionally, a hearing was granted, but aboriginal overtures mainly fell on deaf ears and went unrecorded beyond the limited confines of elite circles. At the cusp of the millennium, heightened global forces of economic and political interdependence, ever more sophisticated forms of information-sharing technology, and a profusion of political movements adept at exploiting these techniques and situations, have swiftly internationalised aboriginal politics. As Coates recalls:

> Indigenous peoples, the most localised of societies before World War II, quickly became foremost citizens of the global community, utilising indigenous contacts, media connections, and pooled resources in a way that few other groups succeeded in doing. (Coates 1998: 35).

Shared resources, networks and common cause were found among international non-indigenous organisations, including the growing number of support groups for aboriginal peoples and formidable global environment lobbyists. Indigenous peoples became 'icons of ecological correctness' (Bordewich 1996: 133), portrayed as oases of traditional, spiritual conservation in a desert of commercial greed. Using these potent symbols and allies, better resourced aboriginal groups were able to wage sustained, effective international political campaigns against local state and/or multinational development projects. More commonly, the less powerful sought some protection under broader umbrella organisations. Regional and national aboriginal associations in Australia, Canada, New Zealand and the United States are now formally affiliated to international organisations like the World Council of Indigenous Peoples, the International Indian Treaty Council and the Inuit Circumpolar Conference. These bodies are seeking to establish international legal and political instruments that will exert some extra-local control over the juridical and cultural recognition of aboriginal people in particular states and territories.

The claims being advanced by indigenous peoples worldwide fall under four broad headings (Nettheim 1998). First, is the demand for physical survival as recognised distinct peoples. Second, is the quest for autonomy of peoplehood, generally speaking within existing states. Control over land, waters and resources is a third vital area, with freedom from racial discrimination and equality of treatment as human, social and political subjects completing the picture. Some of these claims bring the statuses of the poor and powerless, migrant or native, together. Most of them hinge on establishing a special footing for indigenes. Here lies a continued point of friction.

The international status of indigenous peoples still falls 'somewhere between that of states and individuals' (Magallanes 1999: 244). To push for statehood is to run into a wall of opposition where individual state control is still bolstered by international fiat over external intrusion into internal affairs. To settle for individual minority rights is to lose one's grip on the unique lever of aboriginal standing. Initially, the successful pursuit of Third World self-determination seemed to offer hope for Fourth World aspirations. But the newly independent, industrialising states of the South, who bolstered the membership of the UN since the 1950s, have shown no greater support for indigenous peoples than the Northern colonisers they supplanted. The late twentieth-century 'frontier' expansion of development projects in Central and South America, or South East and Eastern Asia, has hardly been more benign than the previous economic and cultural expansion of European settler societies. Nonetheless, by the 1990s, aboriginal peoples seem to have emerged as world subjects and makers of international law and practice instead of objects defined solely by national state edict (ibid.: 238).

The reception of the draft Declaration on the Rights of Indigenous Peoples, initiated by the UN Working Group on Indigenous Populations (in 1982), will be an acid test of world and national opinion. Expectations are still high among indigenous and non-indigenous rights groups that the UN Commission on Human Rights will eventually support prescriptive guidelines for the status and treatment of aboriginal minorities, replacing rhetoric with real legal teeth. Unfortunately, there are ample precedents for believing individual states are likely to jib at what they see as further assaults on their sovereignty. Despite well-established traditions of divided and overlapping sovereignties in Canada and the United States, there is still a general tendency to prioritise domestic over international law, and there is little sympathy with ideas of divisibility in New Zealand. Only the Australian judiciary has demonstrated more willingness to use international instruments, mainly because of the limits on the constitutional powers of the national polity and the entrenched intractability of some individual federal states to recognise aboriginal claims (Havemann 1999: 185).

Given the resistance of global and national state governments, and the fragility of public sympathy, aboriginal minorities are nudging the ceiling of limited concessions. However effective they have proved in using the weapons of global awareness, there are limits to moral suasion, let alone legislative action, in a world where politicians and majority electorates face a barrage of competing images of claims for recognition and resources. The most probable outcome of recent initiatives is a firmer acknowledgement of the entitlement of aboriginal groups, as non-government organisations (NGOs), or, in some cases, special territories, to sit at the bargaining tables of the UN, the ILO, and various international commissions on human rights affiliated with these organisations. The key issue is whether they will have an observer or more weighty roles in such arenas. Having established a reputation as 'liberal nations', our case studies will be loath to lose their legitimacy, so their aboriginal minorities might have a decisive edge in negotiations. The most likely result, however, will be something between hard-edged indigenous demands for swift and outright sovereignty and post-settler state governments' blanket refusal to contemplate any further erosion of their jurisdiction – an inevitable, inconclusive outcome, given a global climate where the still rapid corporate acquisitions of resources, in liberalised markets, place the ability of both local groups and states to control their own destinies into firm perspective. Such corporations seem freer to deal directly with aboriginal peoples under new free trade agreements like NAFTA. This may favour well-organised and resource-rich 'tribes', with multimillion dollar commercial enterprises, seeking international co-franchise agreements, particularly where, as in the United States, they may be freer from state regulation. Equally, it could leave powerless peoples even more at the mercy of external commercial interests.

Globalisation opens up new spaces for aboriginal minorities. For some it offers the prospect of the authority of states being tempered by international regulation, and economic opportunities unbounded by histories of local control. For others, the shift to regional and wider political powers may further undermine the leverage of local Crown treaties and domestic state obligations, while placing them into the more distant, but still controlling hands, of international capital.

Transmigration and new diasporas

If current aboriginal initiatives depict one set of local–global dynamics, recent migration flows portray another. In both cases, or so the globalists tell us, borders are becoming superfluous and the nation-state is losing its dominion. If aboriginality is a cause transcending local boundaries, migration is increasingly sensitive to shifts in a shrinking world connected by a string of 'global cities'. Between these cosmopolitan centres, migrant movements are extensive and often more intermittent, as travellers display a propensity to settle, often briefly, in new places while continuing to maintain their attachment to their countries of emigration.

Within this general picture of fluidity, our case studies still reveal underlying patterns of control. Like the United States, Canada, Australia and, with more caveats, New Zealand, continue to fit the image of classic societies of immigration, recurrent groundswells of popular opposition to increased migrant numbers notwithstanding. Yet their doors are far from wide open. The Mexican and Latin American 'borderland cultures' (Cohen 1997: 190) reaching across the USA are far more attenuated in northern North America, and Australasia can still rely on relative remoteness to protect its shores. Liberal, but selective, immigration is still the order of the day. Business migration is opened up, family renewal and haven seeking are regulated.[1] Legal immigration remains a filtering mechanism, ever responsive to economic, and more recently, humanitarian imperatives, while the welcome mats remain furled for most illegal arrivals.

Australian and Canadian entry policies in the 1990s have been streamlined, but overall immigration policies remain expansive. Broadly speaking, New Zealand fits this image, but here we are reminded how opening borders has two-way repercussions. Some people can leave as easily as they can enter. By the mid-1990s much of the gloss had worn off an Antipodean neo-liberal experiment, which, in truth, was always more radical in trading assets than persons (Kelsey 1999). Poor employment prospects and spiralling tertiary education costs saw skilled New Zealanders flocking across to Australia or further afield, while their, mainly Asian, replacements returned home or moved on to more attractive destinations.

In all of our case studies, possession of capital, employability, English (or French in Canada) language competence, and 'self-reliance', are the screening devices through which controls are retained, while a form of 'global apartheid' (Richmond 1994) segregates and stratifies migrant flows within and between rich receiving and poor sending societies in class, 'race' and gender terms. But these mechanisms only slow, not halt, the inexorable tendency for increasing diversity within the most recent waves of migration, many of which cross the so-called North/South divide. This has given rise to a burgeoning literature on transnationalism and renewed debates about a new breed of globalised diaspora. Transnationalism is 'the process by which immigrants forge and sustain multi-stranded social relations that link together their societies of origin and settlement' (Basch et al. 1994: 6). For these authors, 'transmigrants' maintain links, establish institutions, and transact economic, social and symbolic exchanges having far-reaching political implications for receiving and sending societies. Easier and cheaper travel, plus electronic communication enable, at least more affluent, migrants, to be almost instantaneously 'here' and 'there'. These 'electronic solidarity networks' (Langer 1998: 174) are a far cry from the modes of communication of 'old news' sustaining links between hosts and homelands of earlier arrivals. Indeed, some of the successors of prior generations, from Ireland, Eastern Europe and the Mediterranean, for example, are reactivating past attachments at the same time as migrants from Latin America and the Middle East are devising new connections. The media being used are unquestionably novel, but how original are the movements and the politics of 'new diasporas'?

Globalisation certainly enhances the probability of multifarious movements embracing some diasporic criteria. Migrant movements are increasingly multiple and transnational. But are they enduring? Diasporas, relatively speaking, are formed by settlers not transients. They move, and stay, within established networks of *multi-* (not simply dual) directional dispersal. Those pursuing profits, wages or asylum may transfer between nodal points of settlement stemming from prior diasporic travelling, or they might initiate them, but blanket usage of the term to define temporary and permanent, and uni- and multi-directional travel, confirms my earlier misgivings (in Chapter 3) about conceptual inflation.

A final glance at the fates of British and Chinese diasporas demonstrates the interweaving of both continuance and transformation. The British hegemonic endeavour, you will recall, represented a global imperial diaspora. In settler societies, these transoceanic elite movements were gradually complemented by dominion British diaspora migrations *en masse*. Eventually, the overseas British became natives in post-settler states. In contrast, the Overseas Chinese in the selfsame places, remained circumscribed by discriminatory practices and legal categorisations which constricted migrant and capital transfusion until well into the twentieth century. Currently, the British remain influential regional, economic players, and London continues to operate as a powerful global financial centre. But consider the contrasting, more spectacular growth of the Chinese economy in the 1990s, and the irresistible strengthening of the *huaqiao* by the liberalisation of people and capital movements. Much of the overseas investment China's growth is based on derives from Chinese diaspora capitalists (Lever Tracy et al. 1996). Overseas Chinese communities now control an economy worth roughly as much as the mainland Chinese (cf. Gray 1998: 59). Their presence reflects a historically embedded trading diaspora, whose internal composition, range of activities, and stretch of networks, has been greatly diversified and expanded by globalisation. For archetypical global migrants we need look no further than Hong Kong. Faced with the imminent expiry of Britain's lease, and the marked reluctance of the post-imperial metropolis to offer sanctuary to offshore British subjects, many Hong Kong business people moved their families elsewhere, including North America and Australasia, but continued regularly to revisit 'their' island to maintain commercial interests. As global 'astronauts', literally flying through space, they bolster unparalleled visions of transmigration and problematise distinctions between sojourning and settlement. Yet they also provoke reminders of pre-existing ethnic patterns as well as rapid change. Travelling has been revolutionised, but destinations may remain the same.

The persistence, as well as decline of 'nation-states', is pivotal in understanding the political efficacy of new and renewed transnational forms of identity and community formation (Demetriou 1999). In post-settler societies, narratives of multicultural diversity and heterogeneous migrant contributions to nation-building have replaced assimilationist prescriptions of unwavering conformity. These changes, I have argued, were as much to do with the domestic unfolding of historical ethnic and national tensions, as recent international contingencies. Immigration was a necessary but not sufficient causal factor here. With more liberal and open espousal of multicultural objectives, immigrant minorities, including diaspora, are far more inclined to maintain transnational ties and be less fearful of recrimination for doing so. So while global effects on the intensity of these links are undeniable, local shifts to liberalise still resilient nation-states seem equally influential in creating the *'impression'* (original emphasis) of major differences between old and new migrations (ibid.: 19). More compelling than global versus local arguments, as Langer (1998) illustrates in her study of political refugees from El Salvador in Australia and Canada, is an argument for overlapping multiple sites of political change.

Langer shows how globalisation reduces the distance between sending and receiving societies. Salvadorans, especially the urban middle class, are already immersed in Americanisation *before* they leave El Salvador. A 'global uniform of jeans, T-shirts and sneakers' is far more reminiscent of 'home' than the 'traditional' national costumes worn at Winnipeg or Melbourne multicultural events (ibid.: 170). Different international and local constructions of the 'Salvadoran community' – as victims, dispossessed indigenes, or exemplars of theological or Marxist-Leninist liberation – also represent alternative political garb. These trappings of 'ethnic' distinction are generated or defended by an array of local and international human rights agencies, religious and environmental organisations, and used as cultural boundary markers by identity brokers. Running through the Salvadoran 'community' are divisions, recognisable in some refugee groups across all of our case studies,[2] between those who seek to stay 'in' or 'out' of a history of what they hope is a transition to democracy in their countries of origin. Many welcome the opportunity to exchange a war-torn past for the shelter of even an ambivalent reception 'down under' or in the 'far north'; others maintain an intense political engagement through local and global organisation; no one is immune from the footage of civil war appearing on TV screens.

Immigrant minorities, diasporic or otherwise, always had the potential for divided loyalties: it goes with the territory of chosen as well as forced exile. Globalisation has aided the continuance and reinvigoration of transnational politicisation, most vividly displayed in forms where arms, money and drugs are involved. *Miami Vice*-style melodrama aside, there are also enough incidents of, occasionally violent, influence of diaspora on host and homeland politics to support the thesis of states under threat from forces transcending their borders. Open challenges to state sovereignty in host states, as we noted in the last chapter, remain exceptional however. On the whole, migrant clusters are too small, diverse, and geographically scattered to represent major centres of dissidence. Nor is there convincing evidence that multicultural policies provide anywhere near the institutional support to sustain, let alone encourage, any semblance of self-governing territories, diasporic or otherwise. Immigrant minorities have their own, in some cases, locally powerful, informal political infrastructures, but they tend not to form, individually or in coalition, separate ethnic-based political parties. Representation still tends to remain within the provincial and national mainstream (Kymlicka 1998; Castles 1999). But this is not to cast too complacent an eye over issues of economic, political and social inclusion, nor to ignore the challenges to state sovereignty transnational migrations and multiculturalisms offer.

Global and local citizens

Such challenges, as Joppke (1998: 7) observes, can be viewed in conservative and progressive terms. Some may adjudge globalisation as a threatening force requiring protection of existing borders and long-standing state institutions. Others will detect an attractive prospect for worldwide transformation of conventional political and territorial arrangements. Population movements and multiculturalisms challenge the congruence of political and cultural boundaries. Ultimate, sovereign control over bounded populations and territories is further relativised by domestic and international pressures. If liberal states do not require flows of increasingly diverse migrants to assimilate, and migrants do not want to blend into the social and political landscape, we have, depending on one's inclination, a mutually reinforcing formula for fragmentary disaster or enervating freedoms.

Citizenship plays a leading role in both scenarios as an instrument and object of material and symbolic inclusion and exclusion. As a legal status it stipulates rights and duties and affects who gets what and when. Linked to nationality, it is a tangible, formal marker of state membership, and a more nebulous indicator of whether you belong in 'the nation'. Conservatives are concerned that what they see as a classic link between legal status and identity in the nation-state, is broken. Nation and state are separated out as citizenship seemingly no longer acts as an effective form of closure, and global heterogeneity outweighs local unities. Progressives see these very same conditions as supporting their view of globalisation as an agency for providing flexible statuses and identities in a post-national future (Soysal 1994), where multiple citizenships link immediate political communities to a regional and global cosmopolitan democracy (Held 1999: 107).

Both positions, I believe, understate the current resilience of 'the nation' and the power of 'the state', although one is based on a questionable view of the past, while the other poses a debatable future. Implicit in the conservative stance is a dubious assumption of some golden era of immigration and citizen regulation where states could control who entered their portals, while the progressive perspective draws an over-rosy vision of free-floating migrants in a borderless world where they are protected by supra-state polities and rights norms. A brief tracing of the major steps in the citizenship story of our case studies fleshes out my contentions, while serving to remind us of the main themes of this book.

Although our post-settler case studies are often seen as pioneers in the move to multicultural citizenries, none of them has a history of the supersession of strong national concepts of legal citizenship, and post-national membership featured prior to the onset of recent globalization: although here, admittedly, it related to rather different groups than globalists have in mind. Since their establishment as settler societies, the Anglo-Celtic majority have tended to view citizenship and nationality as indistinguishable. Settlers were part of an international British family sharing the status of monarchical subjects, bound together by kinship ties of blood ('race') and ethnic origin. In Canada, notable concessions were made to French 'relatives', and in New Zealand, Maori were 'intimate Others', but the overriding image of nationhood was a core of British (and Irish) descent recreating British state institutions overseas. Unlike the United States, entry and residence within a colonial diasporic network, rather than indigenously created and embedded notions of legal citizenship, promoted closure.[3] Distinctions between subsequent waves of British kin migrants and local-born settlers soon arose in the assessment of national identity, but citizenship hardly figured in these calculations of belonging.

This model of a core *ethnie* had far-reaching implications for minorities. The key test for offshore 'aliens' was whether they could become assimilated into an Anglo-Celtic people. Most foreigners never made it through the doors of the national club, let alone become accepted as equals if admittance was achieved. The same tests of inclusion were used to measure the status of 'aliens within'. For aboriginal peoples, citizenship was either denied, ignored or viewed as a civilising threshold indigenes had to cross before acquiring marginalised national membership. This passive citizenship model of imperial subjecthood proved highly resilient. Australia, Canada and New Zealand drew no legal distinction between a British and local identity until the 1940s. Even then, the *de jure* difference between kin migrants and the already settled remained relatively minor, until it finally widened in the 1970s after Britain started to conjure with the idea of national citizenship as a means of excluding most ex-colonial family members.[4]

Even when citizenship started to confer some additional rights, many permanently resident British migrants chose not to acquire them. The status was easily achieved if one, for example, wished to seek public office, and, of course, one's children automatically obtained these additional membership criteria if locally born. Also, the holding of British and local passports was thoroughly conventional. Thus, there was a tradition of settler and post-settler denizenship, and dual citizenship, predating the full flourishing of 'globalisation'. But this was embedded within the majority population. What proved challenging were the quickening pace and diversifying origins of non-British arrivals and the vigour of ethno-regional and aboriginal demands for citizenship on their own terms: even to the point of seeking their own separate statehood. These external and internal pressures promoted the emergence of more pluralistic models of citizenship.

The discussion of the shift from assimilative to multicultural policies presented in earlier chapters can be glossed as a nation-state building narrative of settler societies progressing from tightly deployed, ethnocentric and racist regimes, to more flexible, post-settler, deracialised plural frameworks. What you have read is a messier tale of expedience, and a complex mix of domestic and international factors in period- and context-specific terms, constraining individual states' abilities to control their own destinies.

The course of both immigration and aboriginal citizenship policy in settler and post-settler states questions the plausibility of using a Marshallian-inspired, narrative of incremental progress from legal, through civil, to social rights. Marshall provided a (British) context and a set of yardsticks for analysing citizenship rights. His criteria are useful for assessing the form and content of societal and state membership, and acting as a normative metaphor for discussing their full achievement. Comparatively speaking, Marshall's analysis is too place-and-time-bound to serve as a general model or as an actual historical account for our case studies (Colom-González 1996: 96).

Settler subjecthood-cum-citizenship always contained multiple loyalties, most apparent in northern North America. Here, a sense of belonging to Canada coexisted with other possible allegiances to 'the British Empire, to French-Canada, aboriginal nations, to the provinces, and to old homelands' (ibid.). Some of these complementary or contradictory multilayered identities are usable in Australasia, provided one weighs their relative strength in local terms. Historically, this multiplicity was recognised in a variety of formal and informal arrangements designed to accommodate polyethnic and multinational ramifications, but still within an overriding majority elite ideal vision of a singular (in Canada, dual) nation-state. Post-Second World War globalisation, in its various forms, undoubtedly influenced the tensions within and between the settler, aboriginal and immigrant populations commanding our attention, but it did not create them.

With the weakening of motherland connections, and the strengthening of Other belongings, political elites reshaped national ideologies and state institutions to accommodate greater diversity without relinquishing a core framework of ethnic and civic solidarity. Citizenship rules became more inclusive, flexible and democratic, as internal and external 'aliens' were not formally required to seek entry to a white, British (and in Canada, French) family. Using a repackaged multicultural kindred image of 'the nation', post-settler polities sought to modify institutions and 'renegotiate the terms of integration' of ethnic categories into the state (Kymlicka 1998: 59). The old family image was not superseded by the new. They coexisted within elite and popular circles, as alternative symbolic frameworks driving contested political practices. Nevertheless, multiculturalism was ascendant. Admission and naturalisation rules were liberalised, denizenship and dual citizenship rights extended, and assimilatory expectations eased. Migrant strangers started to enjoy some of the privileges only accorded to kin migrants in the past. Citizenship as a legal status was now detached, for long resident and newly settled persons, from any single ethnocultural affiliation. In terms of belonging, 'multicultural citizens' were now free to choose their cultural allegiance, with two important state provisos: the right to maintain one's own culture was balanced by duties, not only to recognise the private cultural rights of others, but also publicly to acknowledge the primacy of national core languages, institutions and values.

Racial and ethnic exclusivity had not dissolved, nor had the disparity between legal and substantive citizenship disappeared. There were wide-ranging discrepancies between a liberalised formal access to citizenship, and the class and gendered achievement of ethnic categories to get jobs, education, social welfare and politically participate on equal terms with others. But a new category of 'cultural' rights had been added to the citizenship bundle, and, particularly in the 1970s, there was a modest commitment to underpin the symbolic role of the new ideology with a modicum of state assistance. The welfare state was still seen as supplementing voluntary aid to migrant settlement, assisting the eradication of ethnic and racial disadvantage, and, more contentiously, supporting cultural maintenance. These measures went some way towards meeting migrant demands for 'polyethnic rights' (Kymlicka 1995). A symbolic endorsement of pluralism, and positive steps to redress questions of distributive rights within a mildly modified liberal individualist view of universalist entitlements and obligation, seemed to offer possibilities of reconciling civic status and ethnic/national belonging.

Since the 1980s we have seen an intensification in the basic contradiction between principles of citizenship espousing the active inclusion of ethnic minorities, and a continued restructuring of welfare states with exclusionary outcomes. Economic rationalist policy regimes, while supporting the freeing up of entry and residence requirements, and supranational citizenship, in the quest for market freedom, produced a widening gap between rich and poor, with old and new ethnic minorities disproportionately disadvantaged. The swelling ranks of the 'socially excluded' or 'underclass' told the story, evoking widespread concern about social cohesion and a predictable scapegoating of minorities by beleaguered working (and middle) classes. One response was a renewed emphasis on citizenship in the 1990s from varied standpoints (Joppke 1999). Drawing on international human rights organisation for legitimacy and sustenance, leftish-liberal commentary and political practice continued to pursue a reconciliation between equal rights, cultural pluralism and recognition of difference. Neo-liberals also espoused the virtues of diversity, but they had different payoffs in mind. An expansion of multicultural citizenship rights would attract desired capital and labour by enhancing transnational linkages, while the possibilities of reviving notions of 'responsible citizenship' would improve social control. The result has been a locally varied mix of free market imperatives and residualist social justice, driving citizenship aims drawn from very different liberal traditions. There have been recent state cutbacks in the bureaucratic infrastructure of multicultural services, a tightening of on-settlement migrant provision, and calls for more commitment to the duties as well as rights attached to full citizenship, but all of our cases exemplify 'the overwhelming trend in Western immigrant-receiving states... (is) towards liberalized citizenship regimes (ibid.: 645) In post-settler states, only part of this story is explainable by globalisation, or, indeed, immigration.

If diasporic or transmigrant minorities seek more flexible supranational arrangements to allow them to move between territories and polities in a global network of external state relations, aboriginal peoples and regional neonationalisms pose even greater challenges to citizenship and sovereignty from within post-settler states. Canadian First Nations, following separatist-inclined Québécois, may see themselves as future sovereign polities with their own separate citizenries reflecting a mix of perceived, past and present customary political practices. Sovereignty and rights talk is equally rife in Australasia. For some aboriginal persons, and fewer members of post-settler elites, indigenous minorities should have collective self-determining rights within domestic states, and supranational recognition as peoples and nations, thus ensuring, not only their distributive rights as individual citizens, and reparation for past exclusion and dispossession, but also their attainment of political autonomy as 'distinct societies' (Havemann 1999: 471–2).

Local variations have always tempered mixed success in meeting these aims. In New Zealand, we have a story of marginalised subjects, eventually acquiring special representation rights as citizens, which currently gives them real political clout. But the infancy of proportional representation leaves a question mark over how much Maori political muscle is required to firm up rather flaccid notions of unicameral partnership.[5] In Canada, there is a tale of reluctant citizens, where the historical hangovers of tutelage still figure in the complexities of the most developed experiment in seeking a differentiated citizenship within an asymmetrical federation. This account has some resonance in Australia, although the themes of exclusionary closure and the policing of citizenship boundaries are even more deeply etched into the story line (Chesterman and Galligan 1997: 212). Despite different historical starting points and pathways, we can discern some points of convergence. Across all three states, individual aboriginal legal citizenship rights have been realised, although not without challenge from within and beyond indigenous groups.[6] Reparative claims, although hardly uncontested, have also progressed within their particular settings. The developments of common law and native title, and the settlement of treaty claims and constitutional reforms, have been lethargic and often acrimonious processes, but they add up to unprecedented steps forward.

Debates about whether aboriginal peoples should have some 'autonomous' and 'self-determinative' control over their destinies have shifted to arguments about what this might mean and how it could be implemented. Yet, mainly philosophical, attempts to reconcile liberal and collective notions of rights and freedoms (see, for example, Kymlicka 1995) still constantly rub up against the intractable gulf between aboriginal and settler perceptions of liberty and obligation. As we have seen, only in a few (Australian and Canadian) isolated regions has aboriginal self-government remotely resembled a form of consociational power-sharing, let alone more radical designs.

For most aboriginal peoples, to extend Cairns' (1995: 254) point about Canada into our other societies, the real issue is not how to break free, but how to become or remain part of the state while 'retaining concurrently a sense of separate selfhood'. Selfhood has individual and collective connotations. Aboriginal persons are individuals. Many of them live and work in towns and cities where their day-to-day lives may be little different from other minorities. The uniqueness of aboriginal status, however, hinges on the survival of social orders, as collectivities, within varying levels of territoriality, under the same overarching state political jurisdiction. Within this broadly integrative agenda, aboriginal minorities strive to eliminate the impediments to their full social membership, while simultaneously struggling to retain and expand rights recognising their separate legal and political status and distinct sense of national belonging. This presses aboriginal claims well beyond those of immigrant minorities. States may accede to migrant demands for transnational citizenship, but they are far more resistant to aboriginal conceptions of a kind of 'double citizenship' (Peterson 1998: 110), particularly where they are still required to subsidise, by tax concessions or welfare payments, the autonomy being demanded. Here lies the nub of the philosophical and practical problems of harmonising Western individual and aboriginal collective rights, and the delicate relation between historical forgetting and a degree of current remembrance, within debates about minority and majority responsibility.

States of unease

Local/global relations are nothing new. Settler societies were forged out of disparate (*not* multicultural) meetings inserting dissimilar populations into new local settings intimately attached to regional and global networks. Multiethnicity was not necessarily invented in the process: it often took a different and more expansive turn. There is much fashionable talk of multiple identities and global hybridity today, but the histories of settler societies embraced both of these conditions from their inception. They were and remain conspicuously 'in-between' societies. Within them, diverse peoples experienced various homes amidst sundry departures and destinations, so the intermingling of bodies and cultural identities inevitably followed, despite, in many instances, strenuous and continued efforts to resist these processes. What needs re-stressing is the differing dynamics of the linkage and disengaging of imperial and dominion diaspora from their origins, and the structuring of relations of syncretism and resistance within and between majority/minority relations. The *privileged* economic and political dependence of settler elites on their motherland was greatly different from the nature of their relations with the aboriginal minorities they dispossessed. So the current tendency, in some circles, to label both the discontinuity of post-settler states becoming detached from their origins, and the continuous process of aboriginal/post-settler engagement as 'post-colonial', is misleading. Far better, as I argued earlier, to keep the hyphen for the former process, and remove it when describing the ongoing, postcoloniality, of the latter. Which still leaves open the query whether 'majority populations' are affected by invasive and complementary global forces *in the same way* as minorities.

There is no conclusive account we can draw upon to predict where globalisation is headed or the weight to be attached to utopian or more sceptical political forecasts, nor, as the Canadian experience tells us, any grand design for dealing with ethnic and national conflict. The excesses of deconstructive fragmentation currently overshadow the certainties of modernising convergence, except in the hearts of nationalists and 'ethnicists' (and the heads of some who study them): many of whom cling stubbornly to preordained myths and destinies of nations, and beliefs in the palpability of ethnic communal boundaries. Hard-line attachment to modernist and post-modernist positions cannot be reconciled. Still, I have sought to inch along a dangerous tightrope, seeking to balance coherence and fluctuation, without falling into the precipice of over-historicisation or plunging into the depths of denial of any historical encoding of national and ethnic political identities and formations. The task has been to devise a framework to explore what I have argued are discernible historical trajectories of settler, aboriginal and immigrant politics while recognising the contextual and constructed nature of each non-linear step along the way. In this approach, ethnicities and nationalisms are neither long-standing primordial relics nor the ephemeral consequence of political manipulation, and there is no simple model of before and after.

In settler society, national unity was never assured, and all is not flux and fluidity in post-settler times. What I have traced is the historical interplay of (mono and dual) shifts from settler to post-settler patterns of dominance, from kin migrant to transmigrant journeying , and from pre-modern *ethnie* to late modern aboriginal 'nations'. In the process a number of still prevalent notions were problematised. Aboriginal peoples are no longer exclusively indigenous. Ethnicity is not confined to migrants or minorities. So, despite their enduring categorical and group differences, common experiences of relative powerlessness and disadvantage place many aboriginal, migrant and post-settler persons in similar positions. As a consequence, ethnic relations, especially in globalised urban settings, are as much a coming together as keeping apart.

In our case studies, the political and economic relations between minorities and 'the majority' were always mediated transculturally, but they eventually resulted in a more explicit recognition and equivocal acceptance of multicultural, multinational states. The recency and rapidity of this transformation has inevitably left unresolved tensions. Most evident is the decoupling of nations from the state by neo-national and aboriginal minorities (and some majority group nationalists); the resistance of settler nativism to post-settler ethnic and national reimaginings; and the trend among some migrant categories and communities to revive or create attachments extending beyond cultural diversity into social and political pluralism. In a nutshell, we are seeing simultaneous drives towards, respectively, secession, reconstituted assimilation, and segmentalism. Australia and New Zealand face the last two pressures, Canada has to resolve all three.

Citizenship as a legal and political status has too much work to do in alleviating these stresses and producing a concerted sense of belonging. As a metaphor for national and state membership it is more successful, pointing to the need for social, economic and symbolic supports for formal juridical and political status. A sturdy inclusive civic culture, or so I believe, relies on adequate provision of public services and public investment, and an economy and welfare system fostering social membership. A sense of belonging in these senses is as important for national identity as ethnic myths and memories. Aboriginal and immigrant minorities (not to speak of some majority members) are at the sharp end of systems of disadvantage, in societies where the wealthy increasingly exhibit a dearth of civic obligation while pointing accusatory fingers at the 'poor' for their lack of responsibility. This sharing of similar fates might, ultimately, prove as important as the different histories they originated from.

Australia, Canada and New Zealand are often, rightly, seen as pacesetters in devising policy frameworks which respect ethnic diversity while promoting social integration. But this position has arisen from piecemeal interventions not far-sighted design. And local patterns of power distribution and stratification reveal the durability of compartmentalised hierarchies of ethnic interests and rewards, as well as the *ad hoc* nature of the policies devised to ameliorate them. Within a play of familiar comparative themes the balance of power between local political actors retains its own character. The Quebec issue still dominates Canadian ethnic and national politics. Aboriginal voices, although much stronger, remain relatively muted in Australia. Maori politics continue to overshadow migrant issues in New Zealand. Our case studies, therefore, cast doubt on the supranational exportability of a complete package of political and socio-cultural arrangements. But, given how much things have changed in the past half-century, I hesitate to foreclose on any forecasts for the next few decades. One thing we can be sure of, the power of ethnicity and nationalism to shape foreseeable future worlds is unlikely to dissolve. So, even in those places where innovative civic/ethnic arrangements might inspire some optimism, people will continue to live in states of unease.

Notes

2. Nations without States

1. The Robinson Treaties were negotiated with the Objibwa in northern Ontario in 1850. The 14 Douglas Treaties were made with various peoples in what was to become the province of British Columbia, during James Douglas's term as Governor in the 1850s and 1860s.
2. A series of treaties, each assigned a number from 1 through 11, were negotiated between 1871 and 1921. Several of them were signed in the 1870s to facilitate the western development of the Canadian state.
3. The federal state became involved directly on a specific regional basis in the Northern Territory in 1911.
4. The Waitangi Treaty was preceded, in 1835, by a politically expedient attempt by the Crown to create 'a confederation of tribes' among thirty-four northern hapu and iwi.

3. States without Nations

1. The Lower Canadian legislature voted by a slender margin of 27 to 21 in favour of Confederation.
2. The term Francophone (and the matching Anglophone) is also of very recent ancestry, having been coined by the Royal Commission on Biculturalism in the 1960s.
3. See Spillman (1997) for a comparison between the Australian and United States centennials, and Buckner (1997) for Canadian (and South African) material.
4. In the 1850s they formed about 5 per cent of the Eastern states' populations. By 1861, 60 per cent of miners in New South Wales and 25 per cent in Victoria were 'Orientals', and later strikes in Queensland (in the 1870s) led to substantial local communities.
5. The dearth of females was particularly striking in Australasia and Canada, less so in the United States.
6. Anthias (1998) provides a recent overview of debate.
7. Historians are divided on whether this sense was nascent in the minds of migrants before they left the 'Old country', whether it emerged on the voyage, or it started to flourish after stepping ashore in the 'New'; see Akenson (1995: 396–7).
8. See interesting discussions in Hastings (1997) and Tarver (1992) on England and America respectively.

4. Migrations

1. The Aliens Act of 1905 and the Aliens Restriction Act of 1914 were the key pieces of exclusionary legislation.

2. Cook Islanders, Niueans and Tokelauans are full New Zealand citizens, and Samoans have a 'special relationship' given their histories as New Zealand colonies or protectorates.
3. A formalised international legal definition of refugees only emerged post-Second World War. The United Nations devised a concept of political persecution in 1951 modelled chiefly on Eastern European experiences, but has since broadened the definition to embrace a wider range of political events.
4. In the mid-1980s, Britain was tenth in a table of European refugee receiving countries, topped by Sweden.
5. In settled Australia in 1986, if the Census is our guide, almost 80 per cent of aboriginal people aged 15 and over lived in urban centres of 10 000 or more persons; the corresponding figure for remote Australia was 28 per cent.

5. Management, Accommodation and Resistance

1. Termination policies, reversing the mood of the IRA era that reaffirmed the federal 'sovereign nation' relation of aboriginal peoples with the state, proposed abolishing reservations and all the legal and bureaucratic provisions according Native Americans a 'special' status.
2. The word 'allophone' refers to settlers without British or French ancestry.
3. Two of the more notable cases were the Calder case, which gave some credence to the claims of the Nisga'a in northwestern British Columbia in 1973, and the James Bay and Northern Quebec Agreement, signed in 1975. The latter gave Cree, at that time, unprecedented levels of self-government, control over hunting and trapping, and a substantial cash settlement.
4. The term 'patriate' refers to a process of completely removing the Canadian constitution from the control of the British Parliament. Successive Canadian governments had sporadically attempted to achieve this since the Statute of Westminster in 1931 recognised Canada's legislative authority, see Webber (1994: 81).
5. Contrary to conventional wisdom of the time (and later) the 1967 referendum did not 'give' Aborigines the vote in federal elections; these were already granted years before in a technical, *de jure* sense. Nor were the constitutional changes arising in 1967 particularly noteworthy in a legal sense. As recent scholarship shows the referendum was far more important as a widely publicised symbolic marker of a sea change in aboriginal and non-aboriginal *perceptions* of the legitimacy of aboriginal *practices* in the areas of citizenship and rights, see Attwood and Markus (1998).
6. Crucial moments in the Australian land rights struggle in the 1960s were the Yirrkala people's 1963 petition, on bark, to Parliament about the excision of their territory by a bauxite mining company, and the Gurindji labour protest and land claim (in 1966).

6. Multi-Culturalisms

1. California attracts, approximately, one-third of legal immigrants, and half of illegal entries to the United States, an overwhelming majority of whom are categorised as Hispanic or Asian, with Los Angeles their main centre of settlement.

2. There is a plethora of literature on Meech and Charlottetown. Russell (1992) and Webber (1994) are good overviews.
3. The regional question was also tackled through wide-ranging proposals for Senate reform, including the formula for representation, the defining powers of provincial and federal authority and economic union. See Webber (1994), especially chapter 5.
4. This report was reinforced by the damning findings of the Royal Commission into Aboriginal Deaths in Custody (1987–91) that painted a sombre picture of the treatment aboriginal and Torres Islander people received in police stations and prisons.
5. For good summaries of the Sealord fisheries deal, and the major land and resource settlements with Tainui (in 1995) and Ngai Tahu (in 1996), see Durie (1998).

7. Nationalisms

1. The 1961 census showed 30 per cent of the total Canadian population claimed French origins; by 1991 this figure had dropped to 23 per cent. But the proportion of French persons residing in Quebec province (80 per cent) remain unchanged over this period (Breton 1998: 73).
2. In the referendum 49.4 per cent voted Yes and 50.6 per cent voted No. Francophones voted 60–40 for Yes, while Anglophones and Allophones voted 90–10 No (Keating 1997: 175).
3. In 1999 the Canadian Supreme Court ruled that subsequent referenda must be more clearly worded, and the level of majority required for a firm resolution could be reconsidered. They did not venture to suggest norms for either eventuality.
4. In 1996 the Nisga'a negotiated agreement in principle with federal and provincial governments to assume a greater level of self-government in the future if they so wished.
5. Other key political recommendations included renewed claims for treaty making, calls for a new Royal Proclamation and for Parliament to remove the 'doctrine of discovery' as the basis for settlement. An enhanced land base, educational reforms and economic development were seen as essential requirements for assuming national powers.
6. In July 1990, a conflict in a village west of Montreal, ostensibly over the encroachment of a golf course onto Mohawk land, spiralled into a months-long armed stand-off between Mohawk 'warriors' and their sympathisers, and Quebec and federal forces, see Fleras and Elliott (1992: 92–9).
7. For example, ATSIC administers the Community Development Employment Projects scheme (dating back to 1977), a kind of 'workfare' programme in which aboriginal persons forgo individual welfare payments and work for local community organisations which are funded mainly through lump sums equivalent to these welfare entitlements.
8. Approximately 80 per cent were urban-based in the 1996 census. Twenty-eight per cent of Maori did not claim a tribal affiliation at this time.
9. A key factor in the referendum was the stipulation, inserted by the pro-monarchist, Australian Premier, John Howard, that if Australians voted for

a republic their President would be chosen by politicians. Given the choice of a popular presidential voting system the republicans would probably have won the day.

8. Beyond Nations and States?

1. In 1998, for example, over half (55 per cent) of the 174 000 migrants entering Canada were business migrants, 29 per cent were relatives of existing citizens, and 13 per cent were refugees.
2. See Labelle and Midy (1999) for Canadian examples, and Sudo and Yoshida (1997) for Oceania.
3. Which is not to say that the United States had 'thick' notions of citizenship either. As Joppke (1999: 632), points out: 'in a society cherishing markets over the state and the open border over bounded community, entry and residence have always been more meaningful than citizenship'. The key distinction between the USA and our case studies, however, is the early republican rejection of British subjecthood in America. The formation of a separate state with its own citizenship made this concept far more central as a status of belonging in the US than Canada or Australasia.
4. For local overviews of this convergent history, see Davidson (1997), Kaplan (1993) and McKinnon (1996).
5. In November 1999, the second election under MMP, a new leftist coalition government was elected, led by the Labour leader, Helen Clark. Labour regained all the Maori seats from New Zealand First. Despite some loss of representation in the new Executive, the combined Maori parliamentary presence (15 per cent) continued to match their total New Zealand population base.
6. For example, see discussion in Kymlicka (1995) about the difficult interface between collective conceptions of Canadian First Nation self-government and individual Charter rights, particularly in relation to women's rights.

Bibliography

Akenson, D. H. (1993) *The Irish Diaspora* (Toronto: P. D. Meany).
Akenson, D. H. (1995) 'The Historiography of English-Speaking Canada and the Concept of Diaspora: a Skeptical Appreciation', *The Canadian Historical Review* 76(3): 377–409.
Alomes, S. (1988) *A Nation At Last?* (North Ryde, NSW: Angus & Robertson).
Altman, J. C. and J. Nieuwenhuysen (1979) *The Economic Status of Australian Aborigines* (Cambridge: Cambridge University Press).
Anderson, B. (1984) *Imagined Communities: Reflections on the Origin and Spread of Nationalism* (London: Verso).
Anthias, F. (1998) 'Evaluating "Diaspora": Beyond Ethnicity', *Sociology* 32(3): 557–80.
Appleyard, R. T. (1988) 'Post-war British Immigration' in J. Jupp (ed.) *The Australian People* (North Ryde, NSW: Angus & Robertson).
Armitage, A. (1995) *Comparing the Policy of Aboriginal Assimilation* (Vancouver: UBC Press).
Attwood, B. and A. Markus (1998) 'Representation Matters: the 1967 Referendum and Citizenship' in N. Peterson and W. Sanders (eds) *Citizenship and Indigenous Australians* (Cambridge: Cambridge University Press).
Ayres, J. M. (1995) 'National No More: Defining English Canada', *The American Review of Canadian Studies* Summer and Autumn: 181–201.
Bacchi, C. L. (1983) *Liberation Deferred? The Ideas of the English-Canadian Suffragists, 1877–1918* (Toronto: University of Toronto Press).
Bach, R. L. (1992) 'Settlement Policies in the United States' in G. P. Freeman and J. Jupp (eds) *Nations of Immigrants* (Melbourne: Oxford University Press).
Ballara, A. (1998) *Iwi* (Wellington: Victoria University Press).
Barkin, J. S. and B. Cronin (1994) 'The State and the Nation: Changing Norms and the Rules of Sovereignty in International Relations', *International Organization* 48(1): 107–30.
Basch, L., N. Glick Schiller, et al. (1994) *Nations Unbound: Transnational Projects, Postcolonial Predicaments and Deterritorialized Nation-State* (Amsterdam: Gordon and Breach Science Publishers).
Beckett, J. (l988) 'Aboriginality, Citizenship and the Nation-state', *Social Analysis* 1(4): 3–18.
Beckett, J. (1989) 'Aboriginality in a Nation-state: the Australian Case' in M. C. Howard (ed.) *Ethnicity and Nation-Building in the Pacific* (Tokyo: United Nations University).
Beckett, J. (n.d.) 'Indigenous Minorities and the Welfare State: an Australian Case', unpublished paper: 1–16.
Behdad, A. (1997) 'Nationalism and Immigration to the United States', *Diaspora* 6(2): 155–78.
Belich, J. (1996) *Making Peoples* (Auckland: Penguin).
Billig, M. (1995) *Banal Nationalism* (London: Sage).
Binzeggar, A. (1980) *New Zealand's Policy on Refugees* (Wellington: New Zealand Institute of International Affairs).

BIR (Bureau of Immigration Research) (1990) *Australia's Population Trends and Prospects, 1989* (Canberra: Australian Government Printing Service (AGPS)).
Blainey, G. (l984) *All For Australia* (Sydney: Methuen Haynes).
Boehmer, E. (1995) *Colonial & Postcolonial Literature* (Oxford: Oxford University Press).
Boldt, M. (1993) *Surviving As Indians* (Toronto: University of Toronto Press).
Bordewich, F. M. (1996) *Killing the White Man's Indian* (New York: Anchor Books Doubleday).
Boreham, P. et al. (1989) 'Semi-peripheries or Particular Pathways: the Case of Australia, New Zealand and Canada as Class Formations', *International Sociology* 4(1): 67–90.
Borjas, G. J. (1990) *Friends or Strangers: the Impact of Immigration on the US Economy* (New York: Basic Books).
Brawley, S. (1993) 'No "White Policy" in NZ: Fact and Fiction in New Zealand's Asian Immigration Record, 1946–78', *New Zealand Journal of History* 27(1): 16–36.
Breton, R. (1984) 'The Production and Allocation of Symbolic Resources: an Analysis of the Linguistic and Ethnocultural Fields in Canada', *Canadian Review of Sociology and Anthropology* 21: 123–44.
Breton, R. (1988) 'The Evolution of the Canadian Multicultural Society: the Significance of Government Intervention' in A. J. Fry and C. Forceville (eds) *Canadian Mosaic Essays on Multiculturalism* (Amsterdam: Free University Press).
Breton, R. (1998) 'Ethnicity and Race in Social Organizations: Recent Developments in Canadian Society' in R. Helmes-Hay and J. Curtis (eds) *The Vertical Mosaic Revisited* (Toronto: Toronto University Press).
Broome, R. (1982) *Aboriginal Australians* (North Sydney, NSW: Allen & Unwin).
Brubaker, R. (1992) *Citizenship and Nationhood in France and Germany* (Cambridge, Mass.: Harvard University Press).
Brubaker, R. (1998) 'Myths and Misconceptions in the Study of Nationalism' in J. A. Hall (ed.) *The State of the Nation* (Cambridge: Cambridge University Press).
Buckley, H. (1992) *From Wooden Ploughs To Welfare* (Montreal & Kingston: McGill-Queen's University Press).
Buckner, P. A. (1997) 'Making British North America British, 1815–1860' in C. C. Eldridge (ed.) *Kith and Kin* (Cardiff: University of Wales Press).
Burke, H. K. (l986) *Review of Immigration Policy 1986 Appendices to the Journal of the House of Representative* (Wellington: Government Printer).
CAAIP (Committee to Advise on Australia's Immigration Policies) (1988) *Immigration: A Commitment to Australia* (Canberra: AGPS).
Cairns, A. C. (l992) *Charter versus Federalism: The Dilemmas of Constitutional Reform* (Montreal & Kingston: McGill-Queens' University Press).
Cairns, A. C. (1995) 'Aboriginal Canadians, Citizenship, and the Constitution' in D. E. Williams (ed.) *Reconfigurations: Canadian Citizenship and Constitutional Changes* (Toronto: McClelland & Stewart).
Calhoun, C. (1997) *Nationalism* (Buckingham: Open University Press).
Cassidy, F. (1994) 'Troubled hearts: Indigenous peoples and the Crown in Canada', *Pacific Viewpoint* 35(2): 173–192.
Castles, S. (l992) 'Australian multiculturalism: Social Policy and Identity in a Changing Society', in G. Freeman and J. Jupp (eds) *Nations Of Immigrants* (Melbourne: Oxford University Press).

Castles, S. (1997) 'Multicultural Citizenship: a Response to the Dilemma of Globalisation and National Identity', *Journal of Intercultural Studies* 18(1): 5–22.
Castles, S. (1999) 'Citizenship and the Other in the Age of Migration' in A. Davidson and K. Weekley (eds) *Globalization and Citizenship in the Asia-Pacific* (Basingstoke: Macmillan).
Castles, S., W. Foster et al. (1998) *Immigration and Australia* (St Leonards, NSW: Allen & Unwin).
Castles, S., M. Kalantzis et al. (1988) *Mistaken Identity* (Sydney: Pluto Press).
Castles, S. and M. Miller (1993) *The Age of Migration* (Basingstoke: Macmillan).
Champagne, D. (1989) *American Indian Societies* (Cambridge, Mass.: Cultural Survival, Inc.).
Chesterman, J. and B. Galligan (1997) *Citizens Without Rights* (Melbourne: Cambridge University Press).
Choy, P. P., L. Dong et al. (1995) *Coming Man: Nineteenth Century Perceptions of the Chinese* (Seattle: University of Washington Press).
Coates, K. S. (1998) 'International Perspectives on Relations with Indigenous Peoples' in K. S. Coates and P. G. McHugh (eds) *Living Relationships* (Wellington: Victoria University Press).
Coates, K. S. (1999) 'The "Gentle Occupation": the Settlement of Canada and the Dispossession of the First Nations' in P. Havemann (ed.) *New Frontiers* (Auckland: Oxford University Press).
Cohen, R. (1994) *Frontiers of Identity* (London: Longman).
Cohen, R. (1997) *Global Diasporas* (London: UCL Press).
Cole, D. (1971) 'The Problem of "Nationalism" and "Imperialism" in British Settlement Colonies', *Journal of British Studies* 10(2): 160–82.
Collins, J. (1984) 'Immigration and Class: the Australian Experience' in G. Bottomley and M. de Lepervanche (eds) *Ethnicity, Class and Gender in Australia* (Sydney: Allen and Unwin).
Collins, J. (1988) *Migrant Hands in a Distant Land* (Sydney: Pluto Press).
Colom-González, F. (1996) 'Dimensions of Citizenship: Canada in Comparative Perspective', *International Journal of Canadian Studies* 14 (Fall): 95–110.
Cornell, S. (1988a) *The Return of the Native* (New York: Oxford University Press).
Cornell, S. (1988b) 'The Transformation of Tribe: Organization and Self-Concept in Native American Ethnicities', *Ethnic and Racial Studies* 11(1): 27–47.
Cornell, S. (1996) 'The Variable Ties that Bind: Content and Circumstance in Ethnic Processes', *Ethnic and Racial Studies* 19(2): 265–89.
Cornell, S. H. and D. Hartmann (1998) *Ethnicity and Race Making Identities in a Changing World* (Thousand Oaks, Calif.: Pine Forge Press).
Crone, P. (1986) 'The Tribe and the State' in J. Hall (ed.) *States in History* (Oxford: Basil Blackwell).
Davidson, A. (1997) *From Subject to Citizen* (Melbourne: Cambridge University Press).
Day, D. (1996) *Claiming a Continent* (Sydney: Angus & Robertson).
Deloria, V. J. (1998) *The Nations Within* (Austin: University of Texas Press).
Demetriou, M. (1999) 'Beyond the Nation-state? Transnational Politics in the Age of Diaspora', *The ASEAN Bulletin* 16 (Winter): 17–25.
Denoon, D. (1983) *Settler Capitalism: the Dynamics of Dependent Development in the Southern Hemisphere* (Oxford: Oxford University/Clarendon Press).
Diamond, J. (1998) *Guns, Germs and Steel* (London: Vintage).

Dickinson, H. and T. Wotherspoon (1992) 'From Assimilation to Self-government: Towards a Political Economy of Canada's Aboriginal Policies' in V. Satzewich (ed.) *Deconstructing a Nation: Immigration, Multiculturalism & Racism in '90s Canada* (Halifax: Fernwood).

Dinnerstein, L., R. L. Nichols et al. (1996) *Natives and Strangers* (New York: Oxford University Press).

Dirlik, A. (1998) 'The Asia-Pacific Idea: Reality and Representation in the Invention of a Regional Structure' in A. Dirlik (ed.) *What Is In A Rim?* (Lanham: Rowman & Littlefield).

Dittgen, H. (1997) 'The American Debate about Immigration in the 1990s: a New Nationalism After the End of the Cold War?', *Stanford Humanities Review* 5(2): 256–86.

Durie, M. (1998) *Te Mana Te Kawanatanga: the Politics of Maori Self-Determination* (Auckland: Oxford University Press).

Dyck, N. (1992) *What is the Indian Problem?* (St Johns, Newfoundland: ISER Books).

Eddy, J. and D. Schreuder (eds) (1988) *The Rise of Colonial Nationalism* (Sydney: Allen & Unwin).

Elliott, J. L. and A. Fleras (1990) 'Immigration and the Canadian Ethnic Mosaic' in P. Li (ed.) *Race and Ethnic Relations in Canada* (Toronto: Oxford University Press).

Esman, M. (1994) *Ethnic Politics* (Ithaca: Cornell University Press).

Farmer, R. (1986) 'International Migration and New Zealand Labour Markets', *International Migration* 24(2): 485–500.

Favell, A. (1998a) *Philosophies of Integration* (Basingstoke: Macmillan).

Favell, A. (1998b) 'Introduction', *Journal of Ethnic and Migration Studies* 24(4): 605–11.

Fincher, R., L. Foster et al. (1994) 'Gender and Migration Policy' in H. Adelman, A. Borowski et al. (eds) *Immigration and Refugee Policy 1* (Melbourne: Melbourne University Press).

Fleras, A. (1998) 'Working Through Differences: the Politics of "isms" in Aotearoa', *New Zealand Sociology* 13(1): 62–96.

Fleras, A. and J. L. Elliott (1992) *The Nations Within* (Toronto: Oxford University Press).

Foster, H. (1999) 'Canada: "Indian Administration" from the Royal Proclamation of 1763 to Constitutionally Entrenched Aboriginal Rights' in P. Havemann (ed.) *New Frontiers* (Auckland: Oxford University Press).

Foster, L. (1998) *Turnstile Immigration* (Don Mills, Ont: Thompson Educational).

Francis, D. (1997) *National Dreams: Myth, Memory and Canadian History* (Vancouver: Arsenal Pulp Press).

Freeman, G. P. (1998) 'The Decline of Sovereignty? Politics and Immigration Restriction in Liberal States' in C. Joppke (ed.) *Challenge to the Nation-State* (Oxford: Oxford University Press).

Freeman, G. P. and J. Jupp (eds) (1992) *Nations of Immigrants* (Melbourne: Oxford University Press).

Fried, M. (1975) *The Notion of Tribe* (Menlo Park: Cummings).

Fryer, P. (1984) *Staying Power: the History of Black People in Britain* (London: Pluto Press).

Gellner, E. (1983) *Nations and Nationalism* (Oxford, Blackwell).

Gibbins, R. and J. R. Ponting (1989) 'Historical Overview and Background' in J. R. Ponting (ed.) *Arduous Journey: Canadian Indians and Decolonization* (Toronto: McClelland & Stewart).
Gibbons, P. J. (1981) 'The Climate of Opinion' in W. H. Oliver (ed.) *The Oxford History of New Zealand* (Wellington: Oxford University Press).
Giddens, A. (1985) *The Nation-State and Violence* (Cambridge: Polity Press).
Glazer, N. (1997) *We Are All Multiculturalists Now* (Ithaca, NY: Cornell University Press).
Grant, G. (1983) *The Concrete Reserve: Corporate Programs for Indians in the Urban Work Place* (Montreal: Institute for Research on Public Policy).
Gray, G. (1998) 'From Nomadism to Citizenship: A. P. Elkin and Aboriginal Advancement' in N. Peterson and W. Sanders (eds) *Citizenship and Indigenous Australians* (Cambridge: Cambridge University Press).
Green, A. G. (1994) 'A Comparison of Canadian and US Immigration Policy in the Twentieth Century' in D. DeVoretz (ed.) *Diminishing Returns* (Toronto: C. D. Howe Institute/The Laurier Institution).
Hage, G. (1998) *White Nation* (Annandale, NSW: Pluto Press).
Hall, J. A. and C. Lindholm (1999) *Is America Breaking Apart?* (Princeton, NJ: Princeton University Press).
Harney, R. F. (1988) 'So Great a Heritage as Ours: Immigration and the Survival of the Canadian Polity', *Daedalus* 117(4): 51–97.
Hartz, L. (1964) *The Founding of New Societies; in the History of the United States, Latin America, South Africa, Canada and Australia* (New York: Harcourt, Brace & World).
Haseler, S. (1996) *The English Tribe* (London: Macmillan).
Hastings, A. (1997) *The Construction of Nationhood* (Cambridge: Cambridge University Press).
Havemann, P. (1999) 'Indigenous Peoples, the State and the Challenge of Differentiated Citizenship' in P. Havemann (ed.) *Indigenous Peoples' Rights in Australia, Canada & New Zealand* (Oxford: Oxford University Press).
Hawkins, F. (1972) *Canada and Immigration: Public Policy and Public Concern* (Montreal: McGill-Queen's University Press).
Hawkins, F. (1989) *Critical Years in Immigration: Canada and Australia Compared* (Kensington, NSW: New South Wales University Press).
Held, D. (1999) 'The Transformation of Political Community: Rethinking Democracy in the Context of Globalization' in I. Shapiro and C. Hacker-Gordon (eds) *Democracy's Edges* (Cambridge: Cambridge University Press).
Heller, T. C. (1997) 'Modernity, Membership and Multiculturalism', *Stanford Humanities Review* 5(2): 2–69.
Hesse, B. (1997) 'It's Your World: Discrepant M/multiculturalisms', *Social Identities* 3(3): 375–94.
Higham, J. (1998) 'Multiculturalism and Universalism: a History and Critique' in M. W. Hughey (ed.) *New Tribalisms: the Resurgence of Race and Ethnicity* (New York: New York University Press).
Hjerm, M. (1998) 'Multiculturalism Reassessed', unpublished paper presented to 1998 Meeting of International Sociology Association, Montreal, Canada.
Holton, R. J. (1998) *Globalization and the Nation-State* (Basingstoke: Macmillan).
Hoogvelt, A. (1997) *Globalisation and the Postcolonial World* (Basingstoke: Macmillan).

HREOC (Human Rights and Equal Opportunity Commission) (1991) *Racist Violence: Report of the National Inquiry into Racist Violence in Australia* (Canberra: AGPS).
Hunn, J. K. (1960) *Report on Department of Maori Affairs* (Wellington: Government Printer).
Huntingdon, S. (1996) *The Clash of Civilizations and the Remaking of World Order* (New York: Simon & Schuster).
Hutchinson, J. (1994) *Modern Nationalism* (London: Fontana).
Hutchinson, J. and A. D. Smith (eds) (1996) *Ethnicity* (Oxford: Oxford University Press).
Inglis, C., A. Birch et al. (1994) 'An Overview of Australian and Canadian Migration Patterns and Policies' in H. Adelman and A. Borowski et al. (eds) *Immigration and Refugee Policy: Australia and Canada Compared* (Melbourne: Melbourne University Press).
Inglis, K. S. (1996) 'Australia' in P. J. Marshall (ed.) *British Empire* (Cambridge: Cambridge University Press).
Irving, A. (1997) *To Constitute a Nation* (Cambridge: Cambridge University Press).
James, P. (1996) *Nation Formation* (London: Sage).
Jenson, J. (1993) 'Naming Nations: Making Nationalist Claims in Canadian Public Discourse', *Canadian Review of Sociology & Anthropology* 30(3): 336–58.
Joppke, C. (1995) *Multiculturalism and Immigration: a Comparison of the United States, Germany and Britain* (Florence: European University Institute).
Joppke, C. (1998) 'Immigration Challenges the Nation-state' in C. Joppke (ed.) *Challenge to the Nation-State* (Oxford: Oxford University Press).
Joppke, C. (1999) 'How Immigration is Changing Citizenship: a Comparative View', *Ethnic and Racial Studies* 22(4): 629–52.
Jupp, J. (1991) *Immigration* (Sydney: Sydney University Press).
Jupp, J. (1992) 'Immigrant Settlement Policy in Australia' in G. P. Freeman and J. Jupp (eds) *Nations of Immigrants* (Oxford: Oxford University Press).
Jupp, J. (1997) 'Tacking into the Wind: Immigration and Multicultural Policy in the 1990s', *Journal of Australian Studies* 53: 29–39.
Juteau, D. (1992) 'The Sociology of Ethno-national Relations in Quebec' in V. Satzewich (ed.) *Deconstructing a Nation: Immigration, Multiculturalism and Racism in the '90s* (Halifax: Fernwood).
Kaplan, W. (ed.) (1993) *Belonging: the Meaning and Future of Canadian Citizenship* (Montreal: McGill-Queen's University Press).
Kaufmann, E. (1997) 'Condemned to Rootlessness: the Loyalist Origins of Canada's Identity Crisis', *Nationalism & Ethnic Politics* 3(1): 110–36.
Kearney, H. (1991) 'Four Nations or One?' in B. Crick (ed.) *National Identities: the Constitution of the United Kingdom* (Oxford: Blackwell).
Keating, M. (1996) *Nations Against the State* (Basingstoke: Macmillan).
Keating, M. (1997) 'Canada and Quebec: Two Nationalisms in the Global Age' in M. Guiberneau and J. Rex (eds) *The Ethnicity Reader* (Cambridge: Polity Press).
Kelsey, J. (1990) *A Question of Honour? Labour and the Treaty* (Wellington: Allen & Unwin).
Kelsey, J. (l993) *Rolling Back the State* (Wellington: Bridget Williams Books).
Kelsey, J. (1999) *New Zealand and the Global Economy: Reclaiming the Future* (Wellington: Bridget Williams Books).
Kibria, N. (1998) 'The Contested Meanings of "Asian American": Racial Dilemmas in the Contemporary US', *Ethnic and Racial Studies* 21(5): 939–58.

Knowles, V. (1992) *Strangers at Our Gates* (Toronto: Dundurn Press).
Kymlicka, W. (1995) *Multicultural Citizenship* (Oxford: Clarendon Press).
Kymlicka, W. (1998) *Finding Our Way: Rethinking Ethnocultural Relations in Canada* (Don Mills, Ontario: Oxford University Press).
Labelle, M. and F. Midy (1999) 'Re-reading Citizenship and the Transnational Practices of Immigrants', *Journal of Ethnic and Migration Studies* 25(2): 213–32.
Lake, M. (1992) 'Mission Impossible: How Men Gave Birth to the Australian Nation', *Gender and History* 4(3): 377–86.
Langer, B. (1998) 'Globalisation and the Myth of Ethnic Community: Salvadoran Refugees in Multicultural States' in D. Bennett (ed.) *Multicultural States* (London: Routledge).
Layton-Henry, Z. (1994) 'The Would-be Zero-immigration Country' in W. Cornelius et al. (eds) *Controlling Immigration* (Stanford: Stanford University Press).
Lever-Tracy, C., D. Ip and N. Tracey (1996) *The Chinese Business Diaspora and Mainland China* (Basingstoke: Macmillan).
Levine, H. B. (1997) *Constructing Collective Identity* (Frankfurt am Main: Peter Lang).
Lind, M. (1995) *The Next American Nation* (New York: Free Press).
Lipset, S. M. (1963) *The First New Nation: the United States in Historical and Comparative Perspective* (New York: Basic Books).
Lopez, D. and Y. Espiritu (1990) 'Panethnicity in the United States: a Theoretical Framework', *Ethnic and Racial Studies* 13: 198–224.
Maaka, R. C. A. (1994) 'The New Tribe: Conflicts and Continuities in the Social Organisation of Urban Maori', *The Contemporary Pacific* 6(2): 311–36.
Magallanes, C. J. I. (1999) 'International Human Rights and their Impact on Domestic Law on Indigenous Peoples' Rights in Australia, Canada and New Zealand' in P. Havemann (ed.) *Indigenous Peoples' Rights in Australia, Canada & New Zealand* (Oxford: Oxford University Press).
Mann, M. (1984) 'The Autonomous Power of the State: its Origins, Mechanisms and Results', *European Journal of Sociology* 25: 185–213.
Markus, A. (1979) *Fear & Hatred* (Sydney: Hale & Iremonger).
Markus, A. (1994) *Australian Race Relations 1788–1993* (St. Leonards, NSW: Allen & Unwin).
McCrone, D. (1998) *The Sociology of Nationalism* (London: Routledge).
McHugh, P. G. (1998) 'Aboriginal Identity and Relations in North America and Australasia' in K. S. Coates and P. G. McHugh (eds) *Living Relationships* (Wellington: Victoria University Press).
McKinnon, M. (1996) *Immigrants and Citizens: New Zealanders and Asian Immigration in Historical Context* (Wellington: Institute of Policy Studies, Victoria University of Wellington).
McRoberts, K. (1984) 'The Sources of Neo-nationalism in Quebec', *Ethnic and Racial Studies* 7(1): 55–85.
Miles, R. (1993) *Racism After 'Race Relations'* (London: Routledge).
Miller, J. R. (1991) *Skyscrapers Hide the Heavens* (Toronto: University of Toronto Press).
Miller, J. R. (1996) *ShingWauk's Vision: a History of Native Residential Schools* (Toronto: University of Toronto Press).
Moran, A. (1998) 'Aboriginal Reconciliation: Transformations in Settler Nationalism', *Melbourne Journal of Politics* 25: 101–32.

Morris, P. (1996) 'Community Beyond Tradition' in P. Heelas, S. Lash and P. Morris (eds) *Detraditionalization Critical Reflections on Authority and Identity* (Oxford: Blackwell).
Nagel, J. (1997) *American Indian Ethnic Revival* (New York: Oxford University Press).
Nagel, J. (1998a) 'Ethnic Nationalism: Politics, Ideology, and the World Order' in M. W. Hughey (ed.) *New Tribalisms: the Resurgence of Race and Ethnicity* (New York: New York University Press).
Nagel, J. (1998b) 'Constructing Ethnicity: Creating and Recreating Ethnic Identity and Culture' in M. W. Hughey (ed.) *New Tribalisms: the Resurgence of Race and Ethnicity* (New York: New York University Press).
Nairn, T. (1981) *The Break-Up of Britain: Crisis and Neo-Nationalism*, 1st edition 1977 (London: New Left Books).
Nettheim, G. (1998) 'The International Law Context' in N. Peterson and W. Sanders (eds) *Citizenship and Indigenous Australians* (Cambridge: Cambridge University Press).
NMAC (National Multicultural Advisory Council) (1995) *Multicultural Australia: the Next Steps Towards and Beyond 2000* (Canberra: AGPS).
Norris, M. J. (1990) 'The Demography of Aboriginal People in Canada' in S. Halli, F. Trovato and L. Driedger (eds) *Ethnic Demography* (Ottawa: Carleton University Press).
Oliver, M. (1993) 'The Impact of the Royal Commission on Bilingualism and Biculturalism on Constitutional Thought and Practice in Canada', *International Journal of Canadian Studies* 7–8 (Spring–Fall): 315–32.
OMA (Office of Multicultural Affairs) (1989) *The National Agenda for a Multicultural Australia* (Canberra: AGPS).
Ong, A. (1993) 'On the Edge of Empires: Flexible Citizenship Among Chinese in Diaspora', *Positions* 1(3): 745–78.
Ongley, P. and D. Pearson (1995) 'Post-1945 International Migration: New Zealand, Australia and Canada Compared', *International Migration Review* 29(3): 765–93.
Oommen, T. K. (1997) *Citizenship, Nationality and Ethnicity* (Cambridge: Polity Press).
Paine, R. (1977) 'The Path to Welfare Colonialism' in R. Paine (ed.) *The White Arctic: Anthropological Essays on Tutelage and Ethnicity* (St. John's, Newfoundland: Memorial University).
Paine, R. (1984) 'Norwegians and Saami: Nation-state and Fourth World' in G. Gold (ed.) *Minorities and Mother Country* (St. Johns, Newfoundland: ISER Books).
Passaris, C. E. A. (1984) 'The Economic Determinants of Canada's Multicultural Immigration', *International Migration* 22(2): 90–100.
Paul, K. (1997) *Whitewashing Britain: Race and Citizenship in the Postwar Era* (Ithaca: Cornell University Press).
Pearson, D. (1990) *A Dream Deferred: the Origins of Ethnic Conflict in New Zealand* (Wellington: Allen and Unwin/Port Nicholson Press).
Pearson, D. (1991) 'Biculturalism and Multiculturalism in Comparative Perspective' in P. Spoonley et al. (eds) *Nga Take Ethnic Relations and Racism in Aotearoa/New Zealand* (Palmerston North: Dunmore Press).
Pearson, D. (1994) *Canada Compared: Multiculturalism and Biculturalism in Settler Societies* (St. John's, Newfoundland, ISER).

Perry, R. J. (1996) ... *From Time Immemorial* (Austin: University of Texas Press).
Peterson, N. (1998) 'Welfare Colonialism and Citizenship: Politics, Economics and Agency' in N. Peterson and W. Sanders (eds) *Citizenship and Indigenous Australians* (Cambridge: Cambridge University Press).
Pettman, J. (l992) *Living in the Margins* (Sydney: Allen & Unwin).
Pettman, J. (1995) 'Race, Ethnicity and Gender in Australia' in D. Stasiulis and N. Yuval-Davis (eds) *Unsettling Settler Societies* (London: Sage).
Phillips, J. (1998) 'Exhibiting Ourselves: the Exhibition and National Identity' in J. B. Thompson (ed.) *Farewell Colonialism* (Palmerston North: Dunmore Press).
Ponting, J. R. and J. Kiely (1997) 'Disempowerment: "Justice", Racism, and Public Opinion' in J. R. Ponting (ed.) *First Nations in Canada: Perspectives on Opportunity, Empowerment, and Self-Determination* (Toronto: McGraw-Hill Ryerson).
Povinelli, E. (1998) 'The State of Shame: Australian Multiculturalism and the Crisis of Indigenous Citizenship', *Critical Inquiry* 24 (November): 575–610.
Price, C. A. (1974) *The Great White Walls are Built: Restrictive Immigration to North America and Australia, 1836–1888* (Canberra: Australia National University Press).
Price, C. A. (1991) 'Environment, Aborigines, Nationalism, Ethnic Origins and Intermixture' in C. A. Price (ed.) *Australian National Identity* (Canberra: The Academy of the Social Sciences in Australia).
Pryor, E. T. et al. (1992) 'Measuring Ethnicity: is "Canadian" an Evolving Indigenous Category?' *Ethnic and Racial Studies* 15(2): 14–35.
Rata, E. M. (1996) 'Global Capitalism and the Revival of Ethnic Traditionalism in New Zealand' (University of Auckland, PhD thesis).
Reitz, J. G. (1988) 'The Institutional Structure of Immigration as a Determinant of Inter-racial Competition: a Comparison of Britain and Canada', *International Migration Review* 22(1): 117–46.
Reynolds, H. (1996) *Aboriginal Sovereignty* (St. Leonards, NSW: Allen & Unwin).
Richmond, A. (1994) *Global Apartheid: Refugees, Racism and the New World Order* (Toronto: Oxford University Press).
Ringer, B. B. and E. R. Lawless (1989) *Race-Ethnicity and Society* (London: Routledge).
Rowse, T. (1994) 'Putting Regions on the Agenda of Indigenous Australian Self-determination', *Pacific Viewpoint* 35(2): 143–72.
Russell, P. H. (1992) *Constitutional Odyssey: Can Canadians Become a Sovereign People?* (Toronto: University of Toronto Press).
Russell, P. H. (l993) 'Attempting Macro Constitutional Change in Australia and Canada: the Politics of Frustration', *International Journal of Canadian Studies* 7–8 (Spring-Fall): 41–62.
Salmond, A. (1997) *Between Worlds* (Honolulu: University of Hawaii Press).
Sassen, S. (1999) *Guests and Aliens* (New York: The New Press).
Satzewich, V. (1990) 'Rethinking Post-1945 Migration to Canada: Towards a Political Economy of Labour Migration', *International Migration* 28(3): 327–46.
Satzewich, V. and Wotherspoon, T. (1993) *First Nations: Race, Class and Gender Relations* (Toronto: Nelson).
Scarman, (Lord) L. (1981) *The Brixton Disorders 10–12 April 1981: Report of an Enquiry* (London: HMSO).
Schlesinger, A. J. (1992) *The Disuniting of America Reflections on a Multicultural Society* (New York: Norton).

See, K. O'Sullivan (1980) 'The Social Origins of Ethnic-National Identities in Ireland and Canada' in J. Dofney and A. Akiwowo (eds) *National and Ethnic Movements* (Beverly Hills: Sage).
See, K. O'Sullivan (1986) *First World Nationalisms* (Chicago: Chicago University Press).
Sharp, A. (1997) 'The Waitangi Tribunal 1984–1996' in R. Miller (ed.) *New Zealand Politics in Transition* (Oxford: Oxford University Press).
Sigurdson, R. (1996) 'First Peoples, New Peoples and Citizenship in Canada', *International Journal of Canadian Studies* 14 (Autumn): 53–76.
Sinclair, K. (1986) *A Destiny Apart* (Auckland: Allen and Unwin).
Sinclair, K. (1988) 'Why New Zealanders are not Australians: New Zealand and the Australian Federation Movement 1881–1901' in K. Sinclair (ed.) *Tasman Relations: New Zealand and Australia, 1788–1988* (Auckland: Auckland University Press).
Smith, A. D. (1986) *The Ethnic Origins of Nations* (Oxford: Basil Blackwell).
Smith, A. D. (1989) 'The Origins of Nations', *Ethnic and Racial Studies* 12(3): 340–67.
Smith, A. D. (1991) *National Identity* (London: Penguin).
Smith, A. D. (1995) *Nations and Nationalism in a Global Era* (Cambridge: Polity Press).
Sorrenson, M. P. K. (1979) *Maori Origins and Migrations* (Auckland: Auckland University Press/Oxford University Press).
Sorrenson, M. P. K. (1981) 'Maori and Pakeha' in W. H. Oliver (ed.) *The Oxford History of New Zealand* (Wellington: Clarendon/Oxford University Press).
Soysal, Y. N. (1994) *Limits of Citizenship* (Chicago: Chicago University Press).
Spencer, S. (1994) 'The Implications of Immigration Policy for Race Relations' in S. Spencer (ed.) *Strangers and Citizens* (London: IPPR/Oram Press).
Spillman, L. (1997) *Nation and Commemoration* (Cambridge: Cambridge University Press).
Stasiulis, D. and R. Jhappan (1995) 'The Fractious Politics of a Settler Society: Canada' in D. Stasiulis and N. Yuval-Davis (eds) *Unsettling Settler Societies* (London: Sage).
Stasiulis, D. and N. Yuval-Davis (eds) (1995) *Unsettling Settler Societies* (London: Sage).
Statham, P. (1999) 'Political Mobilisation by Minorities in Britain: Negative Feedback of "Race Relations"?', *Journal of Ethnic and Migration Studies* 25(4): 597–626.
Sturgis, J. (1997) 'Learning About Oneself: the Making of Canadian Nationalism, 1867–1914' in C. C. Eldridge (ed.) *Kith and Kin* (Cardiff: University of Wales Press).
Sudo, K. and S. Yoshida (eds) (1997) *Contemporary Migration in Oceania: Diaspora and Network* (Osaka: National Museum of Ethnology).
Tarrow, S. (1995) *Power in Movement* (Cambridge: Cambridge University Press).
Tarver, H. (1992) 'The Creation of American National Identity: 1774–1796', *Berkeley Journal of Sociology* 37: 55–99.
Trainor, T. (1994) *British Imperialism and Australian Nationalism* (Melbourne: Cambridge University Press).
Trlin, A. D. (1979) *Now Respected, Once Despised* (Palmerston North: Dunmore Press).
Turner, B. (1986) *Citizenship and Capitalism: the Debate over Reformism* (London: Allen and Unwin).

Turner, D. H. (1980) *Australian Aboriginal Social Organization* (Canberra: Humanities Press).
Van Hear, N. (1998) *New Diasporas* (London: UCL Press).
Vertovec, S. (1996) 'Multiculturalism, Culturalism and Public Incorporation', *Ethnic and Racial Studies* 19(1): 46–69.
Wade, M. (1968) *The French Canadians* (Toronto: University of Toronto Press).
Walker, R. J. (1999) 'Maori Sovereignty: Colonial and Post-colonial Discourses' in P. Havemann (ed.) *Indigenous Peoples' Rights in Australia, Canada & New Zealand* (Oxford: Oxford University Press).
Ward, A. (1973) *A Show of Justice* (Auckland: Auckland University Press).
Ward, A. and J. Hayward (1999) 'Tino Rangatiratanga: Maori in the Political and Administrative System' in P. Havemann (ed.) *New Frontiers* (Auckland: Oxford University Press).
Ward, W. P. (1978) *White Canada Forever: Popular Attitudes and Public Policy Toward Orientals in British Columbia* (Montreal: McGill-Queen's University Press).
Weaver, S. (1985) 'Political Representivity and Indigenous Minorities in Canada and Australia' in G. Gold (ed.) *Indigenous Peoples and the Nation-State* (St. John's, Newfoundland: ISER Books).
Webber, J. (1994) *Reimagining Canada* (Kingston & Montreal: McGill-Queen's University Press).
Webber, M. J. (1992) 'Settlement Characteristics of Immigrants in Australia' in G. P. Freeman and J. Jupp (eds) *Nations of Immigrants* (Oxford: Oxford University Press).
Weitzer, R. (1990) *Transforming Settler States: Communal Conflict and Internal Security in Northern Ireland and Zimbabwe* (Berkeley: University of California Press).
Werther, G. F. A. (1992) *Self-Determination in Western Democracies* (Westport, Connecticut: Greenwood Press).
White, P. M. and T. J. Samuel (1991) 'Immigration and Ethnic Diversity in Urban Canada', *International Journal of Canadian Studies* 3 (Spring): 69–85.
White, R. (1981) *Inventing Australia* (Sydney: Allen and Unwin).
Wievorka, M. (1998) 'Is Multiculturalism the Solution?' *Ethnic and Racial Studies* 21(5): 881–910.
Williams, M. (1997) 'Crippled by Geography? New Zealand Nationalisms' in S. Murray (ed.) *Not on Any Map* (Exeter: University of Exeter Press).
Wolfe, P. (1994) 'Nation and Miscegenation: Discursive Continuity in the Post-Mabo Era', *Social Analysis* 36: 93–152.

Index

Aboriginal Advancement Associations/ Leagues (Aus), 113–14
Aboriginal and Torres Strait Islander Commission (ATSIC), 117, 164, 207
aboriginal peoples
  in Australia, 13, 30–4, 40, 92–6, 113–15, 163–5
  in Canada, 25–30, 35–40, 94–5, 109–11, 139–43, 159–60, 162–3
  economies of, 26, 30, 34–5, 40
  employment of, 92–6
  evangelisation of, 26, 31, 35–6, 39
  migration of, 91–7
  in New Zealand, 34–8, 39–41, 96–7, 165–6
  and population decline, 27, 32, 38–9
  presettlement politics of, 44–6
  in United States, 25–7, 92–3, 160–2
  urbanisation of, 91–7
aboriginality
  defined, 12–14
Aborigines, Australian
  see aboriginal peoples, in Australia
Aborigines Protection Acts/Boards (Aus), 33
Africa, 2–3, 64, 72, 81, 90–1, 103, 134
  migration from, 81, 84, 90
African-Americans, 20, 131–2, 149, 182
Alberta, 94, 110
Aliens Acts (1905, 1914) (Brit), 205
America
  Thirteen Colonies, 27, 30
  see also United States
Anglophone
  see English Canadian
Antipodes
  see Australia, New Zealand
Aranda (Aus), 48
Arawa (NZ), 48
Arnhem Land, 164

Asia, 2–3, 72, 80–1, 83, 90, 98, 103, 130, 187–9
  migration from, 1, 70, 79–84, 90–1, 100, 116, 132–4
  South East, 6, 65, 88, 106, 116
  Western image of, 67, 116, 148
  see also under individual countries
Asia Pacific Economic Co-operation forum (APEC) 187–8
Asian-Americans, 20, 131–2, 182, 206
  aboriginal policies of, 28, 33, 36, 109, 113
  assimilation of, 122–5
  immigration policies of, 108, 113, 118
  political movements of, 132
Assiniboine (Can), 48
Association of Southeast Asian Nations (ASEAN), 9
asylum seekers, 13, 89–91
  see also refugees
Auckland, 1, 89
Australia (Aus)
  aboriginal policies, 33, 95, 113, 163, 206
  citizenship, 117, 144, 200
  as dominion society, 6
  immigration policies, 84–6, 112–13
  labour force, 85, 95
  migration to, 84–7
  as penal colony, 30
  settlement of, 30–2
  see also multiculturalism, nationalism
Australia and New Zealand Army Corps (ANZAC), 12, 61
Australian Labor Party (ALP), 114–15, 141, 144

Banks, Joseph, 31
Basques, 25

biculturalism
  in Canada, 109
  in New Zealand, 118–21, 145–8, 151–2, 171–2
Blainey, Geoffrey, 116
Bloc Québécois, 140
Boer War, 55, 61
Bourassa, Robert, 108
Boxer Rebellion, 60
Bracero Program (US), 79
Bretton Woods, 187
Britain
  and European Union, 183–6
  immigration policies of, 81–2, 134–5
  labour market, 81
  migration flows, 3, 71–3, 84–6, 99, 193
  race relations in, 134–7
  and regional devolution, 185
  United States, influence of, 135–7
British Colonial Office, 35
British Columbia, 65, 95, 159, 205–6
British Empire League, 61
British North America Act, 27, 59
Bureau of Indian Affairs (BIA) (US), 93, 161

California, 20, 65–6, 131, 133, 206
Canada (Can)
  aboriginal policies, 35–6, 113–15, 206
  aboriginal treaties, 27, 205–6
  citizenship, 140, 200
  constitutional experiments, 137–41, 158
  demographic change of, 167, 207
  as dominion society, 6
  English, 56–8, 167–9, 171
  French, 52–6, 157, 167
  immigration policies, 82–4, 208
  migration to, 82–4, 186
  settlement of, 25–30
  see also multiculturalism, nationalism
Caribbean, 4, 30, 52, 65, 81, 88
Catalonia, 155
Catholicism
  in Australia, 60–1
  in Canada, 52–3, 156
  see also Quebec, history
Celtic fringe, 4, 15, 20
census
  categories, 167–8
Charlottetown Agreement (Can), 138–40, 158, 207
Charter of Rights and Freedom (Can), 110, 112, 139–40, 208
Chile, 187
China, 60, 70–1, 188, 193
Chinese
  in Australia, 65–8, 193, 205
  in Canada, 65–8, 193, 205
  diaspora, 70–2, 193
  global economic links, 193
  labour, 1, 65
  migration, 1, 65–8, 70, 193
  in New Zealand, 65–8, 193
  in USA, 65–6, 193, 205
Christianity, 26, 31, 35, 39, 68
citizenship
  aboriginal, 28, 33, 36, 117, 196, 200
  American, 208
  Australian, 117, 144, 200
  British, 82, 134–5, 198
  Canadian, 140, 200
  defined, 23
  global, 195–6
  multicultural, 21, 140, 144
  New Zealand, 36, 148, 200
  in post-settler societies, 196–9
  in settler societies, 22–3, 197
  see also under individual countries
Civil Rights movement, 104–6, 130–3
Clark, Helen, 208
class, 10, 12, 22, 63, 167
  and citizenship, 22–3, 198–9, 203
  and gender, 10, 12, 22, 66, 198
  imagery, 10
  middle, 61
  and racism, 66, 123, 198
  underclass, 199, 203
  working, 23, 63
Clinton, Bill, 161
Closer Economic Relations (CER), 87, 187
Cold War, 79–80, 104, 154

colonies of settlement, 6
  see also settler colonies
colonisation, 9, 38
  British, 3–9, 26, 30–8, 56
  French, 3, 8, 26, 52
  internal, 13, 38
  limited and extensive forms of, 4–5
  Portuguese, 3
  Spanish, 3
Commission for Racial Equality (Brit), 135
Commonwealth, 81, 108
  Games, 176
Conservative Party (Brit), 134–5
Conservative Party (Can), 55
Constitution Act (1791) (Can), 53
Cook, Captain James, 31, 35
Council for Aboriginal Reconciliation (Aus), 144
Cree, 206
Cuba,
  migration to USA, 90
culture, 19–22, 116, 123, 149–52
  maintenance of, 111, 116, 149
  see also biculturalism, multiculturalism

Darwinism, Social, 33, 63, 67
Deakin, Alfred, 59
decolonisation, 21
Department of Aboriginal Affairs (Aus), 117
Department of Indian Affairs (DIA) (Can), 93, 108
Department of Maori Affairs, 97, 119, 121
diaspora
  British, 15–16, 71–3, 166–9, 193
  defined, 68–9
  dominion, 72, 166
  global, 193–4
  imperial, 15–16
  labour, 70
  trading, 70
Diefenbaker, John, 108
dominion societies
  see settler societies
Douglas, James (Governor), 205
Durham, Lord, 54

economies
  global restructuring of, 106–7, 186–7, 199
elites
  role in state making, 4, 9, 51, 122
El Salvador, 91, 194
  migration from, 70–91
  see also refugees
emigration
  see migration
empires
  British, 3, 15, 20, 60, 64, 68
  European, 3
ethnic categories, 13, 41, 124, 131, 160
ethnicisation, 17
ethnicity
  defined, 16–18, 42–3, 48
  and migration, 48
ethnie, 44
ethnification 48
ethnoregional movements, 155–9
  see also nationalism, Quebec; Scottish
European Union (EU), 155, 183–7
  citizenship, 184
  coinage, 1, 183
  migrant policies, 184

federalism, 9
  asymmetrical, 159
  Australian, 59–60
  Canadian, 55, 75
First Nations
  Canadian, 45, 140, 156, 159–60, 162–4, 200, 206, 208
  United States, 44, 49, 160–1, 206
First World, 21
First World War, 55, 61, 63–4, 75, 77, 93, 103
Fordism, 106
  post-Fordism, 106–7
Fourth World, 163, 189
France
Francophone
  see Canada, French; French Canadian
Fraser, Malcolm, 115
Free Trade Agreement (Can/US), 158
fur trade, 26

Index

Gallipoli, 61
gender
　and Chinese migration, 67
　imagery, 10
　and nationalism, 57, 61, 64
Glazer, Nathan, 19, 129
globalisation, 103
　of aboriginal politics, 188–91
　citizenship, 195–5
　international relations, 103, 122, 186–8
　migration, 191–5
goldmining, 1, 29, 65
　see also migrants, Chinese
Grassby, Al, 114
Great Chain of Being, 67
Grey, Sir George (Governor), 36
Gurindji (Aus), 206

Hanson, Pauline, 144
hapu (sub-tribe), 34–5, 45, 147
Hawke, Bob, 115
Hispanic Americans, 20, 131, 182, 206
　political movement, 131–2
Hobson, William (Captain/Governor), 35, 38
Hong Kong, 89, 93, 106, 134, 193
Howard, John, 144, 207
Hunn Report (1960) (NZ), 118

identity, 1, 10–16, 101, 123, 176, 185, 195
　aboriginal, 160–6, 189, 201
　American, 59, 74, 175, 182–3
　Australian, 10, 59–61, 75–6, 171, 173
　British, 59, 64, 71–4, 167, 175,
　Canadian, 10, 55, 75–6, 108
　English, 185–6
　English Canadian, 56–8, 75, 168–9, 171, 175
　French Canadian, 53–5, 58, 75
　hyphenated, 55, 116, 167–8, 174
　Irish, 58–60, 72
　Native American, 160–2
　New Zealand, 10, 62–4, 75–6, 120, 171, 173
　Pakeha, 171–2
　Québécois, 156–7, 177

'white', 76, 172
　see also nationalism
International Labour Organisation (ILO), 190
immigration
　see migration
imperialism, 3–4, 6–7
　see also diaspora, imperial
India, 60
Indian Act (1876) (Can), 28–9, 33
Indians
　American, 1, 13, 26, 92–3, 131, 160–1
　Canadian, 1, 13, 27–9, 94–5, 109, 162
　see also Native Americans, First Nations
indigenous peoples, 14, 124
　claims, international, 188–90
　see also aboriginal peoples
intelligentsia, 75, 120, 130, 167, 171–6
International Indian Treaty Council, 189
Inuit, 28, 111, 159, 162
　Circumpolar Conference, 189
　see also Nunavut
Ireland, 185, 192
　migration from, 60, 80–6
Israel, 79
iwi (tribe), 34–5, 45, 147–8, 165
　urban, 147–8
　see also Maori

James Bay and Northern Quebec Agreement (1975), 206
Japan, 187–8
Jenkins, Roy, 135
Jewish
　diaspora, 15
　migration, 79–81
'Jim Crow' system, 78

Keating, Paul, 142–3
King, Martin Luther, 105
Kipling, Rudyard, 76

Labour Party (Brit), 134–5
Labour Party (NZ), 62, 88, 118–20, 208

land
  dispossession, 13, 27–38, 40–1
  rights, 111, 114, 120–1, 126, 142–3, 147–8, 169, 189, 206–7
  see also reserves
language, 52–5, 71, 171
  see also rights, language
Latin America, 6, 65, 80, 90, 98, 131, 187, 189, 192
  migration from, 90, 191
law, 9, 11, 23, 53
  international, 189–90
Lawson, Henry, 59
League of Nations, 103
Lebanon
  migration from, 70, 91
Lesage, Jean, 108
Liberal Party
  Australian, 115, 144
  Canadian, 55, 109–10, 156
Loyalists, 53, 56

Mabo case, 142–3, 164
Macdonald, John A., 57
majorities
  defined, 14, 18
  identity of, 166–73, 176
  indigenisation of, 166–8, 172
  myths of origin of, 10–11, 73–4, 173, 176
  public opinion of, 121, 173, 190
  see also diaspora, dominant
Manitoba, 29, 55, 94
Maori, 1, 13, 34–8, 45, 48, 63–4, 96–7, 145, 151, 168, 172, 175, 204, 207
  education, 37–8
  kinship units, 34, 45, see also hapu; iwi; whanau
  migration, 96–7
  parliamentary seats, 37, 119, 146, 208
  political movements, 37, 119–22, 146–8
  and proportional representation, 146, 208
  religious movements, 119
  state policies for, 36–8, see also biculturalism
  urbanisation of, 97, 119, 165

Maori Battalion, 119
Maori Congress, 147
Maori Council, 120, 148
Maori War Effort Organisation, 119
Maori Women's Welfare League, 120
Marshall, John (Chief Justice), 49, 160
Marshall, T. H., 23, 197
McCarran-Walter Act (1952) (US), 80–1
Meech Lake Accord (Can), 138–40, 158, 207
Melbourne, 89, 112
Métis, 28, 55, 94, 111, 162
Mexico, 130, 187, 191
  migration from, 48, 79, 98, 131, 191
  see also Bracero Program, Hispanic Americans; NAFTA
migrants
  business, 1, 100, 192–3
  female, 100
  guestworker, 13, 79, 84, 88, 98
  kin, 72–3
  transnational, 191–5
  see also migration
migration, 77–101 passim, 191–5
  Central European, 68, 81, 85, 170
  Eastern European, 68, 79, 81–5, 88, 90–1
  labour, 3–4, 77–101, 184, 187, 191–2
  Southern European, 79, 81, 85, 170
  see also under individual countries
minorities, 12–14, 18, 134, 150, 177
  aboriginal, 12–14, 38–41, 127, 178
  defined, 12
  immigrant, 13–14, 127, 177, 194
  national, 177
  visible, 13, 150
missionaries, 26, 28, 31, 36, 39, 47
  Jesuit, 26
Mohawk (Can), 163, 207
Mulroney, Brian, 110
multiculturalism, 19–21, 127, 129–53 passim, 174, 176, 197–9, 201
  and affirmative action, 131–2, 135–6, 149–50
  in Australia, 20–1, 112–18, 141–5, 150–1, 175, 194
  in Britain, 20, 133–7, 150

in Canada, 20–1, 107–12, 137–41, 150–1, 175, 194
and education policies, 132–3, 136
in Netherlands, 133–4
in New Zealand, 20–1, 118, 145, 148–9, 152
in Scandinavia, 133
in United States, 20, 130–3, 149, 182
Muslims, 136–7
  politics of, 136, 185
  see also Rushdie affair
myths of destiny, 10, 73–4, 172
myths of origin, 10–11, 73–4, 156, 172, 175

NAFTA, 155, 158, 187, 190
National Agenda on Multiculturalism (Aus), 117, 141
National Party (Can), 170
National Party (NZ), 120, 147
nationalism, 9–12, 17, 103, 154–79 *passim*
  aboriginal, 159–66
  Australian, 58–61, 175
  Black, 105
  British, 74, 154, 186
  British settler, 71–6, 174
  Canadian, 56–8, 109, 157–9, 175
  civic, 10, 177–8
  defined, 10, 17
  in Eastern Europe, 103
  ethnic, 10, 177–8
  majority, 166–73
  Maori, 145, 147–8, 165–6
  New Zealand, 61–4
  Pakeha, 171–2
  Quebec, 56, 155–9, see also Québécois
  Scottish, 155–6, 186
  state and counter-state, 174
  symbols of, 11–12, 56–7, 61, 74, 176
  Third World, 103–4
Nationality Act (1981) (Brit), 134
nations, 16–18, 43–4, 46–76 *passim*
  domestic dependent, 49, 160
  and ethnic groups, 16–18, 42–4
  and 'race', 16–17
  reframing of, 173–8

and states, 44, 47, 49, 51–76 *passim*
and tribes, 42–4
see also First Nations; nationalism
nation-states
  formation of, 8–12, 50, 73–6
Native Americans, 20, 105, 149, 160–2
  political movements of, 132, 149, 160–2, 182
  tribal and ethnic, 160–2
  see also First Nations; Indians, American
Native Land Court (NZ), 37–8
Native Title Act (1993) (Aus), 143
Netherlands, 133
New Brunswick, 55
New South Wales, 31, 61, 65, 96, 114–15, 121, 205
New York, 100, 133
New Zealand (NZ)
  aboriginal policies, 45–7, 118–21, 145–8, 171–2, see also Maori
  citizenship, 36, 148, 200
  as dominion society, 6
  immigration policies, 86–9
  migration flows, 85–9
  settlement of, 34–8
  Wars, 37
  see also multiculturalism, nationalism
New Zealand Company, 35
New Zealand First Party, 146, 148, 170, 208
Next Steps programme (1995) (Aus), 142–4
Ngai Tahu, 207
Nisga'a, 206–7
Nixon, Richard, 161
North America
  see Canada, USA
Northern Ireland
  see Ireland
Northern Territory (Aus), 33, 95
Nunavut, 159–60, 164
  see also Inuit

Official Languages Act (1969) (Can), 109
Ojibwa (Can), 205
Olympic Games, 176

One Nation Party (Aus), 144, 170
Ontario, 29, 55, 95, 109–10, 121, 138

Pacific Island societies, 87, 206
  migration to New Zealand, 68, 87
Pacific Rim, 7, 187
Pakeha, 35, 120–1, 145, 151
  see also identity; nationalism
Parizeau, Jacques, 158
Parti Québécois, 108, 156–7
pastoralism, 32
patriotism, 51, 54
Pearson, Lester (Sir), 109
peoplehood, 10, 44
Peters, Winston, 146
pluralism
  cultural, 122–3, 127, 133, 141, 149, 152–3
  social, 123, 169, 199
politics
  aboriginal, 44–6, 125–7
  globalisation of, 188–91
  immigrant, 122–5, 194
  neo-liberal, 107, 110, 199
  New Right, 118–19
post-colonialism, 22, 202
postcoloniality, 22, 202
post-settler society
  defined, 102
Powell, Enoch, 135

Quebec, 2, 27, 29, 57, 69, 95, 109, 112, 138, 206
  compared with Scotland, 156, 159
  history of, 52–6
  and Quiet Revolution, 108
  and United States, 158, 187
  see also nationalism
Quebec Act (1774), 52
Quebec Inc., 156
Québécois, 55, 137, 156, 159, 166, 177–8, 200
Queensland, 60, 65, 68, 144, 205

race
  categories, 16–18, 70, 124, 149, 152, 182
race relations industry (Brit), 135

racialisation
  defined, 17
racism
  and anti-racism, 111, 131–3, 138, 150
  in Australia, 33, 66–7, 76, 113, 142, 144
  in Britain, 76, 81–2, 98, 134–6, 150
  in Canada, 28, 66–7, 76, 94, 110
  and immigration, 68, 76, 82–7, 98, 100, 123
  in New Zealand, 36, 63, 66–7, 76
  and settler nationalism, 40, 76
  in United States, 66–7, 76, 78, 98, 105, 130, 182
Rainbow Coalition, 132
Ratana movement, 119
reconciliation, 172–3
referenda
  Aboriginal citizenship (Aus), 114, 206
  Quebec independence, 158, 207
Reform Party (Can), 140
refugees, 13, 89–91, 206
  see also migrants; migration
representivity, 19, 124
reserves, aboriginal
  Australian, 32, 34, 47, 95
  Canadian, 27–9, 47, 94, 160
  United States, 47, 93, 161
Rhodesia
  see Zimbabwe
Riel, Louis, 55
rights
  civic/political, 21, 23, 111, 114, 130, 195
  European Union national, 184
  fishing, 120, 147, 207
  human, 110, 190
  indigenous, 23, 111, 114, 120, 126–7, 138, 143–4, 160, 189, 200
  international, 184–5, 189, 195
  land, 111, 114, 120, 143, 147, 164, 206
  language, 108–9, 120, 133, 156–7
  legal, 22, 111, 150, 195
  migrant, 127, 185, 197
  mining, 114, 164
  and obligations, 23, 199

polyethnic, 199
social welfare, 126, 170, 199
symbolic, 23
working class, 23
see also Civil Rights movement
Royal Commission on Aboriginal Deaths in Custody (Aus), 207
Royal Commission on Aboriginal Peoples (Can), 162–4
Royal Commission on Bilingualism and Biculturalism (Can), 138–9, 205
Royal Commission on Social Policy (NZ), 121, 145
Royal Proclamation (1763) (Can), 26
Rushdie, Salman, affair, 136–7

Saskatchewan, 55, 94, 110
Scandinavia, 130, 133
Scarman Report (1981) (Brit), 135
Scotland, 80, 155, 159, 185
and EU, 155, 185–6
see also migration, Scottish; nationalism, Scottish
Second World War, 2, 19, 26, 62, 77, 93–4, 97, 103, 107
Select Committee on Aborigines in British Colonies (1837), 35
self-determination
see aboriginal peoples, Third World
settler capitalism, 4, 9, 19, 40
settler societies, 5–8
as colonies of settlement, 6
defined, 5
as dominion societies, 6
semi-peripheral status of, 7
settler state
formation of, 9–11, 51, 59, 73–6
incorporation of aboriginal peoples, 38–42, 46–50, 125
policies of inclusion/exclusion, 18–19
see also state
Siegfried, Andre, 52, 62
slavery
American, 78–9, 151
Caribbean, 4, 30
social movements, 105–6

South Africa, 8, 64, 86, 173, 205
apartheid, 8, 106
migration from, 86
South America
see Latin America
sovereignty
aboriginal, 23, 120, 160–5, 189–90
and globalisation, 189–90, 195
state, 9, 22–3, 117, 120, 195
state
compared with nation, 8–12
defined, 9
post-settler, 186–8
restructuring of, 106–7, 122, 126, 170
welfare, 23, 106, 125–6, 169, 199, 203
subjecthood
see citizenship
Swan Report (1985) (Brit), 136

Tainui, (NZ), 207
Taiwan, 1, 89, 106
Tasman, Abel, 35
Tasmania, 60
terra nullius, 31, 143
Thatcher, Margaret, 135
Third World, 21, 103–4, 160, 163, 189
see also self-determination
tolerance, 176
Torres Strait Islanders, 143, 164, 168
see also ATSIC, Mabo case
transnationalism, 191–4
defined, 196
Treaty of Union (1707) (Scotland/England), 155
Treaty of Waitangi (1840) (NZ), 35–6, 117, 120–1, 145–8, 165, 205
articles, 36
claims, 145, 147
see also Waitangi Tribunal
tribe
defined, 43–4
see also iwi; Native Americans
Trudeau, Pierre, 109–10, 139, 157

United Kingdom (UK)
see Britain (Brit)
United Nations (UN), 90–1, 189–90

United Nations Convention on Refugees (UNHCR), 90–1
United Nations Working Group on Indigenous Populations, 189–90
United States (US)
  citizenship, 208
  and civic unity, 182–3
  civil rights in, 104–6, 130
  demographic change of, 131
  exceptionalism, 7, 181
  immigration policies, 78–81, 92–3
  IRA era, 206
  liberal traditions of, 75, 130, 183
  migration flows, 78–80, 84, 86
  national identity, 74, 133, 182–3
  New Deal, 130

Victoria (Aus), 33, 65, 96, 115, 205
Vietnam War, 106
Vikings, 25

Waitangi Tribunal, 120, 147
  see also Treaty of Waitangi
Wakefield, Edward Gibbon, 35
Wales, 80, 185–6
welfare colonialism, 111, 125–6
West Indies
  see Caribbean
whanau, 45
White Australia Policy, 84–5, 143
White Paper on Indian Policy (1969) (Can), 109, 162
Whitlam, Gough, 114–15, 117
Wilson, Woodrow, 103
women
  and citizenship, 23, 198, 208
  labour force participation, 100, 169–70, 198
  migration of, 100
  and national identity, 57, 61
  see also gender
World Council of Indigenous Peoples, 189

Yirrkala (Aus), 206

Zimbabwe, 8

Augsburg College
Lindell Library
Minneapolis, MN 55454